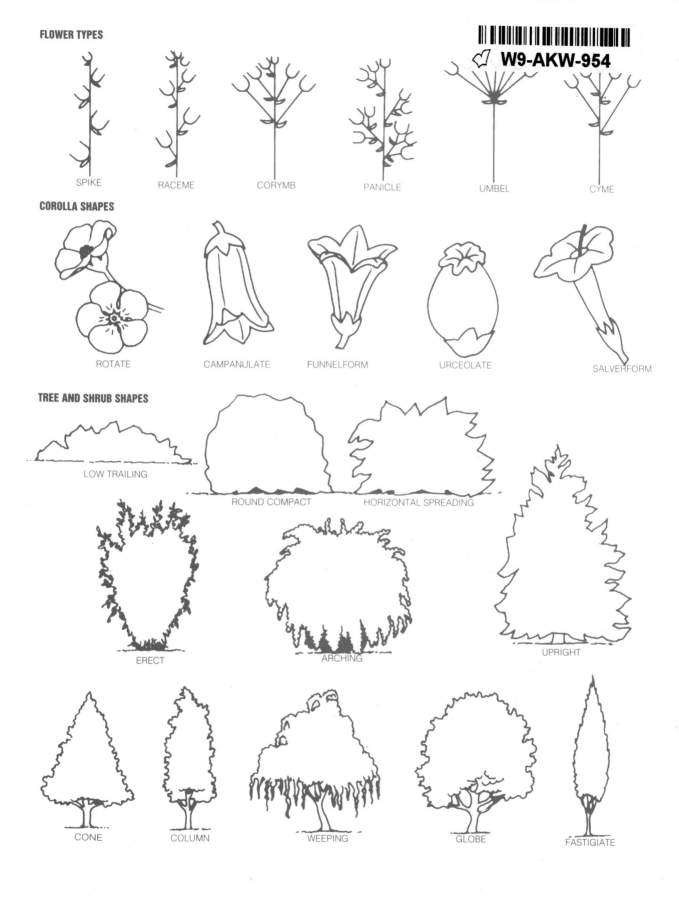

FLOWER TYPES

SPIKE RACEME CORYMB PANICLE UMBEL CYME

COROLLA SHAPES

ROTATE CAMPANULATE FUNNELFORM URCEOLATE SALVERFORM

TREE AND SHRUB SHAPES

LOW TRAILING ROUND COMPACT HORIZONTAL SPREADING

ERECT ARCHING UPRIGHT

CONE COLUMN WEEPING GLOBE FASTIGIATE

THE AMERICAN GARDEN GUIDES

tropical gardening

General Consultants:
Larry E. Beezley, Quail Botanical Gardens, Encinitas, California
Robert Bowden, Harry P. Leu Gardens, Orlando
Linda Gay and Douglas Williams, Mercer Arboretum and Botanical
  Garden, Humble, Texas
Robert Hirano, Lyon Arboretum, Honolulu
Sean Hogan, Portland, Oregon
June Hutson, Missouri Botanical Garden, St. Louis, Missouri
David Price, Bok Towers Gardens, Lake Wales, Florida
Keith Woolliams, Waimea Falls Park, Waimea, Oahu

Botany Consultant: Dr. Lucile H. McCook
Enabling Garden Consultant: Eugene Rothert, Chicago Botanic Garden

tropical gardening

Fairchild Tropical Garden
Miami, Florida

David Bar-Zvi
CHIEF HORTICULTURIST

With Kathy Sammis
Preface by Brinsley Burbidge, Ph.D.
Series Editor: Elvin McDonald

Principal Photography by Chani Yammer
and Albert Squillace

Pantheon Books,
Knopf Publishing Group
New York
1996

Acknowledgments

If one subscribes to the school which says that there isn't a person I've met who hasn't taught me something, as I do, acknowledgment is truly a daunting task. Inevitably, important people are omitted, sometimes for their very obviousness as mentors and teachers.

First are the hardworking, dedicated horticultural and research staff of Fairchild Tropical Garden: Don Evans, Director of Horticulture, a friend and colleague without whose encouragement this would not have been as easy. Horticulturists Craig Allen, Mary Collins, Cathy Ryan and curators Charles "Chuck" Hubbuch and Dr. Richard Campbell generously shared their knowledge and experience in growing bromeliads, flowering trees, vines, ferns, palms, cycads and tropical fruits; Dr. Brinsley Burbidge, director of the Garden who cleared the way for this book, along with associate director Phyliss Shapiro and assistant Linda Lambert.

Along the path have been scores of teachers and sources of inspiration and special friends who have nourished and encouraged my wonder of plants. Several have given me opportunities which made it possible to share some of what there is to know about plants and growing them: Paul Azaroff, my dearest friend to see me through thick and thin; Dr. Gerald B. Straley who has been an inspiration and example; Mary Comber Miles who helped me to understand the beauty of plants; Roy Forster who first opened the door to the world of botanical gardens; Mr. and Mrs. W.R. (Bill) Barnes who planted the seed.

Plantspeople around the world have been a well of information and learning: Gary Baker, Ernie Chew, Paul Gripp, Shlomo Krebs, W. John Kress, Fred Berry, Joseph Fondeur, Mark Collins, Alan Carle, Billie Davis, Alan Meerow, Tim Broschat, Henry Donselman, Stan Wood, David McLean, Paul Drummond, William Theobald, Bill Lessard, Pat, Sue, and Kim Trickel, Steven Slaughter, Garrin Fullington, Ray Baker, August Braun, Tom Wood, Derek Burch, Michael Pursell, Jackie Miles, Kim and Wiess Oei, Bill and Chandra Waggoner, Toby Berg, Mark Levandowski, Shirley Mayotte, Said el Naghif, Kim Chun Lee, David Roberts, Halijah Ibrahim, Mushlim Musa, Suzan Harada, Elsie Horikawa, Helen Kennedy, and many others.

In producing this book, we appreciate the help of all the photographers and consultants who contributed so much to it, Michael Kristiansen of Honolulu Botanic Gardens, Larry Schockman of The Kampong, Dr. Victoria Matthews who lent expert editorial advice, Kathy Grasso, David Pryor, Susan Ralston, Anne Messette, Altie Karper, Barbara de Wilde, Avital and Yaakov Stein, Kirsten Llamos, Sylvia and Steve Sharnoff, Dencie Kane, Mike Mehl, David Steinmetz, Letitia Griffith, Deborah Friel, Brian Erwin, Allan Kellock, Deena Stein, and Michelle Stein.

DAVID BAR-ZVI

Library of Congress Cataloging-in-Publication Data
Bar-Zvi, David.
Tropical Gardening / by David Bar-Zvi, with Kathy Sammis
p. cm. -- (The American Garden Guides)
"Fairchild Tropical Garden."
Includes index
ISBN: 0-679-75863-1
1. Landscape Gardening–United States. 2. Landscape gardening–Canada.
3. Tropical plants–Pictorial works.   I. Sammis, Kathy.
II. Fairchild Tropical Garden. III. Title.   IV. Series.
SB473.B35 1996   95-23964
635.9'52--dc20   CIP

Manufactured in Singapore

First edition

Project Director: Lori Stein
Book Design Consultant: Albert Squillace
Editorial Director: Jay Hyams
Associate Art Director: Chani Yammer

9 8 7 6 5 4 3 2 1

Opposite: Tillandsia capitata

contents

Waimea Falls Park.

3. Garden Design 178

4. Techniques 188

5. Special Conditions 208

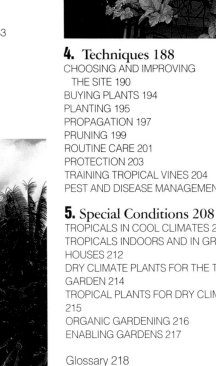

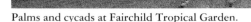
Palms and cycads at Fairchild Tropical Garden.

the american garden guides

The network of botanical gardens and arboreta in the United States and Canada constitutes a great treasure chest of knowledge about plants and what they need. Some of the most talented, experienced, and dedicated plantspeople in the world work full-time at these institutions; they are the people who actually grow plants, make gardens, and teach others about the process. They are the gardeners who are responsible for the gardens in which millions of visitors exclaim, "Why won't that plant grow that way for me?"

Over thirty of the most respected and beautiful gardens on the continent are participating in the creation of *The American Garden Guides*. The books in the series originate with manuscripts generated by gardeners in one or several of the gardens. Drawing on their decades of experience, these originating gardeners write down the techniques they use in their own gardens, recommend and describe the plants that grow best for them, and discuss their successes and failures. The manuscripts are then passed to several other participating gardens; in each, the specialist in that area adds recommended plants and other suggestions based on regional differences and different opinions.

The series has three major philosophical points carried throughout:

1) Successful gardens are by nature user-friendly toward the gardener and the environment. We advocate water conservation through the precepts of Xeriscaping and garden health care through Integrated Pest Management (IPM). Simply put, one does not set into motion any garden that is going to require undue irrigation during normal levels of rainfall, nor apply any pesticide or other treatment without first assessing its impact on all other life—plant, animal, and soil.

2) Gardening is an inexact science, learned by observation and by doing. Even the most experienced gardeners often develop markedly dissimilar ways of doing the same thing, or have completely divergent views of what any plant requires in order to thrive. Gardeners are an opinionated lot, and we have encouraged all participants to air and share their differences–and so, to make it clear that everyone who gardens will find his or her own way of dealing with plants. Although it is important to know the rules and the most accepted practices, it is also important to recognize that whatever works in the long run for you is the right way.

3) Part of the fun of gardening lies in finding new plants, not necessarily using over and over the same ones in the same old color schemes. In this book and others in the series, we have purposely included some lesser-known or underused plants, some of them native to our vast and wonderful continent. Wherever we can, we call attention to endangered species and suggest ways to nurture them back to their natural state of plenty.

Elvin McDonald
Houston, Texas

director's preface

With such a great percentage of the world's species coming from the tropics, the choice of species to feature in this book and also the selection of species to curate and display in a botanical garden devoted to plants of the tropics, such as Fairchild Tropical Garden, is a matter of rigorous selection. We have to miss a great many excellent plants.

The fact that there are so many tropical species is also a strength and should encourage any gardeners with anything from a 10 by 8 foot conservatory in a cooler part of the country to a spacious garden in south Florida or Hawaii to be adventurous and to try new things. It is a sad fact that the majority of nurseries concentrates on a limited number of best-selling ones and that the more unusual plants are difficult to find. But that is where botanical gardens can really help. Most have continuing education programs that provide courses in growing tropical plants; many have plant and seed distribution plans for members. Most display, either outdoors in glass houses (and label with the correct scientific name) a far wider range of correctly named plants than any nursery could think of growing and selling. Botanical gardens are places of tranquility (usually) and provide an ideal environment in which to assess plants that you are thinking of trying as well as places of inspiration for new things you might like to try.

At Fairchild, we solve the difficult problem of too many plants and too few acres by focusing our attention on certain plant groups—in our case, on our world class collections of palms and cycads, on a large collection of tropical flowering trees from all the major tropical families, and on tropical fruit trees. We have an expanding collection of other tropical plants such as heliconias and representative species, often rare and endangered, from Florida and many of the Caribbean islands. We hold classes, distribute interesting and unusual plants to members, and are host to many plant societies who have meetings and shows in our buildings. Our work is based on our collections and focuses on what we can do with them: research, conservation, display, and a strong commitment to education—helping kids in schools to understand plants and helping the community to use plants more imaginatively and more practically in neighborhood plantings. We aspire to be a one-stop shop for anyone who wants to know anything about plants from the tropics.

This book is a great start and will give you the flavor of tropical gardening as well as some exciting ideas. But use it as a starting place. There are many thousands of tropical plants that may be as good or better out there. Visit your botanical garden. The rewarding and intriguing world of tropical plants awaits your discovery.

BRINSLEY BURBIDGE, PH.D
DIRECTOR OF FAIRCHILD TROPICAL GARDEN

Gardeners in the tropics can enjoy the flamboyant, almost unreal, shapes and colors of blossoms that many tropical plants produce. Other plants provide softer texture and form, allowing the gardener to blend elements in sophisticated layered gardens. *Above: Tacca integrifolia,* bat flower.

Preceding pages: Royal palms at Fairchild Tropical Garden.

A venerably twisted coral tree draped in flowering orchids and feathery ferns; a brilliantly striped and quilted croton; a chenille plant covered with drooping, fuzzy ropes of bright red flowers–gardening with tropical plants offers a fascinating array of textures, colors, growth habits, and fragrances. A seemingly endless variety of plants is available to the tropical gardener; over 200,000 species are native to the tropics and subtropics, offering many more varied and interesting forms and textures than exist among plants for temperate regions. In the often swarming growth of the tropics, its native plants are drawn toward flamboyance–in color, size, shape, fragrance–in a competition to attract pollinators or capture available light. Like the pollinators, gardeners too are drawn to these plants, which can provide multiple delights in the home landscape for the senses of sight, touch, and smell.

DEFINITION Strictly speaking, the tropics are the regions of the earth extending 23° north and south of the equator, between the Tropic of Cancer and the Tropic of Capricorn. This region includes places we think of as typically tropical, such as Jamaica, Tahiti, Hawaii, Bali, and Costa Rica. Regions bordering on these parallels of latitude that are generally tropical in nature are termed subtropics or semitropics. (These two terms are used interchangeably, although some people prefer the term semitropical for areas that experience distinct changes in average temperatures.) In the popular concept, the tropics feature uniformly warm, moist growing conditions, but this is only partially correct. Some tropical areas are arid, while tropics in high elevations can be temperately cool. The rainfall pattern in different tropical areas also varies; one location may be uniformly rainy, while another may experience distinct seasonality, with alternating wet and dry periods. Conditions are affected by the presence of mountains, valleys, and oceans.

As a general description, the tropics are warm for most of the year, with a mean annual temperature of 70° F. Freezing temperatures almost never occur. There is little variation throughout the year in the day's length, and the sun lies mostly overhead. Horticulturally, it is only in the tropics that coconut palms and breadfruit trees can produce fruit. The only part of the United States that lies within the true tropics–between the Tropic of Cancer and the Tropic of Capricorn–is Hawaii.

Semitropical conditions are like tropical conditions for much of the year and temperate for the remainder; the subtropics are areas situated outside strictly tropical lattitudes. In the subtropics, the mean temperature during the warmest months is close to 70° F, but can drop to about 45° F during the coldest months. Frosts are infrequent but do occur, so tropical plants grown here need some protection. Mediterranean zones–dry hot summers, cool wet winters, rainfall less than 30 inches a year– are often semitropical in many respects. Horticulturally the subtropics mark the limit for growing oranges. Subtropical areas of the United States include southern California, southern Florida, and southern Texas.

Many tropical (warmth-loving) plants are well adapted to subtropical conditions, while others need extra care; most ultratropicals such as breadfruit will not thrive in temperatures below 50° F. Tropical plants from higher elevations often adapt well to subtropical conditions and even temperate plants can thrive in mountainous tropics.

TYPES OF TROPICAL PLANTS While many plants will grow and survive in the tropics, plants specifically associated with tropical growing conditions and commonly found in tropical gardens include the following:

Palms and Cycads In many people's minds, palms are the symbol of the tropics, and they provide the major and most dramatic objects in many tropical gardens. People unfamiliar with tropical plants may be surprised to learn that there are over 2,500 species of palms, offering the home gardener fascinating flowers and fruit, trunk, and foliage types and textures, and growth habits ranging from knee-high to vining to towering. Cycads are ancient and primitive plants that superficially resemble palms; slow growing, with fronds that grow in a rosette, they are used as decorative specimen plants demanding little care.

Aroids Aroids feature a flower stalk surrounded by a broad protective leaflike sheath. Many aroids have very decorative leaves, and some produce colorful flowers as well. Caladium, anthurium, and philodendron are aroids.

Cacti and Succulents These are certainly not the plants commonly thought of as denizens of a tropical garden, but many are in fact native to the tropics. With good drainage and relatively dry growing conditions, the many cacti and succulents will add very interesting, even remarkable, texture and form to the tropical garden.

Ferns Ferns, prized for their graceful foliage (they do not flower), are familiar to temperate as well as tropical gardeners. Perhaps the best-known fern native to the American tropics is the Boston fern.

Above: Aphelandra sinclariana. Left: a canopy of live oak covers a typically textured tropical garden.

HISTORICAL NOTES

The distant garden we call Paradise must surely have been located in the tropics, in a land where the icy blasts of winter never come, where the sun shines bright every day, and all living things flourish. Paradise was clearly marked on medieval world maps, most often in a far corner to the east, forever inaccessible.

The location of Paradise changed with the expansion of geographical knowledge and Europe's reawakening from the Dark Ages; by the time Columbus set sail, he was searching not for that blessed land but for the riches to be found in its environs. The original wonder expressed by men from temperate climes facing the world of the tropics is still with us. Columbus sailed home laden not just with gold but with seeds and plants gathered in the new lands, and his example became a model for the future: the tropics are still being explored for new plant riches.

The tropical zone includes all the land and water situated between the Tropic of Cancer, the parallel of latitude north of the equator, and the Tropic of Capricorn, the parallel south of the equator. The two imaginary circles on the celestial sphere reflect imaginary lines in the sky marking extremes of the sun's migration and are known as tropics from the Greek word *tropos*, "turn;" when reaching those points the sun seems to stop and turn. The northern tropic became known as Cancer because the sun made its turn at the time of the appearance of the constellation Cancer; the southern tropic was named for Capricorn for its relation to the first appearance of that constellation.

On both sides of the tropical zone are regions of mild climate extending 300-700 miles to the borders of the temperate zone. These regions are known as the subtropics.

Because the tropical zone receives the rays of the sun more directly than areas in higher latitudes, the average annual temperature of the tropics is higher–the monthly average is 65° F–and the seasonal change of temperature is less than in other zones. The seasons in the tropics are marked by changes in wind or rainfall, such as monsoons, rather than temperature. Rain is frequent and evenly distributed throughout the year, and many areas are bathed in dense mist. There is no winter, no frost to restrict plant growth or kill off sensitive species, and there are no droughts to stunt growth.

With a climate ideal for plant growth, the tropical and subtropical zones have the greatest concentration and variety of plant life on earth: more than 200,000 species. Conditions in the tropics vary almost as much as in temperate zones, with various differing microclimates, but in general tropical vegetation is dense, luxuriant, tangled, seemingly impenetrable, and on a gigantic scale. This is the world of the jungle and the rainforest–warm, humid, and green–a steamy environment often teeming with wildlife as well as plants. Trees and shrubs, often flowering and fruited, palms, and tree ferns crowd together and are covered with other plants, mosses, ferns, lianas and other vines, bromeliads, begonias, gesneriads, and epiphytes like orchids. The number of plants growing on other plants is one of the most striking characteristics of tropical growth.

Most of these plants originally existed only in the tropics and became known to Western science following the voyages of exploration that began in the fifteenth century. Like Columbus, the the captains of other ships brought home unknown plants, some of which proved invaluable to agriculture, technology, and medicine, and all of which were full of the romantic appeal of their mysterious homes.

At first, tropical plants were treated much like exotic jungle animals: the animals were put away in zoos, the plants were kept in special structures, glasshouses and greenhouses. When their special needs were understood, many of these plants made the move from greenhouse to parlor window. During the Victorian age, in both Britain and America, these plants attracted enormous popularity, and plant hunters scoured the corners of the globe in search of new specimens. The demanding nature of these plants only increased their value; some boasted other appealing qualities. The monkey puzzle tree had its fun name and the explanation that it was a staple in the diet of distant South American Indians.

Dieffenbachia's attraction was its being poisonous; the insectivorous pitcher plant seemed truly freakish. While outwardly dull, the India rubber tree was appreciated for its noble contribution to the Industrial Revolution. Then there were palms and, perhaps most of all, the orchids. Few plants evoked the sultry heat of the tropics--with its hints of lust–more than the orchid, and their rarity made them all the more desirable and precious. The difficult care of such plants made for a fascinating hobby--no drawing room was complete without its exotic fern or palm--and each new plant's introduction led to a fad. One of the first tropicals to awaken such interest in America was the camellia.

In addition to bringing tropical plants home, Europeans moved them around, taking plants from one area and introducing them to another, usually in the hope of providing a food supply or creating a financially rewarding industry. The most famous event in the history of plant introductions was Captain Bligh's ill-fated voyage on the Bounty; the purpose of his trip was to transport breadfruit trees from the Society Islands in the Pacific to the West Indies. Less famous but more successful was the introduction of the pineapple to Hawaii.

Not all Europeans felt at home in the tropics. The more romantic early adventurers were entranced by the luxuriant plant life around them, but others felt vaguely ill at ease, sensing something immoral and undisciplined in all that riotous growth.

Today, warm-loving tropical plants have been introduced throughout the world, in some places grown only outdoors in others thriving in the local environment. The tip of Florida is only fifty miles from the Tropic of Cancer and thus well within the subtropical zone; the West and Southwest offer other suitable areas for tropical plants. And all the while, the exploration of the tropics goes forward, with new plants being found constantly, each one offering new hopes for medicines and other products. It is arduous work, but as Linnaeus himself wrote (using the Latin he used to name plants): *Botanicus verus desudabit in augendo amabilem scientiam* ("The true botanist will sweat in advancing his beloved science.")

Heliconias and Gingers Heliconias and members of the ginger family (such as alpinias and hedychiums) are potentially huge herbs with large, paddle-shaped leaves similar to those of the banana; they produce dramatic flower stalks.

Orchids As the palm is the tree symbol of the tropics, so the orchid is the tropics' signature flower. The highly prized orchid flowers come in rich variety of forms, scents, and colors, growing as both epiphytic (air) and terrestrial plants.

Vines Vines are abundant in the tropical forest, and less rampant species such as flame vine, jade vine, and bougainvillea can provide drama and interest in the tropical garden.

USING TROPICAL PLANTS In this book, we emphasize the use of plants outdoors in tropical and subtropical areas. Many tropical plants can also be grown outdoors in borderline areas with less-than-tropical growing conditions given some extra care and protection. Alternatively, tropicals can be grown indoors (the tropics and subtropics are the source of most of our house-plants) or in the greenhouse. In cool climates, many plants can be grown like annuals—planted outdoors in the summer and then allowed to die, or dug up and brought indoors for winter. The individual plant descriptions

Some of the plant types available to tropical gardeners (clockwise, from top left): palms (butia); brilliant foliage plants (cordyline); aroids (aphelandra); dramatic flowers (heliconia and alpinia); bromeliads (pineapple); and orchids (vanda).

A BRIEF LESSON IN BOTANY

Plants are living things and share many traits with animals. Plants are composed of millions of individual cells that are organized into complex organ systems. Plants breathe (take in and expel gases) and extract energy from food; to do this they require water, nutrients, and atmospheric gases. Like animals, plants reproduce sexually, and their offspring inherit characteristics through a genetic code passed along as DNA.

Plants, however, can do one thing that no animal can do. Through a process called photosynthesis, plants can capture energy from the sun and convert that energy into compounds such as proteins, fats, and carbohydrates. These energy-rich compounds are the source of energy for all animal life, including humans.

THE IMPORTANCE OF PLANTS

Because no living animals can produce the energy they need to live, all their energy comes from plants. Like other animals, we eat green plants directly, in the form of fruits, vegetables, and grains (breads and cereals), or we eat animals and animal products that were fed green plants.

The oxygen we need to live on Earth is constantly pumped out of green plants as a byproduct of photosynthesis. Plants prevent the erosion of our precious soils and hinder water loss to the atmosphere.

Plants are also an important source of drugs. Fully one-quarter of all prescriptions contain at least one plant-derived product. Aspirin, one of the most commonly used drugs, was originally isolated from the bark of the willow tree.

THE WHOLE PLANT

Basically, a plant is made up of leaves, stems, and roots; all these parts are connected by a vascular system, much like our circulatory system. The vascular system can be seen in the veins of a leaf, or in the rings in a tree.

LEAVES

Leaves are generally flattened and expanded tissues that are green due to the presence of chlorophyll, the pigment that is necessary for photosynthesis. Most leaves are connected to the stem by a stalk, or petiole, which allows the leaves to alter their position in relation to the sun and capture as much energy as possible.

Leaves come in an astounding variety of shapes, textures, and sizes. Some leaves are composed of a single structure, or blade, and are termed simple. Other leaves are made up of many units, or leaflets, and are called compound (see endpapers).

STEMS

Technically, a stem is the tissue that supports leaves and that connects the leaves with the roots via a vascular system. Stems also bear the flowers on a plant. Therefore, a stem can be identified by the presence of buds, which are the unexpanded leaves, stems, or flowers that will develop later.

A single plant can produce more than one kind of stem; the upright, above-ground stem produces leaves and flowers, while a horizontal, below-ground stem can swell and store food products from photosynthesis. Underground stems can overwinter and produce new plants when conditions are favorable.

The stem of a plant often changes as the plant matures. When a tree is young, its stems are green and soft; as the tree grows and ages, however, the stem develops woody tissues. Wood is composed of hardened cells that provide strength to the stem and that allow water, gases, and nutrients to move both vertically and horizontally through the stem. Concentric circles inside a woody stem are called annual rings. The oldest wood is in the center of the rings, and the youngest wood is in the outer ring. Light-colored rings, or early wood, are composed of cells that were added early in the growing season of each year; these cells are larger and are less densely packed together. Late wood is darker in color because the cells are smaller and packed more closely. Each set of a light and dark ring represents one year in the life of the growing plant stem. When a plant grows under constant environmental conditions, with no changes in tem-

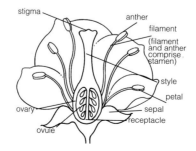

stigma
anther
filament
(filament and anther comprise stamen)
style
petal
sepal
receptacle
ovary
ovule

perature or moisture during the year (like in some tropical rain forests), the wood is uniform in color and lacks annual rings.

Bark forms on the outside of woody stems and is made up mostly of dead cells. This corky tissue is very valuable to the stem because it protects the new wood, allows gas exchange into the stem, and lets the stem grow in diameter. All of the bark is not dead tissue, however; the innermost layer is living vascular tissue. If a stem is girdled or the bark is damaged, this vascular tissue, which moves the food products of photosynthesis around in the plant, will be destroyed, and the plant will die.

ROOTS

Although out of sight, roots are extremely important to the life of the plant. Roots anchor a plant in the soil, absorb water and nutrients, and store excess food, such as starches, for the plants' future use. Basically, there are two types of roots: taproots and fibrous roots. Taproots, such as the edible part of a carrot, are thick unbranched roots that grow straight down. A taproot takes advantage of moisture and nutrients far below the soil surface and is a storehouse for carbohydrates. Fibrous roots are fine, branching roots that often form dense mats, making them excellent agents of soil stabilization. Fibrous roots absorb moisture and nutrients from a shallow zone of soil and may be more susceptible to drought. Roots obviously need to come into contact with water, but they also need air in order to work properly. Except for those adapted to aquatic environments, plants require well-drained soils.

VASCULAR SYSTEMS

Plants have a well-developed vascular system that extends throughout the plant body and that allows movement of water and compounds from one part of a plant to another. Roots absorb water and minerals, and the vascular system funnels them to the leaves for use in photosynthesis. Likewise, energy-rich compounds that are produced in the leaves must travel to the stems and roots to provide nutrition for further growth. The vascular system also strengthens plant tissues.

PHOTOSYNTHESIS

A green plant is like a factory that takes raw

materials from the environment and converts them into other forms of energy. In a complex series of energy transfer and chemical conversion events called photosynthesis, plants take energy from the sun, minerals and water from the soil, and gases from the atmosphere; these raw materials are converted into chemical forms of energy that are used for plant growth. These same energy-rich compounds (proteins, sugars and starches, fats and oils) can be utilized by animals as a source of food and nutrition. All this is possible because of a green pigment, chlorophyll.

Photosynthesis is an extremely complex series of reactions that takes place in the cells of leaves, the byproducts of which are connected to other reactions throughout the cell. The most basic reactions of photosynthesis occurs like this: Energy from the sun strikes the leaf surface, and electrons in the chlorophyll molecule become "excited" and are boosted to a higher energy level. Excited electrons are routed through a chain of reactions that extracts and stores energy in the form of sugars. As a byproduct of electron loss, water molecules are split; hydrogen moves in to replenish the electrons lost from chlorophyll, and oxygen is released, finding its way into our atmosphere. In another photosynthetic reaction, carbon dioxide from the atmosphere is "fixed," or converted into organic compounds within the plant cell. These first chemical compounds are the building blocks for more complex reactions and are the precursors for the formation of many elaborate chemical compounds.

PLANT NUTRITION

Plants require mineral nutrients from the soil, water, and the atmosphere in order to maintain healthy growth and reproduction. Macronutrients, those nutrients needed in large amounts, include hydrogen, oxygen, and carbon–all of which are abundant in our atmosphere. Other macronutrients are nitrogen, phosphorus, potassium, sulfur, and calcium. If macronutrients are in limited supply, growth and development in the plant will be strongly curtailed. Nitrogen is an important component of chlorophyll, DNA, and proteins and is therefore an essential element for leaf growth and photosynthesis. Adding nitrogen to garden soil will generally result in greener, more lush plant growth. But beware of too much of a good thing; too

much nitrogen can burn tender plants. Or, you may have large and lovely azalea leaves, but with no flowers! Phosphorus is also used in building DNA and is important in cell development. Phosphorus is necessary for flowering and fruiting and is often added to garden soil. Potassium is important in the development of tubers, roots, and other storage organs.

LIFE CYCLE

Higher plants (except for ferns) begin life as a seed. Given the right set of conditions (temperature, moisture, light), a seed will germinate and develop its first roots and leaves using food stored in the seed (humans and other animals take advantage of the high-quality food in seeds when they eat wheat and corn, just to name a few). Because of the presence of chlorophyll in the leaves, the small plant is soon able to produce its own food, which is used immediately for further growth and development. As the seedling grows, it also grows in complexity. The first, simple root gives way to a complex root system that may include underground storage organs. The stem is transformed into an intricate system of vascular tissue that moves water from the ground up into the leafy part of the plant, while other tissues transport energy-rich compounds made in the leaves downward to be stored in stem and root systems.

Once the plant reaches maturity, flower initiation begins. Flowers hold the sexual apparatus for the plant; their brilliant colors and glorious odors are advertisements to attract pollinators such as insects or birds. In a basic, complete flower, there are four different parts, given below. However, many plants have incomplete flowers with one or more of these parts missing, or the parts may be highly modified.

1. Sepals. The outermost part of the flower, sepals cover the young floral buds. Although they are often green, they may be variously colored.

2. Petals. The next layer of parts in the flower, petals are often colorful and play an important role in attracting pollinators.

3. Stamens. Stamens are located next to the petals, or may even be basally fused to the petals. The stamens are the male reproductive parts of the flower; they produce the pollen. Pollen grains are fine, dust-like particles that will divide to form sperm cells. The tissue at the end of the stamen that holds

pollen is called the anther.

4. Pistil. The innermost part of the flower holds the plant's female reproductive apparatus. The stigma, located at the tip of the pistil, is often covered with a sticky substance and is the site where pollen is deposited. The stigma is held by a floral tube, call the style. At the base of the style, the ovary holds one to many ovules, which contain eggs that represent undeveloped seeds.

Pollination is the transfer of pollen from an anther to a stigma and is the first step in the production of seeds. Pollen can be transferred by an insect visiting the flower, by the wind, or even by the splashing of raindrops. After being deposited on a compatible stigma, the pollen grains grow into tubes that travel from the stigma, down the floral tube into the ovary, depositing sperm cells to the ovules. If all goes well, sperm cells unite with the eggs inside the ovules, and fertilization takes place.

After fertilization, the entire floral structure is transformed into a fruit. Fruit can be fleshy, like an apple, or dry like a pea pod. Within each fruit, fertilized eggs develop into seeds, complete with a cache of storage tissue and a seed coat.

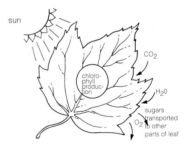

sun

CO_2

H_2O

chlorophyll production

sugars transported to other parts of leaf

O_2

Honolulu Botanical Gardens is comprised of five sites on the island of Oahu, two of which are pictured here. *Above:* Lili'uokalani Botanical Garden, started in 1989, is dedicated to Hawaiian native plants; Queen Lili'uokalani, the last Hawaiian queen, bathed in the pool below this waterfall. Top: Ho'oma-luhia Botanical Garden provides visitors with an escape into a rainforest; up to 60 waterfalls appear after the almost daily rains at this site.

like annuals–planted outdoors in the summer and then allowed to die, or dug up and brought indoors for winter. The individual plant descriptions in Chapter 2, the Plant Selector, give information on these other-than-tropical growing requirements for appropriate plants, in addition to the tropical, outdoor needs.

Tropical landscaping offers more possibilities to the home gardener than what is possible in more temperate, cooler regions. Tropical plants offer a very wide range of foliage colors, from all hues of green to many shades or red, yellow, and purple–even iridescent, in the case of *Strobilanthes dyeranus*. A great range of textures, too, is available, from the finest (as in very fine lawn grasses) to the coarsest (e.g., the giant talipot palm) to the monumentally sculptural (such as agaves). Plant growth habits are more varied than in cooler regions; epiphytes are common; and tropical plants–most notably ficus–often exhibit their roots, which add another element to the aesthetics of the garden.

Because many tropical plants have relatively large, coarse leaves and tend toward individual flamboyance, they can be a challenge to combine in the landscape. However, many combinations are possible. Single-specimen trees or shrubs can be interplanted with groundcovers, less flamboyant flowering and foliage plants, vines, and annuals. Many flowering bedding plants familiar to northern summer gardens–such as impatiens, pansies, petunias, alyssum, and lantana–flourish in the winter tropical garden. The planting season starts in October and some of these plants, though used as annuals in the North, are perennials in the tropics–particularly if they are cut back vigorously every six months to encourage regrowth and new bloom. (However, northern perennials are not suitable for the tropical garden as they require a period of cold or dry weather to induce dormancy.)

NEEDS The basic requirements of tropicals are the same as those of other plants–sunlight, nutrients, and water, plus protection in areas where that is called for. Specific requirements vary for the many different tropical species. Since the plants in your tropical garden (other than annual bedding flowers like impatiens) will be with you for many seasons, you should plan ahead of time what each plant requires, and group plants with similar needs together. When growing tropical plants indoors, or outdoors in containers, keep these basic needs in mind as well.

Nutrients Most plants absorb the water and food they need to grow and thrive from the soil, through their roots. Therefore, a well-conditioned soil, full of nutrient-rich organic matter and providing good drainage, is the best guarantee of success in gardening. Of special note for tropical gardeners are the facts that many tropical plants grow continuously, and organic materials break down swiftly in tropical soils. Therefore, plants in a tropical garden need regular applications of fertilizer.

Well-drained soil is also a necessity, because heavy rainfalls are typical of the tropics and because many tropical plants require generous amounts of water. Quick-draining sandy soils will retain more moisture and slow-

draining clay soils will dry out more quickly with the addition of organic matter. Another consideration is pH, the alkalinity or acidity of the soil. Most plants, including tropicals, grow best in neutral (7.0) to slightly acid (6.0) soil. The addition of organic material to alkaline soil–typical, for example of south Florida–will make the soil more acid.

Not all plants get their nutrients from soil. A unique feature of tropical gardening is the large number of epiphytes, or "air plants," growing on trees. This group of plants needs no soil at all. Attached to the trees by strong roots, the epiphytes–including many orchids, bromeliads, aroids, and ferns–supply themselves with nutrients they extract from atmospheric moisture, airborne dust, and the accumulated debris in which they find their roots.

Sun and Shade Like other plants, the various species of tropicals vary in their need for sun and shade. A large percentage of ornamental tropical plants are those that naturally grow in the filtered light underneath the canopy created by tall forest trees. Few, however, thrive in deep shade; almost all need some direct, although not excessive sun. Strategically placed trees,

Above: The natural area behind Waimea Falls Park in northern Oahu provides a scene typical of the tropics. The lush vegetation includes *Tabebuia donnell-smithii,* travelers palms, erythrinas, and philodendrons.

Above: The rare plant collection at Fairchild Tropical Garden includes begonias, alpinias, ferns, and cyperus. *Right:* An effective use of tropical plants is achieved by combining plants with large, solid leaves such as birds nest anthuriums with lacy ferns, such as holly ferns.

shrubs, and palms can provide the required shade while making their own contribution to overall garden design. Other tropicals, such as cacti and plumeria, thrive in full sun. Some, especially vines like orchid vine, grow decorously in the shade of tropical trees but become rampant aggressors when exposed to sun, as dramatically demonstrated at Fairchild Tropical Garden after Hurricane Andrew ripped away the rain forest garden's canopy.

Water Tropical plants, on the average, like lots of water. While they need water on a regular basis and should never dry out completely, very few tropicals can tolerate standing in water–thus the necessity for well-drained soil. Many plants are native to tropical areas that experience a wet and a dry season, and these plants are well adapted to xeriscaping—water-conserving gardening, a critical concern in many tropical and subtropical areas such as southern California with threatened natural water supply levels. Windbreaks, mulch, and shading protect garden plants from drying out, thereby lessening water demands. In regions that commonly get a lot of rain all at once, plants sensitive to flooding, such as cacti, need to be placed in raised beds or areas with excellent drainage.

Pruning and Weeding These routine garden chores are of particular importance in the tropical garden, where the continuous and rapid growth of both garden plants and weeds needs to be controlled on a regular basis. During cooler periods, rampant growth is not much of a problem, but a few warm nights will produce an onslaught of rapidly growing, potentially large and persistent weeds. Exotic trees have become naturalized and are now pests in many areas.

Leave home for a few months, and you may return to find your tropical garden infested with weed trees such as schefflera, Brazilian pepper, and bischofia. A change in growing conditions, such as additional sunlight, can change tame garden growers into rampant ones, as noted above. Regular pruning and weeding will contain this unwanted growth. A layer of organic mulch will inhibit weed growth while also adding nutrients and humus to the soil; mulch in the tropics needs regular refurbishing, as it breaks down into the soil and the atmosphere relatively rapidly.

Using Tropical Plants Outside the Tropics Enjoyment of tropical plants is not limited to tropical or subtropical climates. Many typically flamboyant tropical plants, like bananas and some palm species, flourish as far north as Mississippi and San Francisco. Some plants that tolerate colder temperatures are root hardy in even colder areas; you can use them if they are not major plants. For areas further north, tropicals are frequently used as annual bedding plants; at the end of the season they are allow to die back or are brought indoors to a protected area. And growing tropicals indoors—old standbys like philodendron and croton, as well as more exotic species like alpinia and hemigraphis—became popular in the 1800s and remains so today.

The world of tropical gardening is fascinating and rewarding, no matter what climate zone you live in. Assess your gardening possibilities, learn each plant's individual requirements, and plunge in!

FAIRCHILD TROPICAL GARDEN is one of the world's preeminent botanical gardens, with extensive collections of rare tropical plants, including palms, cycads, flowering trees and vines. Established in 1938, Fairchild is recognized as a world leader in tropical plant research. The Garden is among Florida's most popular visitor attractions and offers a variety of community programs in environmental education, conservation, and horticulture. The 83-acre grounds, designed by William Lyman Phillips, are a masterpiece of landscape design and horticultural display.

THE GARDENER David Bar-Zvi, Chief Horticulturist at Fairchild Tropical Garden, developed an interest in tropical plants early. He has been growing orchids with an ever-changing fascination since he was ten years old. Palms and the way they grew caught his attention next and he acquired a substantial collection in his garden in Vancouver, British Columbia. Later, working at the Volcani Institute in Israel, at VanDusen Botanical Garden in Vancouver, and at Flamingo Gardens in southern Florida, he concentrated on heliconias, gingers, orchids, palms and tropical flowering trees. Soon after immigrating to Florida, Bar-Zvi became an officer in the newly formed Heliconia Society International; his knowledge of this genus grew as he created a living display collection as curator of plant collections at Flamingo Gardens. At Fairchild Tropical Garden, he is able to share his experiences with an ever-expanding audience, develop an even larger collection of heliconias and related plants, and travel around the world learning more about tropical plants.

SCIENTIFIC NOMENCLATURE

Botanists and horticulturists use a binomial, or two-name, system to label the over 250,000 species of living plants. Because the names are in Latin and Greek, this system crosses both time and language barriers and allows people all over the world to communicate about plants. Occasionally, a scientific name will be changed to reflect additions to our knowledge about plants. A scientific name consists of the genus (singular; genera is plural) and the species—as in the scientific name for Canary Island date palm, *Phoenix canariensis*. The genus name is always first and always capitalized; the species name follows and is generally not capitalized.

Cultivated plants are often selected for a particular attribute, such as leaf or flower color or fruit size. These selections are given a cultivar, or cultivated variety, name in addition to the species and genus. Cultivar names are capitalized and placed within single quotes, such as *Heliconia hirsuita* 'Jamaica Spikey' or *Alpinia purpurata* 'Eileen McDonald'. A particular plant may have many common names—yesterday-today-tomorrow and lady of the night are both used for *Brunfelsia americana*, for example—but it has only one correct scientific name.

Varieties are arranged alphabetically, according to their Latin names; bromelliads, ferns, orchids, palms, and seasonal flowering plants following other entries. See the index or contents page for translations of Latin names.

Some common tropical plants and their genus names:

African tulip tree: *Spathodea*
Amaryllis: *Hippeastrum*
Avocado: *Persea*
Banana: *Musa*
Banyan: *Ficus*
Bat plant: *Tacca*
Bird of Paradise: *Strelitzia*
Bottlebrush: *Callistemon*
Cassava: *Manihot*
Coral tree: *Erythrina*
Croton: *Codiaeum*
Elephant ears: *Alocasia*
Ginger, pineapple: *Tapeincheilos*
Ginger, shampoo, beehive, edible: *Zingiber*
Ginger, torch: *Etlingera*
Ginger, spiral: *Costus*
Ginger, blue: *Dichorisandra*
Ginger, red, shell: *Alpinia*
Gold tree: *Tabebuia*
Lobster claw: *Heliconia*
Orchid tree: *Bauhinia*
Parrot's beak: *Heliconia*
Peregrina: *Jatropha*
Pothos: *Epipremnum*
Powderpuff: *Calliandra*
Queen's Wreath: *Petrea*
Rattlesnake plant: *Calathea*
Screw pine: *Pandanus*
Shrimp plant: *Justicia, Pachystachys*
Spider lily: *Hymenocallis*
Starfruit: *Averrhoa*
Swamp lily: *Crinum*
Taro: *Colocasia*
Ti Plant: *Cordyline*

Though gardening is essentially a hands-on endeavor, some of its greatest pleasures are vicarious: for most gardeners, nothing surpasses the joy of discovering a new plant. Since thousands of different plants are currently under cultivation—and nurseries, botanists, and private gardeners the world over are dedicated to finding and introducing more—there will never be a shortage of horticultural treasures from which to choose. Gardeners in the tropics will find a particularly—almost intimidatingly—vast selection of plants, since conservatative estimates place the number of plants that grow in tropical regions at 200,000.

This chapter is designed to help you sift through those treasures and make a choice. Our authors have selected more than 150 plants that work well for them, mixing common, easy-to-find varieties with others you might not know about, but should; experts from other botanic gardens around the country then added plants that thrive in their own regions. Because most of the gardeners couldn't bear to leave out their favorites, we've included additional recommended plants at the end of the chapter.

The first part of the Plant Selector lists varieties according to size, growth habit, ornamental features, and requirements for sun. Following that is the main portion of the chapter—detailed "plant portraits" describing the plants' qualities, the best conditions for the plants' health, routine care, propagation, pest and disease tolerance, and uses in the landscape. Two hundred of the recommended plants are illustrated, with captions noting their mature size and hardiness zone.

There are only a few keys to successful gardening; choosing the right plant is among them. If a well-tended plant refuses to thrive or succumbs to disease, it probably doesn't belong in its present site. Before deciding on a plant, you need to understand the special conditions of your own garden. Is it sunny, shady, or a combination of both? Is rainfall abundant, or nearly nonexistent? Is the soil sandy, loamy, heavy? How much organic matter does it contain? Does it drain well? What is your soil's natural pH? Information on how to answer these questions is located in Chapter 4; your local nursery, botanical garden, or agricultural extension service can also help. But don't forget that your site is unique, with a microclimate of its own created by the contours of the landscape, shade, and natural barriers; it may be different from those next door, let alone at a nursery ten miles down the road.

To help match plant and gardener, each plant portrait includes information on the following:

Sun and shade In the tropics, most plants benefit from a least a bit of shade from brightest afternoon sun. But there are plants that will thrive in every conditions, from brutal sun to deep shade.

Soil You make minor adjustments in your soil so that the plants can establish itself or survive an unusual drought. But don't try to grow a plant that thrives on nutrients in poor, dry soil; you'll spend the rest of your life pampering it and it will never do as well as a more practical choice.

Water There are plenty of tropical plants that thrive in dry climates—and not all of them are cacti. Notations throughout this chapter point out plants that are adapted to dry climates; see page 214 for information on gardening with tropical plants in dry climates. Because water supplies everywhere are becoming more scarce, all gardeners would do well to heed the basic principles of xeriscaping: proper garden design, maintenance, and especially plant selection.

Hardiness Consider your area's general climate, but keep in mind too that planting in a protected area might allow you to gain one warmer zone–if you don't mind the risk of perhaps, in some years, experiencing winter damage. See page 210 for information on gardening in cooler climates. In the West, climate zones are not as important as summer highs and rainfall.

Pests and diseases We've noted problems that are common to particular plants; if these pests or diseases are rampant in your area, avoid the plants in question. See pages 206-7 for more information on pests and diseases.

Most tropical plants can be used outdoors in only a small section of the United States. For the rest of the country, we've included information on which plants will survive in cooler regions, and which do well as houseplants or as bedding plants that can be planted outdoors when the weather is warm and brought indoors before frost.

The map below was created by the United States Department of Agriculture. It divides the United States and Canada into climate zones. Most nurseries (and this book) use these classifications to advise where plants will be hardy. Although this is a useful system, it is not foolproof; it is based on average minimum temperature, and a particularly cold winter might destroy some plants that are listed as hardy in your climate zone. More often, you will be able to grow plants that are not listed as hardy in your zone, particularly if they are in a sheltered area.

There are other climate-zone classifications; the Arnold Arboretum's is also used quite often. The climate zones referred to in this volume are those of the USDA.

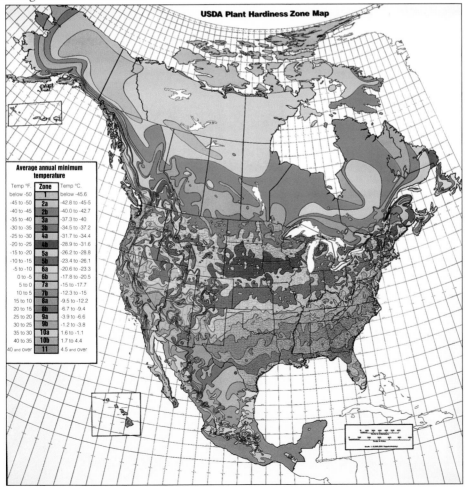

USDA Plant Hardiness Zone Map

Average annual minimum temperature

Temp °F.	Zone	Temp °C.
below -50	1	below -45.6
-45 to -50	2a	-42.8 to -45.5
-40 to -45	2b	-40.0 to -42.7
-35 to -40	3a	-37.3 to -40
-30 to -35	3b	-34.5 to -37.2
-25 to -30	4a	-31.7 to -34.4
-20 to -25	4b	-28.9 to -31.6
-15 to -20	5a	-26.2 to -28.8
-10 to -15	5b	-23.4 to -26.1
-5 to -10	6a	-20.6 to -23.3
0 to -5	6b	-17.8 to -20.5
5 to 0	7a	-15 to -17.7
10 to 5	7b	-12.3 to -15
15 to 10	8a	-9.5 to -12.2
20 to 15	8b	-6.7 to -9.4
25 to 20	9a	-3.9 to -6.6
30 to 25	9b	-1.2 to -3.8
35 to 30	10a	1.6 to -1.1
40 to 35	10b	1.7 to 4.4
40 and over	11	4.5 and over

WHERE CAN TROPICAL PLANTS BE GROWN?

In the United States, only Hawaii lies within the tropics. The southern tip of Florida also lies within Zone 10, and most tropical plants can be grown there without protection. Several other areas can be considered subtropical:

CENTRAL FLORIDA Bok Tower Gardens is located in Central Florida, in a a climatic zone that is subtropical. The garden receives a light freeze (25-32° F) every five to ten years. The gardens are situated on top of a ridge that gives excellent air movement. Often, on cold nights, the temperature in the Gardens is six to eight degrees warmer than surrounding lands. Many tropical plants can be grown in the Garden, but require special treatment every so often to deal with the cold. Planting under a tree canopy provides protection from light frosts. In the event of a harder freeze, plants are mulched with a heavy layer of pine straw to protect stems and roots of tender plants.

Some plants, such as the terrestrial orchid *Phaius tankervillea* are worth protecting with extra care, such as covering it with special cloth; it takes only a few minutes to cover a bed. The cloth can remain on the plants during the heat of the day or in the rain without damage due to its porous nature. Temperatures under the cloth can be 20° F higher than outside temperatures. The Garden's policy is not to plant tender plants that grow large (like trees) or masses of smaller ones. By minimizing use and maximizing the effect of tropicals, the design integrity of the Garden is not lost in the event of a periodic freeze. Placement of herbaceous tropicals behind lower-growing evergreen coldhardy plants allows everyone to enjoy the beauty of the tropicals in a good year and hide the carnage in a bad year. Most often, cold-damaged plants rebound in a month or two.

THE GULF COAST Mercer Garden, in Humble, Texas is located in the Gulf Coast region (along with parts of Florida and Louisiana); it is in climate Zone 8b, though some areas of the Gulf Coast, like Galveston, are Zone 9. Warm southerly winds off the Gulf push arctic fronts away, keeping winters warm; hard freezes occur only about once every seven years. Temperatures go down to about 30° F for a week or so each winter, but most plants seem to recover from that. Many palms and other tropical plants thrive in the area. One limiting factor is high humidity, which, coupled with brutal sun can "cook" plants.

SOUTHERN CALIFORNIA, particularly in areas along the coast, falls into Zone 10; most inland areas are in Zone 9, and areas in higher altitudes can be much colder. Quail Botanical Gardens, in Encinitas (near San Diego and only about a mile from the coast) finds that tropical plants are quite happy in their Zone 10 garden. The major climate problem they encounter is the fact that most of their rain (about 15 inches per year) falls in the winter when plants are dormant and causes roots to rot. Nights are not cool enough to freeze plants, but sometimes a long period (eight to ten weeks) of 45° F nights impedes their growth and weakens them. They find that even light protective devices help a great deal. The area is kept humid by the transpiration of the large collection in the microclimate of the garden, and by winds off the ocean; mistheads hung high in trees help, too. Plants benefit from the fact that temperatures rarely exceed 90° F. For more information on gardening with tropicals plants in dry areas, see pages 214-215.

OUTSIDE THE TROPICS

Many tropical plants can be grown in areas bordering the tropics. In the Southeast, bananas and small palms can be grown through Zone 8 with some protection. In coastal California through Oregon, and in parts of Pacific Canada that warmed by trade winds, palms are common. Sean Hogan, formerly of San Francisco and currently of Portland, Oregon reports that frost of any consequence is rare along the immediate coast (especially south of the Central Oregon Coast), but lack of summer heat can hinder growth. The cool nights and foggy mornings of summer don't allow the plants to accrue enough heat to stimulate plants from tropical climates. He suggests acquiring species from the cloud belt or high mountainous areas of the tropics. Inland areas west of the Willamette Valley bake enough to spur growth in summer, but the occasional invasion of cold air from the interior, often not preceded by a hardening off period, limits the choice of plants. For more information on growing tropicals outside the subtropics, see pages 210-213.

At Fairchild Tropical Garden, chenille plant is a wide-spreading 15-foot-tall hedge that flowers profusely through much of the year. It can also be grown indoors or in a greenhouse in a sunny location (top) or outdoors in cooler regions, where it will grow to about 2 feet tall in a season and then die back to the ground unless it is brought indoors.

ACALYPHA CHENILLE PLANT *Euphorbiaceae*

Several species of this Pacific islands native are commonly grown as ornamental shrubs up to 15 feet tall. **A. hispida,** chenille plant, is grown for its long ropes of tiny red, fluffy flowers produced continuously. **A. wilkesiana,** copper leaf, with inconspicuous flowers, earns its place in the tropical garden for its variegated foliage in a range of colors and patterns. Use as specimen plants, as part of a mixed border, or as an informal hedge.

CULTURE Grow chenille plant in partial shade, with some sun so the flowers develop. Copper leaf needs full sun to develop its full foliage colors; it will drop leaves in cold weather and needs water during the dry season. Prune to maintain shape, and periodically prune older shoots back to the ground to encourage leafy new growth.

OUTSIDE THE TROPICS Acalypha will not survive winter outside Zone 10, but it makes an excellent bedding plant in cooler climates. It grows to a clump about 2 feet across and flowers throughout the summer. May be grown as a houseplant in cooler climates, in a sunny window; water before soil dries out completely. Acalyphas will flower indoors if given bright light and plenty of fertilizer and water.

ADANSONIA DIGITATA BAOBAB TREE, MONKEYBREAD TREE

Bombacacea

Named for French botanist Michel Adanson who was the first to describe it (in the eighteenth century), baobabs are native to Africa and Madagascar. They are oddly shaped trees with immense swollen trunks; they ususaly grow to 75 feet tall with trunks about 30-60 feet in diameter, but one specimen was measured at 85 feet across. When bare, the thick, tapering branches resemble roots, leading to the legend that baobabs grows upside down. The tree bears compound leaves arranged like the digits of the hand, fragrant, pendulous five-petaled showy white flowers and large woody fruit. Baobab trees are an unusual—some gardeners call them ridiculous—specimen in the garden. They also serve as shade trees. In Africa, the tree has many economic uses as well; the pulp of the fruit is used as animal feed and for a citrusy beverage; strong fibers can be made from the bark; and the hollowed trunk can be used for storage and shelter.

CULTURE The swollen trunk of the baobab tree acts as a reservoir for water, which the tree uses in copious amounts—its foliage is sparse to avoid water loss through transpiration. Baobabs need full sun and very warm climates; they are hardy only in the very southern end of Florida and in Hawaii. They thrive in any type of soil as long as it is deep. When planting, protect for the first few years and water generously during any dry periods. Propagate by seed.

AGLAONEMA CHINESE EVERGREEN *Araceae*

Thirty or more species of aglaonema grow wild in forests from their native China and southeast Asia to New Guinea and the Philippines. Typically, they are erect to straggling forest-floor plants, low-growing, with thick, unbranching stems arising from ground level. Grown for their effect as shade plants or indoor potted plants, many species have variegated and highly ornamental leaves. The greenish white, callalike flowers appear only rarely on potted plants. Berries are usually an

ACALYPHA HISPIDA (CHENILLE PLANT) Shrub, to 15 feet tall, with long ropes of small fluffy red flowers produced much of the year. Partial shade, generous water, rich soil. Zone 10.

ACALYPHA WILKESIANA (COPPER LEAF PLANT) Shrub, to 10 feet tall; variegated foliage in shades of brown, bronze, and red, inconspicuous flowers. Full sun for best color, generous water, rich soil. Zone 10.

ADANSONIA DIGITATA (BAOBAB TREE) Tree, to 75 feet tall, with thick, swollen trunk, compound leaves, and fragrant white-petalled flowers. Full sun, high moisture, any deep soil. Zone 10.

AGLAONEMA 'SILVER KING' (CHINESE EVERGREEN) Low-growing foliage plant, to 2 feet tall; narrow light green leaves with silver markings. Moderate to deep shade, generous water, mulch. Zone 10.

VIEWPOINT

PLANTS FOR DEEP SHADE

Aspidistra and ardisia are without question two of the best plants for deep shade. The variegated forms of aspidistra are splendid plants to use in fresh flower arrangements as well. The ground-hugging varieties of ardisia show great great promise for use in small landscapes.
ROBERT BOWDEN, HARRY P. LEU GARDENS, ORLANDO, FLORIDA

In deep shade, we like *Eucharis grandiflora* (Amazon lily) *Clivia miniata*, and *Kaempferia* species.
LINDA GAY, MERCER ARBORETUM AND BOTANICAL GARDEN, HUMBLE TEXAS

In deep shade we use *Anthurium* species, *Setaria palmifolia*, *Philodendron* species, and many other aroids.
KEITH WOOLLIAMS, WAIMEA FALLS PARK, OAHU

We've had success with *Aspidistra elatior* (cast iron plant). *Pogostemon* species (patchoulli) in deep shade.
LARRY E. BEEZLEY, QUAIL BOTANICAL GARDENS, ENCINITAS, CA

Shade-loving groundcovers are easy to maintain because they simply outcompete weeds. Several family member that have the appearance of dark green grass and grow lush in heavy shade, including *Liriope muscari* 'Giant Evergreen' and *L. m.* 'Christmas Trees' with huge flowers spikes that look like purple Christmas trees. *L. spicata* is a lower-growing species. *Ophiopogon japonicum* has shorter but finer leaves.
DAVID PRICE, BOK TOWER GARDENS, LAKE WALES, FLORIDA

There are many leafy herbaceous plants that work well in shade, but fewer with flowers. Dieffenbachia, aglaonema, and spathiphyllum all work well in shade and have variegated foliage with light spots that brighten dark areas; spathiphyllum produces a white flower as well. Some gingers, including *Hedychium coccineum* will grow well in shade; bloom is rare, but the foliage is attractive.
DAVID BAR-ZVI, FAIRCHILD TROPICAL GARDEN, MIAMI, FLORIDA

attractive bright red. Chinese evergreens are ideal as a major groundcover, as contrast statements in tropical forest-type landscapes, and as clumped feature plants in cool, shady spots. They blend well with mossy rocks. With a good selection of cultivars available, aglaonemas can add considerable and varied interest and beauty to the garden. They are also wonderfully reliable, undemanding, low-light houseplants.

CULTURE Does well in a wide range of temperatures and humidity, provided it is grown in moderate to deep shade and has plenty of moisture. Grows well in cooler (55-80° F), wet, tropical forest conditions. Soil should be well drained, with plenty of organic matter. When purchasing, ensure true-to-type coloration on variegated cultivars. Propagates easily from cuttings, or from stems with roots removed and then planted or potted. Seeds of some species will grow quite easily. Set out about 18-24 inches apart; you can bury plants deeper than they were in the original container, as they will root from stems. Keep moist, as plants do not tolerate drought well when young; although they are remarkably adaptable when mature, moisture will produce best results. Once established, little fertilizer is needed if mulch is provided, as it should be constantly. Liquid feed can be beneficial if a boost is needed. Cut back to control shape and spread. Indoors, sponge leaves to keep them clean and fresh. Plants can become hosts to scale insects and mealybugs; this may be a sign the plants are growing in stressful conditions–usually too hot and dry. Control with soft soap sprays, but test first.

OUTSIDE THE TROPICS Chinese evergreen is a popular and attractive houseplant. Potted plants grow slowly in low light, so repotting is seldom needed, although an increased demand for water indicates a need for repotting. They can be brought outdoors–in pots or planted in the ground–when the weather is reliably over 50° F.

SELECTIONS Several beautiful species and cultivars are available; it is a matter of personal taste as to which appeal most. **A. costatum** is very low-growing to prostate, with dark green leaves spotted and mottled white or ivory; in the best forms, the midrib is white. Harder to grow than the following plants, as it prefers plenty of shade, constant moisture, and high humidity. **A. commutatum** grows 2 feet tall, and longer as a groundcover; leaves are all green or blotched and spotted with lighter green. A tough species, useful for a forest setting. Colorful cultivars include **'Malay Beauty',** with green foliage brightly spotted with paler green and white, and **'Pseudobracteatum'**, valued for its narrowly oblong, foot-long, dark green leaves brightly variegated with blotches of lighter green and ivory white; when well grown, this is a striking plant and very useful for color accent. **A. modestum** grows to 2 feet tall with tapering, wavy-edged green leaves; it is popular in the East as a symbol of good luck and in the West as an attractive landscape plant and for its cut stems. Adaptable and tough. **A. pictum** grows 18-24 inches tall, with oblong, metallic blue-green leaves, variously marked with paler green or silver in cultivars; attractive and popular, it adapts to quite variable temperatures.

ALEURITES MOLUCANNA CANDLENUT, KIKUI NUT *Euphorbiaceae*

Aleurites molucanna, native to southeast Asia and naturalized in many tropical areas, is called candlenut because its fruits are so rich in oil that they can be threaded onto string and lit to provide illumination; the oil is also used as a furniture oil and, in Indonesia the grated nut is used in cooking, but only after it has been heated to drive out toxins. This fairly fast-growing tree achieves a height of 60 feet or more. Althought its white flowers are not flamboyant, they are particularly attractive when set off by the white cast of juvenile foliage. For the first year of the tree's life, leaves resemble those of the maple tree; they later become oval. The nuts are about 2 inches across and light green.

CULTURE Mature candlenuts require full sun; they will grow in any soil, so long as it is not boggy. Warm, humid conditions are best, but the tree will tolerate occasional light frost. Look for plants that are not rootbound, with straight trunks and dull, olive green leaves. Plant from containers at any time. Irrigate until the tree is established, then only during periods of drought. Candlenuts do not require fertilizer unless the soil is particularly poor; in that case, use any orchard fertilizer, but avoid fertilizer with very high nitrogen levels. A layer of mulch over the root zone will keep weeds to a minimum. Pruning of this naturally well-shaped tree is usually not necessary; prune only to remove errant branches or dead wood. Propagate by sowing seeds in the area in which the trees are to be grown.

Aleurites flower.

ALLAMANDA *Apocynaceae*

Allamandas comprise approximately 12 species of shrubby or vining plants native to tropical America. With their showy, usually yellow, funnel-shaped flowers produced continuously in warm weather and their glossy green foliage, allamandas are used throughout the tropics as ornamentals. All contain a milky sap; the leaves and bark irritate some people's skin; the prickly fruits are toxic. Vining species can readily be trained to disguise an unattractive fence or to enhance a pergola. The shrubby species are fine accent plants or, grouped, a low screen or informal hedge. Certain species are useful as a shrubby groundcover.

CULTURE Allamandas are easy to grow, in organically rich and moist but well-drained soil and warm, humid conditions. Position in full sun, although they will appreciate some protection from the hottest direct summer sun. Allamandas are easy to propagate, principally from cuttings; when purchasing plants, look for glossy green foliage. Plant out any time, and irrigate to establish and also during dry weather. Feed liberally during the growing season with a balanced fertilizer; mulch is very desirable. Vines must have support; tie the stems while still soft. Prune vining species in winter to remove weak growth and to control size. Prune shrubby species in late winter or early spring to control size and shape and again, lightly, in summer to remove fruits and encourage heavier bloom, followed by fertilizing. Scale or mealybugs may sometimes be a problem; pruning off particularly badly affected parts is helpful. Light pruning for better air circulation will help avoid or control fungus spotting during times of high humidity and low air circulation.

OUTSIDE THE TROPICS Allamandas are sometimes available as houseplants in cooler areas, but controlling their size can be a problem. They require a great deal of humidity and are more suitable for greenhouses than living rooms. They can be planted outdoors if temperature does not fall below 60° F.

SELECTIONS *A. cathartica* is a vigorous vining species, growing to 15 feet, whose various sports produce yellow flowers ranging from large single ones to smaller double ones, some with interesting markings, some fragrant. *A. neriifolia* is a shrubby

ALEURITES MOLUCCANA (CANDLENUT TREE) Large tree, to 60 feet tall, long light green leaves, small white flowers, light green oil-rich nuts. Full sun, any soil except very wet soil, warm humid conditions are best. Zones 9-10.

ALLAMANDA CATHARTICA (GOLDEN TRUMPET) Vigorous vine, to 15 feet; 2-inch yellow single or double flowers, glossy green foliage. Full sun (some protection), rich soil, generous water during growing season. Zones 9-10.

ALOCASIA WATSONIA (ELEPHANT'S EARS) Foliage plant, with huge lobed leaves to 3 feet long and 2 feet wide, dark green with white veins and borders; undersurface is reddish. Partial shade, generous water and humidity, very rich soil. Zone 10.

ALOCASIA 'HILO BEAUTY' (ELEPHANT'S EARS) Foliage plant, with large lobed leaves to 2 feet long and 1 feet wide, dark green with yellow or white markings. Partial shade, generous water and humidity, very rich soil. Can be used in water gardens. Zone 10.

4- to 5-foot bush with yellow flowers. **A. violacea** is a shrub-type vine with showy mauve flowers. A sprawling allamanda, **'Silvern Gold'**, makes an unusual groundcover shrub, with gray or silver foliage and golden yellow flowers.

ALOCASIA ELEPHANT'S EAR PLANT *Araceae*

In the South Sea islands where alocasias are native, they are an important food crop, producing a starch similar to taro that is combined with coconut milk in many dishes. Take note that improper preparation can result in illness; only those experienced in cooking with alocasias should attempt it. In the garden, they are valuable for their immense size and bold patterns. As mass plantings, specimen plants, or accents in large borders, alocasias combine well with other plants and add a bold, tropical look wherever they are planted.

CULTURE The most important factor in choosing a site for alocasias is avoidance of wind. They prefer shade (notably on the Gulf Coast), humidity, warm temperatures, and rich, well-drained, moist organic soil. Look for well-rooted plants without any signs of rot; provide adequate space for their sprawling habit. Keep well watered but not wet; fertilize with a general garden fertilizer such as 14-14-14. Remove dead or dying leaves as necessary and cut back when the plants become leggy. To propagate, remove offshoots (or pruned tip portion) and set in garden. Alocasias can also be propagated by cutting rhizomes into pieces, laying the pieces on their sides in soil, and covering them halfway up. Seeds can also be used, but they will not produce exact replicas. Though usually problem-free, alocasias are sometimes attacked by thrips, slugs, snails, and mealybugs.

OUTSIDE THE TROPICS Although they are hardy only in Zone 10, alocasias do well if planted as annuals, then dug up and stored for winter. The immense leaves combine well with small, brightly colored flowers. Alocasias are difficult to grow indoors because they require more humidity than most homes can provide. They do well in humid greenhouses.

SELECTIONS *A. sanderiana* has arrowhead-shaped, highly glossy dark green leaves, deeply lobed, with curly edges margined in silver. **A. amazonica** has dark green leaves with pure white veins. **A. macrorrhiza** (giant alocasia) has leaves that can grow to 2 feet across. **A. cucullata,** winter hardy on the Gulf Coast, bears arrow-shaped leaves that grow from a large stem; will grow at water's edge. **A. 'Metallica'** has large dark shiny green leaves with purple stems and purple undersides; it grows to 4 feet tall. **A. wentii** has golden green triangular leaves.

ALPINIA RED GINGER, SHELL GINGER *Zingiberaceae*

Lush foliage–with many leafy stems arching from the soil–and showy splashes of flowers are characteristic of many alpinias, which range in height from 1-2 to more than 25 feet. Several species of this herbaceous native of tropical Asia are used in regional folk medicines, and *A. galanga* rhizomes are a culinary spice. Some species bring a texture like seedling palms to the landscape; others provide a yellow tone with their showy, variegated foliage; many are attractively aromatic; many are valued as cut flowers. Alpinia creates a lush, tropical atmosphere with its abundant attractive flowers, usually produced over a long period. One petal of the often conspicuous flower is enlarged and frequently ornately marked and colored. Alpinias flower from spring through summer.

CULTURE Grow alpinias in full sun, with some semishade during the day's hottest

New alocasia introductions, by Robert Hirano of Lyon Arboretum in Honolulu. *Top:* 'Black Beauty'. *Above: Alocasia cuprea.*

GINGER

Zingiberaceae is the Ginger family, a group of tropical rhizomatous herbs often cultivated for its ornamental foliage and growth habit. Most have leafy, arching stems arising from the ground and growing up to 8 feet tall, and conelike, often very showy flower stalks. The ginger we purchase for culinary use is *Zingiber officinale,* used in cooking and medicine for millennia. *Zingiber* ssp. is the species ginger, with common names of shampoo ginger, beehive ginger, or edible ginger. Other commonly grown gingers are alpinia (red or shell ginger), ettlingera (torch or tulip ginger), and hedychium (butterfly ginger).

Other plants with the common name of ginger aren't really gingers: blue ginger (*Dichorisandra thrysiflora*), spiral ginger (costus) (although some botanists include this in the Zingiberaceae family), pineapple or Indonesian wax ginger (*Tapeinocheilos annanasae*), wild ginger (asarum).

Alpinia zerumbet 'Variegata' is valued for its attractive foliage and often used as a groundcover.

hours. Organically rich, moist, well-drained, and slightly acidic soil is best. Most alpinia revel in warm, humid sites protected from wind. Freezing temperatures are not well tolerated by most species. Propagate by seed or well-rooted clump division. Purchase vigorous, actively growing plants. Placing slow-release fertilizer in the planting hole is beneficial, as are regular, light applications of granular palm fertilizer, with some extra potassium added; overfeeding may result in rampant new shoot growth. Regular watering is needed if the weather is at all dry; mulch heavily to maintain moisture. Every few years, cut all or part to ground level to obtain new, fresh growth. Keep up with clump-size containment—some get out of hand quite quickly. Divide and replant as needed. Alpinias have few pest or disease problems.

OUTSIDE THE TROPICS Smaller species of alpinias can be grown as pot plants, *A. zerumbet* 'Variegata' (which produces white flowers) is often chosen for this purpose. Provide bright light, keep evenly moist, and prune frequently to limit size.

SELECTIONS *A. purpurata* is the species commonly known as red ginger, often used in cut-flower arrangements; it prefers light shade. Ornamental variations with conelike flower clusters usually about 1 foot long include the pinks '**Eileen Macdonald**' and '**Jungle Queen**' and the larger '**Jungle King**' and '**Tahitian**', which produces gigantic heads of red bracts. The large, dark green, spreading plants of ***A. zerumbet***, shell ginger, produce striking, pearly shelllike flowers with a highly ornamental lip veined with reddish brown and gold. ***A. z.*** '**Variegata**' is smaller, with yellow and green foliage. Both of these will tolerate temperatures to around 40° F for short periods. ***A. fomosana*** features pin-striped foliage on a 5-foot plant. ***A. mutica,*** also called shell ginger, produces flowers of white, yellow, and red. ***A. vittate,*** variegated ginger, has leaves striped white from midrib to leaf edge; a very attractive light shade lover with pink flowers.

ALTERNANTHERA FICOIDEA JOSEPH'S COAT *Amaranthaceae*

Alternanthera is a low, South American bushy perennial used as a groundcover or contrasting foliage plant throughout the tropics and as a summer bedding plant in temperate regions. The stalkless oval leaves grow only about 4-8 inches high and can be found in dark red, bright red, rosy pink, bright gold, light green, olive green, and dark purple selections, often blotched and veined.

CULTURE Alternanthera grows best in full sun and moist but well-drained soil of average fertility; in very hot climates some protection from afternoon sun helps avoid bleaching of color. Plant rooted cuttings 4-5 inches apart and water well. Propagate by taking 2- to 3-inch cuttings from established plants; rooting is rapid. If desired, the plant can be clipped or sheared to 4-5 inches high for a more formal effect.

OUTSIDE THE TROPICS A bedding plant popular for its high-contrast foliage, Joseph's coat is often used in containers that are brought indoors in winter. Or, overwinter stock plants under glass to produce cuttings the following spring; plant out as soon as danger of frost has passed.

SELECTIONS *A. f.* '**Brilliantissima**' has bright red leaves, '**Aurea-nana**' golden, '**Magnifica**' bronze red, '**Parrot Feather**' bright green with yellow and pink markings, '**Bettzickiana**' green with red and yellow markings. ***A. dentata*** '**Rubiginosa**' has rich purple leaves.

ALPINIA ZERUMBET (SHELL GINGER) Large, dark green, spreading plant with nodding, pearly shelllike flowers. Light shade, high water and humidity, very rich soil. Zone 10.

ALPINIA PURPURATA (RED GINGER) Spreading plant with dark red conelike flowers up to 1 foot long. Light shade, high water and humidity, very rich soil. Zone 10.

ALPINIA PURPURATA 'EILEEN MCDONALD' (RED GINGER) Spreading plant with upright pink flowers up to 1 foot long. Light shade, high water and humidity, very rich soil. Zone 10.

ALTERNANTHERA FICOIDEA (JOSEPH'S COAT) Spreading foliage plants, 4-8 inches tall, with leaves of various colors, some with interesting markings, insignificant flowers. Full sun (some protection), moist soil of average fertility. Zones 9-10.

AMHERSTIA NOBILIS (AMHERSTIA) Small tree, usually under 30 feet in cultivation; green leaves to 3 feet long (red or purplish when young); very showy flowers. Rich, moist soil, high humidity, semi-shade. Zone 10.

ANNONA MURICATA (SOURSOP, GUANABANA, PRICKLY CUSTARD APPLE) Small, spreading, open-branched tree, to 25 feet tall; fuzzy light green fruit in late winter. Very rich, moderately moist soil, high humidity, full sun. Zone 10.

ANTHURIUM 'LADY JANE' (TAILFLOWER) Small plant, 1-2 feet tall and wide, with heart-shaped bright green leaves and showy bright pink flowers. Rich, moist soil, high humidity, light to deep shade. Zone 10.

ANTIGONON LEPTOPUS (CORAL VINE) Vigorous vine, to 40 feet, with heart-shaped bright green leaves and showy racemes of small pink, red, and white flowers over a long season. Moderately moist, moderately fertile soil, full sun; tolerates drought. Zones 8-10.

AMHERSTIA NOBILIS AMHERSTIA *Fabaceae*

If you find an amherstia plant or seed for sale, buy it; it is difficult to obtain and has been called the finest flowering tree in the world. It was discovered in 1826 in a neglected monastery garden in India by John Crawford and named in honor of Lady Amherst, wife of Lord Amherst, and her daughter Lady Sarah, both ardent botanists. The sixth duke of Devonshire read a description of the tree and in 1853 sent one of his gardeners, John Gibson, to India with the sole purpose of obtaining a specimen. Amherstia produces exquisite coral flowers and attractive 3-foot-long leaves that emerge purple or red and turn green. Native to Burma, it is the only species in its genus. If you are lucky enough to obtain one, give it a place of prominence as a specimen.

CULTURE Grow in semi-shade and moist, well-drained soil. Warm to very warm temperatures and high humidity are required. Keep the tree well watered and do not allow the soil to dry out at any time. Propagation, which is accomplished by seed or layering, is not easy. An annual application of 10-30-10 (or monthly applications of 14-14-14) fertilizer help keep the plant thriving; mulching helps keep the soil moist. This tree produces its flowers on terminal growth, so prune only when necessary to remove dead wood. It is rarely attacked by serious pests and diseases.

ANNONA X ATEMOYA CUSTARD APPLE, BULLOCK'S HEART
Annonaceae

Custard apple is a small, spreading, open-branched semi-deciduous tree that bears large, apple-sized, reptilian-looking light green fruit in February. The flesh of the fruit, embedded with black seeds, is fragrant and has a sweet, luscious texture and flavor. This small tree, suitable for a dooryard garden, is a hybrid between *A. squamosa* (sweetsop) and *A. cherimola* (cherimoya). Native to tropical America.

CULTURE Grow in full sun to partial shade in moderately moist, organically rich soil that is well drained; plants are not tolerant of waterlogging. Growing conditions should be warm to very warm and humid, although trees will tolerate a light freeze. When purchasing, be sure container-grown plants are not potbound. Propagation is by grafting a chosen variety onto *A. squamosa* or *A. cherimola*. Trees are best planted out at the beginning of the growing season while still dormant. Do not fertilize immediately, as the roots are tender. Do irrigate regularly to establish, and stake. Mulch the root zone, but keep mulch away from the trunk to avoid collar rot, signaled by a sappy secretion around the trunk's base. Continue to irrigate during droughts, and maintain good soil moisture while trees are flowering. Once plants are established, broadcast a 6-10-16 fertilizer in spring, summer, and fall. Mealybugs and scale are sometimes a problem.

SELECTIONS Good varieties include **'Page', 'Bradley', 'Island Beauty', 'African Beauty', 'Geffner', 'Cherimata',** and **'Finny'**.

ANTHURIUM *Araceae*

Anthuriums are terrestrial or epiphytic aroids native to tropical America, widely grown for their ornamental foliage and their colorful "flowers," which are typical of the Arum family: the spadix, a fleshy spike with flowers embedded in it, is surrounded by a protective spathe, a brightly colored leafy bract. The three main hot

JOSEPH PAXTON'S GLASSHOUSES

When John Gibson brought a specimen of *Amerherstia nobilis* from India to his employer the sixth Duke of Devonshire in England, he was able to protect it well. Also in the duke's employ, as head gardener, was Joseph Paxton, destined to become the most famous glasshouse designer, such structures being essential for the survival of tropical plants. His Great Conservatory at Chatsworth (1836-40), the largest glass-covered area in the world, was wide enough for Queen Victoria to ride through in her carriage. Paxton also built a smaller glasshouse to protect the *Victoria regia* water lily (later renamed the *Victoria amazonia*); he was the first to cultivate this plant, successfully growing it in 1849. Paxton was knighted for his creations in glass.

AROIDS

Aroids are characterized by having a spadix, a fleshy spike with very small and simple flowers embedded in it, surrounded by a protective spathe, a brightly colored and broad leafy bract. Many aroids have decorative, even dramatic, leaves and very colorful spathes in shades of red, pink, white, green, or purple and are popular as indoor plants in cooler climates. Widely grown aroids include philodendron, aglaonema, alocasia (elephant's ear), anthurium, caladium, epipremum (pothos), and dieffenbachia. Growth habits include ground covers and climbers; bird's nest anthurium will grow on trees and rocks, trapping moisture and nutrients in its thick mass of roots.

groups of anthuriums are bird's-nest types, ornamental- foliage types, and colorful flower types. The bird's-nest anthuriums have large, broad leaves with short leaf stems arranged on a stout, erect stem to form a rosette, or "bird's nest." Many of these anthuriums are 3 or more feet across; the leaves of some species emerge in shades of red or burgundy, and the leaf margins are sometimes ruffled. Bird's-nest anthuriums often grow on trees or rocks; the leaf arrangement traps and funnels debris and rainwater to the dense mass of roots, providing a continuous source of nutrition and moisture. The large, dramatic leaves can provide a wonderful textural contrast with finer-leaved plants such as ferns; a dell of bird's-nest anthuriums is a lovely sight. The ornamental-foliage and flower anthuriums are small to medium-sized plants (1-3 feet tall). Their foliage often is heart-shaped, with long stems. Some are interestingly quilted or colored. These anthuriums are fine accent plants grown among other species, and those with dramatic foliage make excellent specimen plants. Some make attractive borders or even groundcovers, and many are grown as houseplants in cooler climates. The colorful flowering types can brighten a gloomy corner in a shaded garden.

CULTURE Grow ornamental-foliage and flower types in light to deep shade, and provide some shade from at least the hottest sun for bird's-nest anthuriums. Soil should be light, open, and well drained and, for ornamental-foliage and flower types, kept moist. The best climate is warm, with high humidity. Purchase bird's-nest types with clean, medium to dark green foliage and ornamental-foliage and flower types with good color and rigid stems and leaf bases. Propagate from seed in a moist environment or divide mature ornamental types. When planting out a young bird's-nest anthurium, provide a moisture-retentive material for the root zone so new roots establish readily. Do not plant ornamental-foliage and flower types out too deeply, and provide some short support. Maintain a moist but not sodden environment and soil. Regular application of liquid fertilizer monthly or semi-monthly will produce large, beautiful plants. Maintain a heavy layer of non-compacting mulch. Pruning consists of removing spent flowers and dead leaves. Snails and slugs can be destructive; hand-pick or bait. Spider mites can be a nuisance in low-humidity conditions; wash leaves regularly to control. In poor drainage, fungus diseases can be serious.

OUTSIDE THE TROPICS Most anthuriums are easy to grow as houseplants if they are provided with low light and high humidity. Use coarse, fast-draining soil.

SELECTIONS Bird's-nest anthuriums: ***A. superbum, A. salviniae,*** and ***A. schlectendalii*** are large and available. ***A. guyanense*** is a more modest size (2-3 ft.) with dark green foliage that emerges as deep burgundy red.

Ornamental-foliage and flower anthuriums: ***A. andreanum,*** flamingo flower, has multitudes of cultivated varieties raised for cut flowers in a range of colors. ***A. scherzeranum,*** the small flamingo flower, offers brilliant orange or red flowers; it will flower in the home if watered carefully and provided with adequate humidity. ***A. lilacina*** hybrids such as **'Lady Jane'** bear pink to purple flowers on small plants; useful as a border. ***A. ornatum*** and ***A. chrystallinum*** have beautiful, subtly colored foliage. ***A. veitchii*** features dramatic, 3-inch-long, quilted leaves.

ANTIGONON CORAL VINE *Polygonaceae*

Antigonon comprises 2-3 species of vigorous, tendril-bearing vines that produce showy racemes of flowers over a long season in colors ranging from white through hot pink to reds. Leaves are medium green and usually heart-shaped; the tubers are said to be edible. These colorful vines are very useful as a decorative screen or wall cover; choose the flower hue with the background color in mind. This native of Mexico and Central America has become naturalized in some waste places in Florida, growing rankly.

OUTSIDE THE TROPICS Antigonon thrives in Zone 8, and in Zone 7 in a protected area. It can be planted in containers and brought into a sunny greenhouse or patio during cold periods.

CULTURE Grow in full sun in warm, humid conditions; plants will tolerate occasional light frost. Infertile soil suits this vine well, but good drainage is necessary. Buy flowering-size plants to be certain what color blooms you will have. Propagate by seed or cuttings. Plant out from containers at any season, and provide support for the vines. Water to establish, and irrigate during the warm months. A balanced fertilizer is beneficial during the growing season, but avoid high-nitrogen fertilizer. Prune hard in the late winter to remove dead wood and spent flowers and to control the vine's growth. Vines are not particularly prone to pests or disease. Fungus leaf spotting sometimes occurs when the foliage is too dense and air circulation is poor; some pruning to open up the vine will help. It is quite drought-tolerant (it may die back during dry seasons, but will grow back quickly) and recommended for warm areas of the Southwest.

SELECTIONS *A. leptopus* grows to 40 feet and produces clouds of flowers through much of the year. *A. guatemalense* is similar, with larger, thicker, and more hairy leaves.

APHELANDRA APHELANDRA *Acanthaceae*

This tropical American genus of evergreen shrubs and subshrubs grows to a height of 3-15 feet. They are grown for their showy flower spikes and bracts of red, orange, yellow, or white, and for their handsome variegated leaves. These valuable, tolerant landscape plants produce abundant flowers throughout the year and often most abundantly in fall and winter.

CULTURE Aphelandra does best in light shade to full sun and in tropical and subtropical landscapes with temperatures of 65-85° F. It grows well in soils ranging from drier, organic types to those with ample moisture. Purchase actively growing, strong-rooted plants. Propagate from seed and from heel cuttings of half-ripe wood of nonflowering shoots. Set out during the wet season, spacing about half the diameter of mature plants. Apply granular fertilizer at planting time and as needed to maintain active, healthy growth while plants are young; you can reduce fertilizing once plants are mature and established. Although mature plants can tolerate some dryness, you should keep young plants moist. Mulch is beneficial. Prune to about half the length of branches after flowering to promote healthy new growth; this will also keep plants relatively free from pests and diseases.

OUTSIDE THE TROPICS *Aphelandra squarrosa,* zebra plant, is often offered as a houseplant, but it is difficult to grow indoors because it needs hight humidity.

SELECTIONS *A. aurantiaca* **var.** *roezlii* is low-growing (to 12 inches); it has 8-inch leaves of an unusual metallic blue color with silvery veins, flower spikes and bracts and tubular flowers of a brilliant orange-scarlet. It does best in moist to wet conditions and in temperatures from 50-85° F; space 8-10 inches apart. A very

ACANTHS

The family Acanthaceae consists of 250 genera and over 2,500 species, most of which are herbaceous, some woody shrubs, and a few trees; their nativity is spread through every continent except Antarctica. The family is characterized by color flower bracts, which is among the reasons so many acanths are popular garden plants; but there the similarity ends, for size, season, and cultural requirements differ greatly within this family; actually, taxonomists have a great deal of trouble with this family. Among popular acanths: Aphelandra. barleria, hemigraphis, justicia, megaskepasma, pachystachys, thunbergia, and ruellia.

The term "not fit to eat" (when applied to things non-poisonous) is indefensible except as a personal opinion of the speaker. For there are no scientific standards in the realm of the palate; in fact, it has no nomenclature comparable to that of the realms of sound or color. When we are newborn babes, the taste buds of our tongues give us the first glimmer of consciousness, and all our lives remain one of our most intimate contacts with the outside world; yet we cannot describe in accurate terms the flavor of a tomato or an apple or any other delicacy further than to say that it is sweet, bitter, spicy, or salty, and continue to ring the changes on these words.

David Fairchild,
The World Outside My Door,
1957.

attractive plant for the forest-type landscape and for specimen plantings.
A. sinclairiana is a shrub that grows to about 15 feet tall with leaves to 13 inches long; its terminal flower clusters feature shiny mauve flowers and magenta bracts; space 4-6 feet apart.

ARDISIA CRENATA CORALBERRY *Mysinaceae*

Coralberries, native to tropical Southeast Asia, are part of a large genus of evergreen shrubs and trees with alternate, simple leathery leaves, clusters of fragrant white flowers, and very ornamenal, long-lasting red berries. It grows to about 3 feet tall and can be used as a hedge or an accent in a border, where it makes an excellent Christmas plant with its dark green foliage and bright red berries.
CULTURE Grow coralberries in fertile, moist, well-drained soil; they prefer light shade, particularly in hot climates, and are hardy in Zones 9-10. Before planting, amend soil with organic matter unless it is naturally rich. Water during dry spells and apply balanced fertilizer if needed. Propagate by seeds, cuttings, or air layering. Scale insects are sometimes a problem.
OUTSIDE THE TROPICS Ardisia is a choice houseplant that grows well in average light and evenly moist soil; repot only when roots fill the pot and fertilize regularly with liquid fertilizer. Some species, such *A. japonica,* are hardy as far north as Zone 7; most other species are hardy to Zone 9.
SELECTIONS A. japonica is a low-growing subshrub with deep green leaves, nodding white flowers, and small bright red fruits that persist into winter.

ARTOCARPUS HETEROPHYLLUS JACKFRUIT, JAKFRUIT *Moraceae*

This quick-growing evergreen tree, native to India and Malaysia, grows 25-60 feet tall, with dense and glossy, dark green, leathery foliage. The yellowish brown fruits that develop on the trunk and branches can grow amazingly large–heavier than 50 pounds is not rare–after 7-10 years. The fruit's tough outer rind is covered in short, hard, leathery spines. Inside are many olive-sized seeds, edible if cooked, embedded in rubbery fibers and surrounded by a sweet, crunchy aril that is a refreshing raw food. A close relative, *A. altilis,* breadfruit, is the famous plant that precipitated mutiny on the infamous *Bounty,* which was bringing slave food from the Pacific Ocean to the West Indies; the ship's crew set Captain Bligh adrift when water rations went to irrigate breadfruits at the expense of the sailors.
CULTURE Grow in full sun or with high canopy shade in warm to hot and humid conditions; mature trees will tolerate light frost. Deep, well-drained, slightly acid, and moist soil is ideal, but trees will tolerate a wide range of soil conditions. When purchasing, be sure container-grown plants are not too rootbound; a new plant should be full, with leaves in good condition. Can be propagated from seed, but named varieties are grafted. Plant out during the warm, wet months. Water well and shade while establishing, then irrigate during drought conditions. Apply a granular, slow-release 10-10-10 fertilizer three or four times a year; farm manure applied with mulch is also beneficial. Little pruning is needed except to remove dead wood. Maintain a good layer of mulch over the root zone to conserve moisture. Scale and mealybugs are sometimes a nuisance.
SELECTIONS Where a medium to large, densely foliated tree with a more or less upright habit is needed, jackfruit is useful. Plant away from walkways or parking

APHELANDRA AURANTIACA VAR. ROEZLII (APHELANDRA) Low-growing subshrub, to 12 inches tall; 8-inch metallic blue leaves with silvery veins; brilliant orange-scarlet flower spike of bracts and tubular flowers. Partial shade, moist to wet conditions, rich soil. Zone 10.

ARDISIA CRENATA (CORALBERRY) 3-foot tall evergreen shrub with glossy dark green leaves and bright red berries. Fertile, moist, well-drained soil; light shade, particularly in hot climates. Zones 9-10.

ARTOCARPUS ALTILIS (BREADFRUIT) Evergreen tree, 25-60 feet tall, with large, glossy dark green leathery foliage, yellow-brown fruits. Full sun or high-canopy shade, deep, well-drained, slightly acid soil is best but adapts to other soils; needs water during establishment, then only in drought. Zone 10, Zones 8-9 for established trees.

AVERRHOA CARAMBOLA (CARAMBOLA, STARFRUIT) Small to medium-sized low-branching trees, usually under 20 feet tall, with tiny pink flowers and abundant five-ribbed yellow fruit. Full sun, rich, slightly acidic soil, well-drained and moist but not wet. Zone 10.

Bauhinia variegata 'Candida' a rare
white form worth seeking.

areas, as the very large fruits can be damaging if they fall. **A. altilis,** breadfruit, is
more strictly tropical; it cannot tolerate any cold and needs deep, rich, and moist
soil. It is a large, handsome, spreading tree with dark green, shiny, and deeply
lobed leaves. Its hard, green fruits are 9 inches or more in diameter, soft and sweet
when ripe, and cooked as a vegetable.

AVERRHOA CARAMBOLA CARAMBOLA, STARFRUIT *Oxalidaceae*

Carambolas are small to medium, low-branching trees with a dense crown that
bears abundant crops of five-ribbed yellow fruits more than once a year; slices of
the fruits are star-shaped. Carambolas mature at a small size and begin fruit-bear-
ing when only 4-5 feet high. These natives of tropical Asia have only recently
become popular and available in the West. A fully fruited carambola is very
attractive, suitable as a small specimen tree or integrated into a large mixed bed
of shrubby and herbaceous plants. Prior to fruiting, the tiny pink flowers add
interest. Fruits are produced throughout the year, most heavily from spring
through fall.

CULTURE Carambolas require full sun. Soil should be slightly acidic, open and well-
drained, moist but not saturated. You can plant container-grown plants any time;
rainy season is best. Trees prefer warm, humid conditions (although they have tolerated brief hours into the 30° F range), and they need protection from cold, dry
winds. During drought conditions, water regularly, and apply a citrus fertilizer
two to four times a year. Mulch regularly to control weeds; prune only to shape.
Fruits should be removed as they ripen and begin to fall. If you thin fruits, those
that remain will grow larger. Rust mites can discolor fruits.

SELECTIONS Varieties produce fruits ranging from sour to delicious; sampling fruit
before choosing a tree is best. **'Arkin'** is grown commercially for its large, golden
yellow fruits that are pleasingly acid/sweet. **'Star King'** is very similar, perhaps a
more prolific bearer. **'Fuang Tung'** produces nonacidic, pale yellow to nearly white
fruit, rated by some as superior and sweet and by others as insipid.

BARLERIA *Acanthaceae*

Barleria is a handsome evergreen shrub, growing to about 5 feet high, with showy
blue, pink, white, or red flowers borne in terminal clusters. These undemanding,
easily grown plants make quick, colorful dividing hedges and fine specimen plants
in shrubberies and large rock gardens, set against boulders of appropriate size.
They are native to the Old World tropics and subtropics.

CULTURE Grow in full sun to light shade; excessive shade results in spindly, poorly
flowering plants. Barleria tolerates soils ranging from drier to amply moist, and it
grows well in temperatures from 65-85° F in the tropics and subtropics. When
purchasing, avoid plants with scale insects in the leaf axils. Easily propagated from
seed and from softwood or semihardwood cuttings. Plants are best set out during
the wet season; set about 2 feet apart. Water well to establish. Fertilize plants
when young or when nutrient deficiencies are apparent. Pinch back tips from
time to time when out of flower to make plants bushy; they also respond well to
being cut back about half the branch length after flowering. With pruning,
plants will flower several times a year and will be relatively pest-free. Scale insects
may be a problem; spray with a soft soap solution.

OUTSIDE THE TROPICS Barleria is a popular houseplant that will flower profusely in a sunny site and benefits from a summer outdoors in a pot or in the ground. It is hardy in Zone 8b–even during harsh winters in the Gulf Coast area–if planted in filtered light. In Houston, it grows 6-8 feet tall, self-seeds abundantly and blooms in late fall.

SELECTIONS *B. cristata* is 4 feet tall, evergreeen, with dark or pale blue flowers; there are also pink and white forms. It makes an excellent hedge or specimen. *B. repens* is a vigorous, sprawling shrub to 2 feet tall with conspicuous green bracts and attractive red flowers; it needs to be kept under control, but makes a splendid, colorful groundcover.

BAUHINIA ORCHID TREE *Fabaceae*

Several members of this genus are useful and available. The Hong Kong orchid tree (*B.* x *blakeana* 'Hong Kong') is a popular street tree in Hawaii and Florida, covered with large orchidlike blossoms for several months; it grows up to 40 feet tall. Other species have vining or shrubby habits; the shrubby types can be espaliered, and vining varieties work well against houses or trellises.

CULTURE Bauhinia will survive in any ordinary garden soil and needs full sun. Fertilize annually if soil is poor. Prune lightly to retain size and shape. Propagate by seeds, layering, and grafting; cuttings rarely succeed. No serious insect pests or diseases.

SELECTIONS *B.* x *blakeana* 'Hong Kong', the Hong Kong orchid tree, grows 20-40 feet and has fragrant purple or pink blossoms, up to 5 inches in diameter, over a four-month period.

B. tomentosa is a shrub with yellow leaves and bell-shaped flowers. It grows up to

Hong Kong orchid tree is available in both shrub (above) and tree (below) forms.

BARLERIA CRISTATA (BARLERIA) Evergreen shrub, to 4 feet tall, with dark or pale blue flowers. Full sun to light shade (too much shade brings poor results); dry to moist soils. Zones 9-10.

BAUHINIA PURPUREA (BUTTERFLY TREE, ORCHID TREE) Small partially deciduous tree, to 20 feet tall, with fragrant 4- to 5-inch pink or purple orchidlike flowers; flowers earlier than most species. Full sun, any ordinary soil (fertilize annually if soil is poor). Zones 9-10, Zone 8 with protection.

BEAUCARNEA RECURVATA (BOTTLE PONYTAIL) Tree to 30 feet tall with thin trunk, long ribbonlike leaves, swollen base. Full sun, well drained gravelly or sandy soil, warm to hot conditions. Zones 8-10, but will suffer damage from frost.

BEGONIA POPENOEI (BEGONIA) Rhizomatous plant with irregularly shaped bright green leaves tinged with red, and large, upright panicles of white flowers. Partial to deep shape, moist rich soil. Zones 8-10.

10 feet tall and can be used as a hedge.

B. corymbosa is a tendril-bearing vine that is covered with panicles of pink or purple flowers from spring through fall.

B. galphimii, nasturtium bauhinia, has a shrubby weeping habit and orange nasturtiumlike flowers all summer; recommended for the Gulf Coast.

BEAUCARNEA RECURVATA BOTTLE PONYTAIL, ELEPHANT FOOT TREE *Agavaceae*

These treelike natives of Mexico have tall, thin trunks arising from a swollen base that, oddly, has few roots; the round base looks very much like an elephant's foot. Leaves are long and ribbonlike and arch gracefully. Both common names are particularly apt. This is a sculpturally interesting plant that can grow into an effective large specimen. It is well suited for dryish, xeriscape landscaping, as the swollen trunk stores water.

CULTURE Grow in full sun in well-drained sandy or gravelly soil. Plants require warm to hot conditions; freezing temperatures will kill whole branches. Propagate by soaking seed for a day or two, then pressing into a sandy growing medium placed in a bright, warm location. Set plants out as the swollen base develops, just nestling the base into the soil. When buying plants, look for a firm, swollen base and erect rather than floppy branches, with healthy-looking foliage. Water to establish and thereafter only during extreme drought; this tree stores water in its trunk, so water it infrequently but deeply. Palm fertilizer with micronutrients is beneficial. Organic mulch is not desirable; gravel mulching, however, can be attractive and useful.

OUTSIDE THE TROPICS Grown indoors, ponytail palm does best in high light and warm temperatures, with the soil drying out between soakings; plants do well in low indoor temperatures only if watered very infrequently. Acclimate them to changes in temperature gradually.

BEGONIA *Begoniaceae*

Begonias are native to many tropical regions around the world, and numerous forms have been developed for use as bedding and houseplants in cooler regions, appreciated wherever they are grown for their handsome foliage and lovely flowers.

CULTURE Most begonias prefer at least some shade, dislike extremely dry conditions, and thrive in a loamy soil enriched with organic matter. Plants may be fibrous-rooted, rhizomatous, or tuberous-rooted. Propagate by stem or root cuttings or by division of new plants from tubers or rhizomes.

SELECTIONS Rhizomatous begonias produce large leaves and can be used as border plants in shaded gardens. **'Joe Haydon'** has dark maroon-black, star-shaped leaves with pink stalks and pink and white flowers. **'Beatrice Haddrell'** has dark green star-shaped leaves with lighter green midribs and stalks of small white flowers. They do fairly well in Hawaii, and are recommended in the Gulf Coast area as well. Rex begonias, which are rhizomatous, are best in the shade; they will usually rot in other locations.

B. foliosa is a shrublike plant with small leaves producing white flowers; it works well as a groundcover or in hanging baskets.

Cane begonias are often tough and need little care except period cutting back.

Bauhinia corymbosa.

Begonias and ferns both thrive in shade; begonias provide solid leaves and colorful flowers, ferns add lacy texture.

'Looking Glass' has beautiful silver leaves that can reach 5-6 feet in containers. Tuberous begonias rarely flourish outdoors in the tropics; they usually flower once and then decline or die. They are best suited to temperate regions, where they are used in hanging baskets.

Fibrous begonias, such as wax begonias, are best-suited to use as winter-flowering bedding plants in the tropics. ***B. semperflorens* 'Scarletta'** is the only begonia that flourishes in full sun on the Gulf Coast. It has green leaves with red margins and red flowers.

BIXA ANNATTO, LIPSTICK PLANT *Bixaceae*

This tree, up to 20 feet tall, is grown as an accent plant for its large, heart-shaped leaves that are sometimes tinged with red, its long-lasting clusters of pink or white 2-inch flowers, which bloom in late summer or fall, and its clusters of spiny red, reddish brown, or orangey seedpods; blooms are produced when the tree is only two years old. The aril surrounding the seeds in these pods is used as a food coloring and a dye; it has also been used in lipstick and as body paint by the indigenous peoples of its native Central America. The flowers and pods are attractive in fresh and dried arrangements.

CULTURE Grow in full sun; bixa adapts to any reasonably fertile soil. If you are growing bixa as a specimen plant, you may want to prune so it develops from a single main stem. Bixa is also suitable as a tall hedge, in which case you may allow it to develop from several ground-level stems. Plants will stand very hard pruning. Propagate by seeds or cuttings, both of which are easy.

BLIGHIA SAPIDA AKEE, SESO VEGETAL *Sapindaceae*

This native of tropical West Africa was introduced to the West Indies by African slaves. The scientific name honors Captain Bligh of *Bounty* fame. The trees are handsome, medium-sized, and evergreen, growing to 30 feet; with proper pruning, they can be used as shade trees. The ornamental red or yellow fruits are leathery and pear-shaped at maturity; they are produced in late winter and spring after four to five years and split open to reveal three shiny black seeds, partially enclosed by a cream-colored fleshy aril. Caution: Although the fruits are well-liked in the West Indies, they must be eaten with care, as underripe or overripe fruit can be toxic. The correct stage for eating is just after the fruit naturally splits open and the arils are still firm; it is the arils that are eaten, as all other membranes plus the seeds are toxic.

CULTURE Grow in full sun and moderately warm and humid conditions; trees are not particular about soil. Propagate from seed or from cuttings of ripe shoots. When purchasing, avoid plants that are potbound. Water to establish and during very dry periods. Apply a top dressing of a balanced fertilizer with micronutrients three or four times per year, and mulch the root zone. This tree has no notable pest problems.

BOMBAX CEIBA RED KAPOK, RED SILK COTTON TREE
Bombacaceae

Red kapok, native to India, Malaysia, and Australia, is very tall—up to 100 feet—and clothed in numerous spines along its trunk and branches. Although it drops its leaves when winter arrives, it then covers itself in waxy red flowers, fol-

BIXA ORELLANA (ANNATTO, LIPSTICK PLANT) Small tree, to 20 feet, with large, heart-shaped leaves, long-lasting clusters of pink or white flowers, and spiny seed pods. Full sun, moist, rich soil. Zone 10.

BLIGHIA SAPIDA (AKEE) Medium-sized evergreen trees to 30 feet tall with pear-shaped leathery yellow or red fruit, glossy green leaves. Full sun, any rich, moist soil. Zone 10.

BOMBAX CEIBA (RED KAPOK) Large deciduous tree, up to 100 feet tall, with waxy red flowers and woody seed pods filled with woolly seeds. Full sun, moist rich soil. Zone 10.

BOUGAINVILLEA GLABRA 'PURPLE QUEEN' (PAPER FLOWER) Vigorous woody vine with large, papery bracts surrounding small white flowers. Full sun, moderately fertile moist but not wet soil; bougainvillea flowers best in dry weather. Zones 8-10.

lowed by seedpods in April and May. Kapoklike fibers are produced in the seeds.
CULTURE Grow red kapok in well drained soil and full sun. The soil should be kept evenly moist when the tree is young. When the tree is mature, it is tough and tolerates dry conditions, though it prefers moisture. It is easily propagated by seeds.

BOUGAINVILLEA PAPER FLOWER *Nyctaginaceae*

Bougainvillea is a showy, flowering vine (and can be trained to tree form), woody and usually spiny, highly evocative of the tropics. The nonfragrant, visible "flowers" produced through the year (particularly abundantly during dry periods) in large clusters at and toward the ends of branches are really colorful, persistent papery bracts surrounding small, inconspicuous true flowers. The color range, particularly of the abundant hybrids, runs from white to deep magenta to orange and red. In more temperate climates, the visual effect is often that of a climbing rose. Bougainvillea has many uses in the landscape: as a luxuriant cascading vine clothing a wall or fence or screening a patio, trained as an eye-catching specimen shrub or tree, or grown as a showy container plant or in other situations where the roots must be confined. It is native to South America, mostly Brazil.
CULTURE Grow in full sun, in warm conditions with moderate to high humidity. Soil should be moderately fertile and not stay overmoist. Some species and their hybrids need an occasional dry spell to do well. When purchasing plants, look for dark green, not mottled, foliage and thrifty growth that is not too soft or weak. Propagate from softwood cuttings in late winter or hardwood cuttings in summer. Plant out from containers at any time; however, plants will establish faster if set out at the beginning of a warm, wet period. Place near a strong support, and avoid planting near automatic irrigation, as bougainvillea prefers dry conditions and is a good xeriscape plant. Even so, water to establish, and irrigate later if plants show signs of drought stress. Apply a granular slow-release fertilizer in early spring and midsummer; avoid high-nitrogen fertilizers which encourage lush growth but few flowers. Light mulching with gravel helps control weeds. Deadhead when flowers are spent, and control size and shape by cutting back in mid- or late summer, removing water sprouts. Remove errant branches at any time. Scale, mealybugs, and aphids can be a problem; hosing will remove light infestations. Caterpillars occasionally need to be controlled. Heavy infestations of tent caterpillars may need pruning to remove.
OUTSIDE THE TROPICS Bougainvilleas do well in cooler climates—to Zone 9 or Zone 8 in a protected spot—and as houseplants as long as they have strong light. Choose compact varieties for indoor growing, and allow soil to dry out between waterings for best bloom.
SELECTIONS *B. glabra* flowers continuously and can be a fairly compact grower; purple to white; ***B. g.* 'Variegata'** has variegated leaves and ***B. g.* 'Carmencita'** has double lavender-mauve flowers. ***B. spectabilis*** flowers more heavily after a dry period; purple, pink, white. ***B. peruviana*** flowers in dry weather; magenta, pink, rose. ***B. x buttiana*** comes in a wide range of colorful hybrids; one industry standard is bright red ***B.* 'Barbara Karst'**. **'Fascell Purple'** is large, deep red-purple. **'Jamaican White'** is white with a flush of pink. **'Blushing Beauty'** has variegated foliage, light blush pink bracts. **'Ms. Helen Johnson'** is a dwarf; fuchsia red. **'Alice'** is very large, with white bracts that stand up well to wet weather. **'O-La-La'** is compact and low; bluish pur-

ple to red. **'Rosenka'** is compact; dusty orange fading to dusty rose. **'Braziliensis'** is compact; medium purple. **'Elizabeth Angus'** is bright; deep purple with extended flowering. **'Silhouette'** has large, lavender bracts that hold up well in wet weather. **'Mary Palmer'** has both white and magenta flowers on the same plant.

BREYNIA DISTICHA SNOW BUSH *Euphorbiaceae*

Named for John Breyne, an early nineteenth-century German botanist, breynia is grown for its striking, mottled pink, green, and white foliage and for its easy nature. It will grow to 8 feet tall, but can also be sheared back to act as a groundcover. Breynia can be used as groundcover under tall trees, as a hedge, or as a backdrop to other plants.

CULTURE Breynia will thrive in sun or light shade in any moderately rich garden soil. Moderate additions of fertilizer and water speed growth. Prune to desired shape at the beginning of the season; no other care is necessary. Stem and root cuttings root easily. In greenhouses, breynia is prone to red spider mite; outdoors it is usually free from insects. It sometimes produces hard-to-eradicate suckers, so don't plant it close to special or delicate plants.

OUTSIDE THE TROPICS Fast-growing breynia works well as a bedding plant in climates where it does not overwinter. It grows to a 3-foot-tall bush in a single season. Take cuttings at the end of the season to use the following year (4- to 6-inch slips of semihardwood; treat with rooting hormone). Breynia does not adapt well as a houseplant, but does well in humid greenhouses. Bury pots up to their rims.

SELECTIONS **'Roseopicta'** has the best coloration. **'Thimma'** has variegated yellow and green leaves; Keith Woolliams finds it even more striking than 'Roseopicta'.

The bougainvillaea was a dark tangle against the sky, and the pine tree black beyond the roof. All the arches were lit, a lantern in each one; a man came around and lit small candles and set them in niches. . . . We had supper there, looking out against the sky and the bougainvillaea against it . . . . It was so perfect, so magical, so unreal–those small niches lighted, the lanterned arches, the cloudy moon half hid behind the bougainvillaea.

ANNE MORROW LINDBERGH,
BRING ME A UNICORN, 1972

BREYNIA DISTICHA 'ROSEOPICTA' (SNOW BUSH) Shrub to 8 feet tall with small green leaves attractively mottled with red, pink, and white. Full sun or light shade, moderately rich moist soil. Zones 9-10.

BROWNEA COCCINEA (SCARLET FLAME BEAN) Compact tree, to 20 feet tall, with branches leaves, and scarlet flowers. Partial sun to full shade, deep, fertile soil that is not allowed to dry out. Zone 10.

BRUGMANSIA VERSICOLOR (ANGELS' TRUMPET) Graceful tree, to 15 feet tall with large, pendulous flowers to 20 inches long. Full sun is best; rich, moist but not waterlogged soil. Zones 8-10.

BRUNFELSIA AUSTRALIS (YESTERDAY-TODAY-TOMORROW) Small to medium-sized shrub with summer flowers that turn from blue-purple to light purple to white. Full sun, slightly acid, rich moist but not wet soil. Zone 10.

BROWNEA ROSE OF VENEZUELA *Fabaceae*

Brownea is a spectacular group of low, spreading trees native to tropical America, for the woodland/forest setting. Almost all species produce showy orange-red to red flowers in large, ball-like clusters 6 inches or more across along the branches and trunk in spring and early summer. The long, narrow leaves are pendulous when young, almost transparent or colored pink or reddish bronze, before gradually stiffening and changing color to a normal green. This transformation is a major attraction of brownea in the garden. At least some species of *Brownea* are pollinated by birds; red flowers are especially attractive to hummingbirds.

CULTURE Grow in warm, humid conditions in partial shade to full sun (in Hawaii, it needs protection from afternoon sun), in fertile, deep soil that is always moist; slightly acid soil is best for most species. Tropical forest conditions of high humidity with day temperatures in the upper 70° F to 80° F and nights in the low to mid-60° F are especially good. Propagate from seed, which germinates rapidly when fresh, or from air layering. When purchasing plants, look for a strong main stem, signs of a tendency to branch freely, and active growth. Plant at the beginning of the rainy season, watering in well and later keeping evenly moist. Give trees plenty of room, as they can spread to be quite wide. Support for the low branches helps to provide visual access to the blooms, which are usually produced on the undersides of the branches. Acid fertilizer is beneficial, as are nutritional sprays if your soil is alkaline. Prune trees only to train the basic skeleton. Regular mulching, particularly in thin soil, helps to retain moisture and the slightly acidic root environment. Brownea is not particularly prone to insect or disease problems.

SELECTIONS *B. capitella* bears 11-inch clusters of 20 or more red-orange flowers. *B. grandiceps*, rose of Venezuela, also produces large, showy clusters of flowers. *B. coccinea,* scarlet flame bean, has spreading, pendant branches and produces large flowers. *B. ariza* is the most vigorous species but has smaller, 6-inch flower clusters. In Hawaii, the plant produces huge heads of 50 or more orange-red flowers.

BRUGMANSIA ANGELS' TRUMPET *Solanaceae*

This soft-wooded shrub or small tree offers frequent, spectacular displays of large, hanging, delicate pastel-colored trumpets that become intoxicatingly fragrant at night. An angels' trumpet tree can be a traffic-stopper used as a specimen in a small garden. These natives of tropical America can also form a large, informal hedge, and they are a very suitable addition to a hummingbird or butterfly garden or wherever evening fragrance would be appreciated. These plants contain toxic compounds used in some tropical Native American religious practices to induce hallucinations; flowers, fruits, and foliage are all poisonous. Brugmansia flowers throughout the year, particularly when evenings are cool.

CULTURE Full sun is best, but light shade is acceptable. Angels' trumpets need organically rich soil, moist but well drained. Waterlogging will cause immediate wilting; if this happens, prune back hard. Growing conditions can range from temperate to warm and humid. Angels' trumpets will not tolerate frost, but they enjoy cool weather, especially at night. When buying, choose plants with strong growth and dark green foliage; pale, misshapen leaves with small holes may indicate the presence of a virus. Propagation from semihardwood cuttings is very reliable; misting and rooting hormone help. Layering of low branches also works

Breynia disticha 'Roseopicta' will grow to 8 feet tall, but takes shearing well.

well. Set out when plants are about 3 feet tall, with a slow-release fertilizer in the planting hole. Water well to establish; thereafter, irrigate only if the plant seems to be in drought stress. Regular light applications of a flowering-shrub fertilizer will keep plants looking vigorous, and a permanent layer of organic mulch is beneficial and discourages nematodes. Spider mites are occasionally a problem; they can be controlled by moving the plant to a cooler, shadier location. If a plant contracts a virus, it is best to discard it.

OUTSIDE THE TROPICS Brugmansia is root hardy in Zone 8b, and is often used on the Gulf Coast. A closely related plant, *Datura metel,* is used as an annual throughout the temperate region and allowed to die back. It grows to a height of about 2 feet, with very large—up to a foot long—trumpetlike flowers. They can be allowed to die back or can be brought indoors for the winter.

SELECTIONS *B. arborea* has white flowers; *B. aurea*, golden yellow to orange-yellow; *B. x insignis* and *B. x candida*, pastel pink, peachy, and orange. *B. suaveolens* has white flowers; *B. suaveolens* **'Plena',** double white. All grow to about 20 feet tall.

BRUNFELSIA YESTERDAY-TODAY-TOMORROW, LADY OF THE NIGHT *Solanaceae*

Brunfelsia, native to tropical America, comprise about 40 species of attractive, fragrant shrubs of modest to moderate size, seasonally covered by successions of showy flowers. The name yesterday-today-tomorrow applies to the most intriguing of the species, whose flowers open blue-purple, fade to a light purple the next day, and become almost white the third day. Brunfelsias, which will flower in winter, serve well in the landscape as showy specimen shrubs or as a large hedge and are best placed so their clove scent can be appreciated, particularly at night.

CULTURE Brunfelsias need full sun for at least five hours daily. They prefer slightly acid, organically rich, moist soil, but they do not like wet feet; some thrive in poorer, sandy soils. Warm, humid conditions suit them best; while various species have a wide range of temperature tolerance, they will defoliate if exposed to cold. Propagate from seeds or from semihardwood cuttings using rooting hormone. Plant when well rooted, in permanent location, allowing room for the plant to grow as wide as it will be tall. Water during drought; do not allow plants to dry out severely. Feed with a balanced fertilizer every third month, plus chelated iron. Mulch regularly to maintain soil moisture. Two annual heavy prunings, preferably in May and late July, will encourage bushy growth and more prolific flowering, since blooms occur in winter on the previous season's growth. Scale insects are occasionally a problem.

OUTSIDE THE TROPICS Brunfelsia does well as a houseplant, flowering abundantly over most of the year, if it is given bright light in winter and some shade in summer, generous water from spring to fall (less in winter), and a place where it will not suffer from sudden shifts in temperature. *B. calycina* is most often used for this purpose.

SELECTIONS *B. americana*, lady of the night, has fragrant 3-inch-long white flowers fading to cream-yellow; because the blooms have an especially strong, sweet smell at night, specimens are often planted near house windows; can grow to about 8 feet tall. *B. australis* features a succession of purple, blue, then white flowers. *B. pauciflora* is similar; **'Macrantha'** has very large flowers.

BULNESIA ARBOREA VERAWOOD *Zygophyllaceae*

This is a charming, pleasantly shaped tree with dark green, compound foliage that effectively sets off the showy, bright yellow flowers produced in spring, summer, and fall. David Fairchild introduced the drought-resistant *B. arborea* to south Florida from its native Venezuela. Trees grow to 25-30 feet. *B. arborea* is used for crossties and fence posts; *B. retama* is the source of retamo wax, used in shoe polish; a tree species is the source of resinous heartwood used for incense in churches.

CULTURE Grow in full sun in a warm climate; temperatures below 40° F may cause defoliation. Plants are not particular about soil but do need good drainage. Purchase a plant with a straight trunk, grown in full sun if possible, and not potbound; if the roots have become coiled around themselves in the pot, the root system will always be weak, and the tree will be easily blown over. Propagate from seed when the winged pods are turning brown; germination takes about a month. Once established in the landscape, additional watering is not needed; this is a good xeriscape plant. Apply a balanced fertilizer twice yearly. Mulch is beneficial, but do not bury the trunk.

SELECTION *B. arborea* is little known but very worthwhile in the landscape. The tree is gradually becoming more available in the nursery trade.

BURSERA SIMARUBA GUMBO LIMBO TREE *Burseraceae*

The gumbo limbo tree has beautiful, smooth reddish bark that peels in a very ornamental way. This softwood, native to south Florida, Central America, and the West Indies, grows to 50 feet. The name is said to derive from the tree's gummy resin; the sap was once used to make glue. Gumbo limbos can be useful as solitary landscape specimens, but they are far more interesting in a copse, planted where the often massive trunks can be seen to best advantage. The clusters of red fruit are attractive to parrots and parakeets.

CULTURE Gumbo limbos are adaptable to a variety of soil conditions. Grow in full sun or partial shade in a warm, humid climate. This is one of the famous fencepost trees of the tropics; whole limbs (the larger the better) may be cut and planted (set firmly into the soil) and, if watered regularly, will root. This is best done at the beginning of the rainy season. Once established, extra water is not needed; trees are drought-tolerant. No special fertilizing is required. Prune only to establish a good form. Light mulching away from the trunk is considered beneficial but doesn't seem essential. Trees sometimes become leafless for a brief period until new growth appears.

CAESALPINIA PRIDE OF BARBADOS, DIVI-DIVI, LIVING FENCE
Fabaceae

This is a large genus of flowering shrubs and small trees native to tropical and subtropical America, many showy and evergreen. *C. pulcherrima,* pride of Barbados, earned its name of living fence from its use as a thorny barrier hedge. It is also known as flowering fence because it can flower virtually all year. Other *Caesalpinia* species make fine specimens, even tub plants, in a small garden.

CULTURE Grow in warm, humid conditions in full sun; almost any soil is fine. Purchase plants with healthy, dark green foliage, or propagate from seed. Water plants well to establish; mature plants are salt- and drought-tolerant. Caesalpinias

A garden full of sweet odors is a garden full of charm not to be implanted by mere skill in horticulture or power or purse, and which is beyond explaining. It is born of sensitive and very personal preferences yet its appear is almost universal. Fragrance speaks to many to whom colour and form say little, and it "can bring as irresistibly as music emotions of all sorts to the mind." Besides the plants visible to the eye there will be in such a garden other comely growths, plain to that "other sense," such as "faith, romance, the lore of old unhurried times." These are infinitely well worth cultivating among the rest. They are an added joy in happy times and gently remedial when life seems warped and tired.

Louise Beebe Wilder
The Fragrant Garden, 1932

are not heavy feeders, but organic mulch around the roots is beneficial. *C. pulcher-rima* may be grown as a shrub or a tree; drastic pruning after flowering encourages more prolific blooming, which occurs on the new growth. Other species do not require regular pruning. Boring weevils will occasionally infest a growing tip, destroying the flower bud.

OUTSIDE THE TROPICS Most caesalpinias are hardy to Zone 8 and are important landscape plants throughout the Southwest. **C. gillesii,** bird of paradise bush, is particularly drought-tolerant and is particularly recommended for the Gulf Coast.

SELECTIONS **C. pulcherrima** has a showy abundance of orange, pink, yellow, or red flowers in large clusters at the tips of new growth; shrub grows to 10-12 feet. **C. granadilla,** bridal veil tree, is medium-sized, with a somewhat spreading crown and beautiful, exfoliating bark. **C. mexicana** is a shapely small tree with yellow flowers through much of the year. **C. coriaria**, divi-divi, is a small, shrubby tree of the coastal areas of tropical, low-rainfall islands; as the plants seem naturally inclined to grow strongly horizontal branches, this species is a favorite of bonsai enthusiasts.

CALATHEA *Marantaceae*

The name *Calathea* was given to this genus in reference to the basket-shaped flowers that appear in some species; the word *kalathos* means basket in Greek. However, most species are usually grown not for their flowers, but for their exquisitely patterned foliage, often including blues, red, greens, purples, white, and silver; the markings on calathea leaves are among the most intricate and ornamental of any in the plant kingdom. These herbaceous plants vary from 6-inch groundcovers to 12-foot specimens. The plants have economic uses as well. Columbus reported finding crops of topee tambou (*C. alluia*) grown for its edible tuber on his first landing in the Caribbean islands; leaves of *C. discolor* are woven into baskets and those of *C. lutea* are used for thatching cottages.

CULTURE Most species are native to the forest floor; they do best in semi-shade and in highly organic, well drained, loose soil. Temperatures should be warm and humidity high; temperatures over 50° F may result in browning of leaves. Buy pest-free plants and place them closely; they are most attractive when pressed together. It is important that the soil be kept constantly moist, but not wet; daily watering is usually necessary. Very little fertilizer is necessary and the plant is easily damaged by the fertilizer; in poor soil a slow-release fertilizer like Osmacote can be used. Mulching helps keep soil moist. After each growing season, cut foliage back. Calatheas are susceptible to mealybugs; control with Malathion. Propagate by seeds, tissue culture, or replanting suckers.

OUTSIDE THE TROPICS Calatheas are popular houseplants; they thrive in low light if high humidity is present. Among the best species for indoor culture are *C. albertii* (which has gray-green leaves feathered in olive green) and *C. roseo-picta* (which has large round dark green leaves with red midribs and undersides).

SELECTIONS Excellent choices for groundcover are **C. zebrina** var. **humilior,** with velvet green leaves, paler green veins and midribs and purple undersides and **C. pseudoveitchiana. C. crotalifera** and **C. libbyana** are recommeneded as specimens. **C. burlemarxii** '**Blue Ice**' (and a new cultivar, '**Green Ice**') are grown for their exotic, gingerlike flowers.

Below: A striking new calathea cultivar under testing at Lyon Arboretum. *Bottom: Calathea insignis,* rattlesnake plant, displays the coloration that is characteristic of this species.

BULNESIA ARBOREA (VERAWOOD) Graceful tree with dark green compound foliage and showy bright yellow flowers from spring to fall. Full sun, any soil with good drainage, tolerates dry conditions. Zones 9-10.

BURSERA SIMARUBA (GUMBO LIMBO TREE) Softwood deciduous tree to 50 feet tall with attractive reddish peeling bark and clusters of red fruit. Full sun to partial shade, adapts to many soil types. Zones 9-10.

CAESALPINIA PULCHERRIMA (PRIDE OF BARBADOS) Flowering shrub, 10-12 feet tall, covered with very showy pink, yellow, and red flowers through much of the year. Full sun, any soil (adapts to dry conditions). Zones 8-10.

CALATHEA MAKOYANA (PEACOCK PLANT) Tuberous foliage plant, to 20 inches tall, with long narrow to broad leaves mottled in a variety of colors. Partial shade, deep loamy soil, humidity and good drainage. Zone 10 with protection.

CALATHEA BURLE-MARXII 'ICE-BLUE' (ICE BLUE CALATHEA)
Herbaceous evergreen plant to 5 feet tall with large bright
green leaves and waxy ice blue inflorescences consisting of
large ice blue bracts surrounding white or lavender flowers.
Moist soil, shady, protected location. Zone 10 with protection.

CALLIANDRA INAEQUILATERA (POWDER PUFF) Shrub or small tree
to 10 feet tall with 3- to 4-inch flowerheads on leafy
branches. Full sun or light shade, any well-drained soil;
best in fertile moist soil but adapts to poor, dry soil.
Zones 8-10.

CALLISTEMON RIGIDUS (STIFF BOTTLEBRUSH) Erect, spring-
blooming shrub or small tree (to 20 feet tall and wide) with
spikes of bright red flowers. Full sun, any soil, dry conditions best. Zones 8-10.

CARICA PAPAYA (PAPAYA) Small, fast-growing tree to 15 feet,
deeply lobed leaves, abundant fruit. Full sun, rich, moist
soil. Short-lived. Zone 10.

CALLIANDRA POWDER PUFF *Fabaceae*

Calliandra comprises about 200 species of shrubs to small trees with pinnate leaves composed of small leaflets. Several species are grown in the landscape for their distinctive bottlebrush or powder-puff-type flowers—a mass of long, colorful stamens with no petals, borne freely in loose clusters during the warm months, typically pink, red, or white and followed by thick-edged seedpods. Calliandras are frequently tough, pioneer species that will tolerate extremes of moisture and temperature; several species are used for firewood and as cover crops to return nitrogen to the soil. Native to the United States, Mexico to South America, Madagascar, and India.

CULTURE Calliandras are sun lovers, though several species do well in light shade. Soil can be poor and stony or rich and organic; good drainage is more important than high fertility. Some species are adapted to very dry conditions, but all do best in moist, fertile soils. Adaptable to various temperatures and humidity levels, with most doing well in temperatures up to around 80° F. Moderate humidity, ample sunlight, and free air movement provide healthy conditions that deter harmful insects. Do not purchase plants with mealybugs or spider mites. Propagation from seed is usually easy, though chipping or soaking is helpful to speed up germination. Large cuttings frequently grow quite easily and are used as living fenceposts. Set out plants firmly and a little deeper than they previously grew to ensure that they do not move in windy conditions. Once plants are established, little routine care is needed. Mulch to maintain soil moisture, apply a balanced all-purpose fertilizer if needed, and prune to shape and rejuvenate.

OUTSIDE THE TROPICS Several calliandras are hardy to Zone 8, including **C. californica,** red fairyduster, which is very drought-tolerant.

SELECTIONS C. inaequilatera is an exceptional tropical plant that forms a shrub or small tree 4-10 feet tall with flower heads 3-4 inches in diameter. Flowers are composed of several conspicuous flowers, each with a mass of long, red stamens borne at the end of leafy branches. A rare white form is also beautiful. Mix the two together for a unique and truly lovely display. Tough and suitable for full sun or light shade.

CALLISTEMON BOTTLEBRUSH *Myrtaceae*

The 20-odd species of these spring-blooming shrubs and small trees native to Australia bear cylindrical spikes of bright red flowers that look remarkably like bottle brushes. *C. citrinus* is an upright form whose leaves smell citrusy when crushed; it can form a useful screening hedge. *C. viminalis* resembles a weeping willow, with long, arching, drooping branches.

CULTURE Grow in full sun in areas with warm to hot summers and cool, drier winters. Callistemon is not particular about soil. When purchasing plants, check to see that the root system in the container is not girdling, and therefore weakening, itself. Plant at the beginning of the warm, wet season. Irrigation is needed only to establish plants, which are otherwise fairly drought-tolerant. An application of granular citrus fertilizer at the beginning of the rainy season will enhance growth. Light mulching to control weeds is helpful but not essential. Routine pruning is not required, and pests are not usually a problem.

OUTSIDE THE TROPICS Callistemon is an interesting novelty houseplant that flowers in summer; it thrives in dry but bright areas.

Top to bottom: Calliandra portoriensis, Calliandra inaequilatera, Callistemon rigidus.

Above: Cassia surattensis.
Top: Senna polyphylla.

CARICA PAPAYA PAPAYA *Cariacaceae*

Papaya is a very popular treelike herb for home gardens, as it is fast-growing and not large (10-15 feet tall) and bears fruit early, prolifically, and continuously. The large leaves are deeply lobed; the delicious fruits, orange or yellow when ripe, are borne just under the tree's crown.

CULTURE Grow in full sun. Set out young plants in well-dug soil with manure added, and apply manure twice a year thereafter. Fruits will be produced within a year, but trees will live for only about 15 years. Replace a tree with a new young plant when production ceases. Plants are male, female, or bisexual, so if you have a female tree, you need a male or bisexual companion for fertilization; neighbors' trees may take care of this problem for you. Propagate from seed.

CASSIA SENNA *Fabaceae*

Cassia is a very large genus, including 500-600 species, many of which are useful, highly ornamental shrubs, small trees, annuals, and perennials that thrive in the tropics and in dry climates. Many of the plants are commonly called shower trees, indicating their profuse production of small flowers, usually in some shade of yellow from pale to bright.

CULTURE Grow in full sun. Some cassias prefer moist soil, but most are drought-tolerant as well and require little care or watering. Propagate by seeds or cuttings taken in early spring and planted in peat in the greenhouse. Hard pruning encourages bloom.

OUTSIDE THE TROPICS Some species, including **C. artemesioides,** are hardy to Zone 8 and very drought-tolerant.

SELECTIONS C. fistula, golden shower tree, is among the most ornamental of the genus; it grows to about 30 feet tall and has 1- to 2-inch fragrant yellow flowers. **C. javonica** and **C. nedosa** have pink flowers and grow 20-50 feet tall. **C. surattensis** is a spreading evergreen shrub, to 8 feet tall and 12 feet wide. It has a graceful natural shape and does not need pruning.

CITRUS *Rutaceae*

Generally, *Citrus* and closely related genera are evergreen, shrubby, small- to medium-sized, and often spiny trees native to tropical and subtropical Asia. *Citrus* species are among the most versatile and ornamental of warm-climate trees. Their naturally pleasant shape and deep green, fragrant foliage make the plants ornamental year-round, and the trees are especially treasured for their fragrant show of white or pinkish blossoms followed by the abundant crop of attractive and desirable orange or yellow fruit. Citrus trees can fit into any tropical garden, with plants ranging from bushes less than 10 feet tall with golf-ball-size fruits to 30-foot trees with basketball-size fruits. Citrus trees may be used as naturally shaped specimens, as tightly pruned and shaped topiary, as dividing hedges, or as a screen for a sunny wall. Many species will thrive and bear fruit when grown in a container.

CULTURE Grow in full sun in fertile, well-drained soil with moisture available. Frost-free and moderately humid conditions are best. Temperatures below 50° F help to color maturing fruit; high temperatures all year produce fruit that is green even when ripe. When purchasing, choose plants with dense, deep green foliage, free of insects or sooty mold, and not potbound. Plants may be grown from seed,

CASSIA FISTULA (GOLDEN SHOWER) Semi-evergreen, fast-growing tree to 35 feet, compound leaves, 12- to 15-inch-long clusters of bright yellow flowers in late summer to early fall. Full sun, rich, moist soil is best, but adapts to dry conditions. Short-lived. Zone 10.

CITRUS x 'CALOMONDINE' [C. RETICULATA x FORTUNELLA SP.] (CALOMONDINE ORANGE) Columnar tree, 8-10 feet tall produces abundant small (½- to 1½-inch) sour oranges. Full sun, fertile, well-drained soil with generous moisture. Zones 9-10.

CLERODENDRUM QUADRILOCULARE (CLERODENDRUM) Twining evergreen vine with simple dark green leaves and very showy large (to 4 inches across) red and white flowers. Partial to full shade, rich, moist soil. Zones 9-10.

CLIVIA MINIATA (KAFFIR LILY) Evergreen plant, to 20 inches high with dark green straplike leaves and tubular orange or pink flowers in clusters; flowers in spring and winter. Light shade to full sun, moist, rich, well-drained soil; adapts to dry climates. Zones 9-10.

Above: *Citrus maxima* 'Haiku' (Pomelo).
Top: Citrangequat, a hybrid of *Citrus* 'Fortunella' x 'Citrange'.

but select varieties are grafted. Set out container-grown plants at any time of year. Irrigate to establish, being sure plant does not dry out, and during dry weather; soil must not become soggy, however. Fertilize with a special citrus formulation. In Florida, you may have to provide a micronutrient spray. Mulching, if done carefully to avoid keeping both the roots too wet and the tree base buried, is beneficial to conserve water and fertilizer while controlling weeds. Pruning is needed only to remove dead wood or shape the tree. Fruit flies and virus diseases are of concern mostly for commercial growers; the home gardener should be more alert for citrus scale and root rot. Sooty mold and scurrying ants may indicate scale.

OUTSIDE THE TROPICS Citrus trees define the subtropics, which are limited by areas in which citrus trees will bear fruit outdoors. Many small citrus trees can be grown indoors or in greenhouses; the greenhouse craze of the Victorian era was started to grow oranges. Site in the sunniest spot available, and provide water generously year-round. Lemons, limes (with protection), oranges, and grapefruits are important shade and fruit trees in the Southwest.

SELECTIONS For the home garden, grow citrus that will provide something different from the commonly available commercial fruits. For example, choose a variety that will bear small amounts of fruit over a long period, such as **Meyer** lemon, which bears continuously. **'Isle of Pine'** grapefruit is too seedy to be grown commercially but is unbelievably deliciously sweet. Kumquats, both round (**'Marumi'**) and oval (**'Nagami'**) types, are small trees or shrubs, colorful in the garden, and provide an unusual, special treat to share. Harder to find but interesting to grow would be a **'Buddha's Hand'** citron, featuring strange and fragrant fruits.

CLERODENDRUM GLORYBOWER *Verbenaceae*

Clerodendrum is a genus of deciduous or evergreen shrubs and trees native to the Pacific islands and tropical Africa grown for their often showy clusters of white, red, or violet flowers, some followed by ornamental berries.

CULTURE Clerodendrums are easy to grow in moist, well-drained soils. Occasional addition of organic matter and fertilizer if beneficial. The plant needs no special care except training or restraining the vines and shaping the bushes or small trees. It propagates readily from suckers or tip cuttings or side shoots taken with heels. Severe pruning may result in an outburst of growth and suckers.

OUTSIDE THE TROPICS *C. trichotomum,* harlequin glorybower, a dieback shrub, is hardy to Zone 6 (one specimen at The Holden Arboretum has thrived in Zone 5 for 60 years). Its flowers are not as abundant, but they do impart a tropical feeling. Clerodendron vines are often used in greenhouses and will flower profusely in rich soil and bright light. It produces clusters of pink buds that open to wonderfully fragrant white starlike flowers, followed by black fruit.

SELECTIONS *C. fallax (C. speciosissimum)*, native to Java, grows to 12 feet, with large, velvety leaves and profuse foot-tall clusters of red flowers. *C. fragrans* is a small shrub that produces very fragrant pink-tinged white flowers, excellent for cutting. *C. splendens*, native to tropical Africa, is an evergreen climber with bunches of bright red flowers in summer; spreads rapidly via root suckers and is a fine choice for the shade garden. *C. thomsoniae*, bleeding heart, is another very ornamental evergreen twiner often grown in pots; the striking flowers have bright crimson petals contrasting with large white calyces; black fruits may develop that split to show black seeds set in a bright orange lining; as a container plant, provide sup-

Left: Clerodendrum splendens.
Above: Clerodendrum thomsoniae,
bleeding heart glorybower.

port and lots of sun during the summer flowering season, followed by a winter of cool, shady, rather dry conditions.

CLIVIA KAFFIR LILY *Amaryllidaceae*

Clivia is an attractive group of evergreen, herbaceous plants, usually growing to about 20 inches high, nearly or completely stemless. Dark green, strap-shaped leaves are 18-28 inches long and up to 2 inches wide, arranged in two ranks. Flower stems bear many tubular, stalked flowers, usually pink or orange with a yellow base; one very rare form is pure golden yellow. Kaffir lily is winter- to spring-flowering, excellent for woodland-type gardens with light shade or gardens that don't receive much direct sun. Plants are tough and can tolerate short dry periods. Native to South Africa.

CULTURE *Clivia* does best with slight shade, or at least no direct afternoon sun, and in organically rich, well-drained, and moist soil. It is tough; in very hot conditions, it will grow fairly well but will not flower prolifically. Temperatures not exceeding 80° F are best, but plants can tolerate temperatures in the 40° F range for short periods. Purchase plants with more than one crown (growing point) and deep green leaves; if plants have been grown from seeds, you should see them in bloom before buying, because flowers will vary from parents. Propagate from division; seeds start easily but take many years to reach flowering size. Do not set out more deeply than plant was previously growing; you must not bury the growing point. Having the root crowns a bit above ground will not harm the plants. Keep plants moist during the growing season for best flowering; drier conditions are fine for the summer when growth slows or stops. Clivia responds well to a thin mulch and a light, general fertilizer applied at the beginning of the growing season. Remove old flower clusters. When clumps get large, divide and replant,

CLUSIA ROSEA (AUTOGRAPH TREE) Bushy tree, 20-50 feet tall with thick leathery sea green leaves, large pearly pink flowers and aerial roots. Full sun to partial shade, warm, humid conditions, any soil from wet to rocky. Zones 9-10.

COCCOLOBA UVIFERA (SEA GRAPE) Small tree with large, leathery red-veined green leaves, to 8 inches across, that may turn red and drop in fall; clusters of dark purple fruit. Full sun to partial shade, rich, sandy, moist but well-drained soil. Zones 9-10.

COCHLOSPERMUM VITIFOLIUM (BUTTERCUP TREE) Slow-growing medium-sized tree (to 35 feet) with small, rounded crown, bright yellow flowers in early spring. Full sun to very light shade, adapts to poor, stony, or dry soils. Zones 9-10.

CODIAEUM VARIEGATUM (CROTON) Bushy shrubs from 1-10 feet tall with leathery leaves in a variety of shapes and sizes from 1-9 inches across in a variety of color combinations. Full sun gives best color, adapts to shade, deep, moist, rich soil is best, but adapts to other conditions. Zones 9-10.

spacing about 10-18 inches apart to give a good display; because clivias resents disturbance, divide at the beginning of a vegetative growth cycle in mild, moist weather. In unfavorable conditions, mealybugs may be a problem; avoid this by moving plants to a more suitable microclimate, a position providing 20 percent shade, or more favorable, slightly acidic pH.

OUTSIDE THE TROPICS Clivias are traditionally used as houseplants; they will flower year after year if allowed to go dormant over the winter.

SELECTIONS *C. miniata* is the common species, with compact heads of erect to arching, scarlet-orange, broad and tubular flowers, each with a yellow base; several cultivars exist, usually variants of color or size. **'Aurea'** is a very desirable golden yellow-flowered form, with darker petal bases. *C. x cyrtanthiflora* is a hybrid of *C. miniata* with *C. nobilis,* featuring attractive 3-inch-long pink to orange, narrow and tubular flowers and 2-inch-wide leaves to 28 inches long.

CLUSIA ROSEA AUTOGRAPH TREE *Clusiaceae*

Clusia is a large group of ornamental 20- to 50-foot bushy trees, with sea green leaves, large flowers, and aerial roots; most species are epiphytes that often begin life in tree branches and sometimes become stranglers. *C. rosea* is the only species commonly available. The attractive, pearly pink, male and female flowers are borne on separate trees. The thick, leathery leaves callous when wounded, so a message or a name scratched on them remains for a long time–hence the name autograph tree. The sticky resin produced by the seeds has been exploited as gutta percha, a nonshrinking, salt-resistant material useful for caulking boats. Plantings of *C. rosea* are useful to screen a wall. Native to the West Indies and from southern Mexico to northern South America.

CULTURE Grow in full sun to semishade; warm, humid conditions are ideal. Clusia is not particular about soil–it will grow on rocks, it will thrive in wet and alluvial soil, and nice specimens can sometimes be seen growing in parking-lot conditions. Purchase a plant with a full, bushy habit with some sign that it will produce aerial roots. Propagate from seed or from hardwood cuttings. Transplant to the same depth as grown in the container, and water to establish. This is a good xeriscaping subject; plants are also salt-tolerant. Applications of granular fertilizer three or four times a year are beneficial. When soil is shallow and rocky, mulch is helpful but not essential. Restrict pruning to removal of selected branches for shaping purposes. Pests and diseases pose no particular problem.

COCCOLOBA SEA GRAPE, PIGEON PLUM *Polygonaceae*

Coccolobas are native to tropical and subtropical America; sea grape is thought to have been the first New World plant spied by Columbus and his crew upon landfall. Sea grape, **C. uvifera,** is a characteristic tree of sandy dunes near tropical shores with large, leathery, red-veined leaves, 8 inches or more across (**C. pubescens,** which grows to 80 feet tall, produces 3-foot leaves). The black-purple fruits, produced in hanging clusters on female trees, are edible and often used to make jelly. Sea grape is very salt- and drought-tolerant. It can be grown as a large specimen; its spreading growth habit also makes it valuable as a screen for privacy or as a wind barrier. Pigeon plum, **C. diversifolia,** is a small, dense tree with large, dark green foliage that changes shape as the tree matures; its edible plumlike fruit is prized

Above: Gloriosa superba.

HEDGES

I define hedges as plants that define a border or create a barrier. We use two types of hedges: formal, that are often clipped and sheared to straight lines and informal, that are allowed to grow loosely. For formal hedges, try citrus, murraya, and gardenia, which also flowers, or any other fine-leaved plant. For an informal hedge, crotons and ti plants are excellent; acalypha also can be used as a hedge. Russellia is a more unusual choice that works well.
DAVID BAR-ZVI, FAIRCHILD TROPICAL GARDEN, MIAMI, FLORIDA

Calliandra makes a perfect hedge, as do *Viburnum odoratissium, Tabaermontana divaritaca, Podocarpus* species, *Pittosporum tobira,* and *Ilex vomitora.* Other plants that can be used as hedges in central Florida are gardenia, eglaeagnus, and carissa, ligustrum, and illicium.
ROBERT BOWDEN, HARRY P. LEU GARDENS, ORLANDO

We've used *Thunbergia erecta, Tibouchina urvilleana, Acalypha wilkesana,* hybrid crotons, heliconias, and hibiscus as hedges.
LINDA GAY, MERCER ARBORETUM AND BOTANICAL GARDEN, HUMBLE, TEXAS

Good plants for hedges in our area include *Thunbergia erecta, Plumbago auriculata, Murraya paniculata, Graphtophyllum pictum* cultivars, *Codiaeum variegatum* cultivars, and *Scaevola serica.*
KEITH WOOLLIAMS, WAIMEA FALLS PARK, OAHU, HAWAII

Malpighia glabra, Illicium floridanum, Cestrum species, and *Hamelia patens.*
DOUGLAS WILLIAMS, MERCER ARBORETUM AND BOTANICAL GARDEN, HUMBLE, TEXAS

by birds, hence the plant's common name. Pigeon plum, with its smooth, light-colored and mottled trunk and branches, makes an attractive specimen tree. In autumn, the leaves may turn a rich red–particularly in coastal areas, where temperatures fall–and some may drop, though the tree is never totally leafless.

CULTURE Grow in full sun to partial shade in rich, sandy, moist, but well-drained soil. Growing conditions should be warm to very warm and humid; trees are somewhat tender to cold. When purchasing, look for a plant with a good branching pattern and not too overgrown in the container. Propagate by seed, layering, or hardwood cuttings with rooting hormone under fog or mist. Transplant from container at any time. Do not root-prune field-grown plants prior to transplanting. Water to establish; thereafter, excessive watering is not necessary. Coccolobas are not heavy feeders, although occasional application of liquid fertilizer such as 20-20-20 will give a boost to containerized plants. Prune to shape just before new growth; selective removal of branches will help to reveal the beautiful trunk. Mulching is generally beneficial, especially on sandy soil. Leaf miners are sometimes a problem on pigeon plum.

OUTSIDE THE TROPICS Although rarely grown indoors, sea grape makes a fine, slow-growing houseplant; provide bright light and keep evenly moist.

COCHLOSPERMUM BUTTERCUP TREE *Cochlospermaceae*

This native of Mexico and tropical America is an outstanding medium-sized feature tree with a small crown; it is most suitable for larger landscapes. Leaves are deeply lobed, 8-12 inches long. Bright yellow camellialike flowers appear in March and April as the last leaves fall, on dormant, mature growth; later, velvety seedpods appear. This is a slow-growing tree, so it can be planted in a more confined area and enjoyed for many years. For best effect, branches should be allowed to spread; the double form in particular makes some large side branches low down on the tree. The carpet of fallen flowers on a lawn or groundcover is an added bonus.

CULTURE Buttercup tree is not very demanding and needs little care. Grow in full sun or very light shade. Trees seem to adapt to poor, stony soils and tolerate dry conditions, but they also do well in evenly moist, deep, fertile soil. Good drainage is important. Temperatures ranging from 70° F to 80° F (or higher), with occasional minimums in the 50° F range suit buttercup tree well. Humidity may be high or low. Purchase a tree with a strong stem and root system. Propagation is easy from seed, and moderately easy from both cuttings and air layering; the sterile double form is grafted or air layered. While buttercup tree does not need high nutrition, is does respond with increased growth to application of a balanced fertilizer. Mulching is beneficial. No pruning is needed other than shaping if desired; hard pruning could result in growth at the expense of flowers. Pests and disease are not problems.

SELECTIONS *C. vitifolium* grows 20-30 feet high, with single, golden yellow flowers, 3-4 inches in diameter; the brown, felt-covered, 3-inch-long fruit is also attractive. The double form is outstanding, with huge, fully double, golden yellow flowers 4½-5 inches in diameter. *C. religiosum* is similar, though smaller in stature, leaves, and flowers.

CODIAEUM VARIEGATUM CROTON *Euphorbiaceae*

Croton is a popular, characteristic plant of warm countries, due to its extreme ease of cultivation and care and its highly ornamental foliage. Crotons are bushy shrubs ranging in height from only 1-2 feet to over 10 feet. Their leathery leaves range in shape from linear and twisted to narrow and ovate and in length from only a few inches to over 9 inches. Leaf color combinations are almost endless, and frequently juvenile and adult leaves are of different colors and shapes on the same bush. Tiny flowers are borne on long axillary stems. As colorful feature, background, and filler plants, as hedges, and for areas needing little maintenance, crotons are outstanding, giving year-round color and interest and needing very little attention. They are especially valuable for those hard-to-fill places and for areas where flowering plants will not give adequate color. Smaller crotons make interesting houseplants. Native to the western South Pacific.

CULTURE Croton grows best and develops best leaf color in full sun, but it will grow and give a good show even in relatively shady spots. At Mercer Botanic Garden, near Houston, gardeners find that the sun bleaches out color and that the best color is achieved with afternoon shade. Although tough and drought-tolerant once established, croton does best in deep, moist, rich soil, preferably with good drainage. It grows exceptionally well near the coast and in sandy soil with

The brilliant leaves of crotons can be used to brighten less colorful plants, or combined with other bold specimens, as shown here with coleus and Jerusalem cherry (*Nertera granadensis*).

CODIAEUM VARIEGATUM 'SPIRALE' (CROTON) Bushy shrubs to 2 feet tall with stringy twisted leaves in red, yellow, and green. Full sun gives best color, adapts to shade, deep, moist, rich soil is best, but adapts to other conditions. Zones 9-10.

COLOCASIA ESCULENTA 'FONTANESIA' (VIOLET-STEMMED TARO) 3- to 6-foot-tall plant with very large purple-veined heart-shaped leaves and purple stems. Full sun or afternoon shade; fertile, moist soil. Zones 9-10.

CONGEA TOMENTOSA (ORCHID SHOWER) Shrubby vining plants covered in velvety lilac to pale pink flower bracts. Full sun, warm climate, adapts to many soils but not overly wet or overly dry. Zone 10.

CORDYLINE FRUTICOSA 'BABY DOLL (CABBAGE TREE, TI PLANT) Shrubby plant, 3-5 feet tall with narrow, hot pink-edged green leaves forming loose rosettes. Partial shade, well-drained rich soil. Zone 10.

organic matter added. It is tolerant of widely variable temperature and humidity conditions. When purchasing, watch for scale insects and mealybugs, especially deep in the leaf axils. Choose plants in active growth. Frequently, juvenile plants have green or minimally colored leaves, so look for older plants with more typical, mature leaves already present. Propagation from cuttings is very easy. Growing from seed can be fun; rarely are the results like the parent plant. Keep soil moist with routine watering and mulch; frequently hose or fog the leaves to highlight the color. Croton responds well to general fertilizer applications. No pruning is required other than for shaping; you can cut plants back hard every three to five years to rejuvenate if needed. Scale insects and mealybugs can be a problem and spider mites are problematic on the Gulf Coast; well-grown, healthy plants do not get attacked as much.

OUTSIDE THE TROPICS Grown indoors, croton requires good light, medium to warm temperatures, and high humidity. They benefit from being taken outdoors in summer, in pots or planted in the ground.

SELECTIONS *Croton* is also the botanical name of a large genus within *Euphorbiaceae*; do not confuse the two, as they are very different. Hundreds of named and unnamed cultivars of all kinds of *Codiaeum* are available, and all are excellent landscape plants. **'Volutum'**, also called ram's horn, is 4-6 feet; rarely seen, with sharply outward-curled and narrow leaves, dark green with a broad yellow band down the midrib and yellow veins. **'Interruptum'** is 6-10 feet; very unusual, with very narrow, often twisted leaves of green, red, and orange, often interrupted along the midrib. **'Gloriosa'** is a very common landscape plant with large, broad, ovate leaves, dark green with a network of golden yellow that turns crimson. **'General Paget'** is very robust, 16-20 feet tall, with leaves 16 inches long, 4 inches wide, dark green with veins and vein and midrib areas yellow, cream, or ivory; some upper leaves may be all clear yellow, and midrib may be pink; very striking as feature and accent plant. **'Maculatum Katoni'** is compact, to 8 feet, with unusual three-lobed leaves, oval changing to oblong and pointed, green densely covered with yellow or cream spots.

COLOCASIA ELEPHANT'S EAR, TARO *Araceae*

One of the oldest cultivated food crops of the world, grown for over 10,000 years in Asia, taro is little used today. The tubers, or corms, are an excellent non-allergenic source of nutrition, used in the Hawaiian dish poi, but need to be prepared thoroughly by a knowledgeable cook or they can be toxic. Eight species of this terrestrial herb are native to the the old-world tropics from western India to southeast Asia and Polynesia; they spread by underground tubers, which make them hardier on the Gulf Coast than alocasias. Many are attractive and ornamental garden plants with huge leaves and striking green or purple colors in foliage and/or stems. They are used as fillers in borders and usually replanted annually. Colocasias do well in water and are striking additions to pond gardens.

CULTURE Grow colocasias in full sun (afternoon shade on the Gulf Coast), in fertile, moist, slightly acid soil, under hot, humid conditions. Choose cultivars according to their use for food or ornament. Space 2-2½ feet apart; if you plan to use the corm, you must plant 12 inches deep and keep mulching as the plant the grows; the corm will grow up, not down, and needs to be covered with mulch. Keep soil constantly wet and fertilize with 10-30-10 fertilize every three to four months. Mulching is essential. Propagate by planting offshoots or by cutting the mother corm with leaf sheaths attached. Colocasia is susceptible to nematodes and fungus diseases; control by rotating planting sites and keeping leaves as dry as possible.

OUTSIDE THE TROPICS Colocasias are hardy throughout the Gulf Coast region and do well in areas with rich soil and plenty of moisture. Though sometimes used as houseplants, they require more humidity than easily provided.

SELECTIONS Recommended cultivars of *C. esculenta* include **'Elepaio, 'Uahiapele',** and **'Lumi Eleele';** most grow 3-7 feet tall. **'Fontanesia' [*C. violaceae*],** violet-stemmed taro, has purple-veined leaves and purple stems. **'Illustris',** black caladium, imperial taro, has purple leaves and stems. *C. affinis* **'Black Princess'** has heart-shaped green leaves with black centers.

CONGEA TOMENTOSA ORCHID SHOWER, SHOWER OF ORCHIDS *Verbenaceae*

This shrubby, vining plant produces a generous spring display of velvety, lilac to pale pink or white flower bracts, borne in sprays that sometimes completely cover the plant. This native of Burma and Thailand is useful in the landscape as a supported climbing vine, especially striking when grown up into a tree, as a sprawling shrub in a large open area, or as a trailing, erosion-controlling cover for a sloping bank.

CULTURE Grow in full sun in warm to very warm conditions. Plants are adaptable to varying degrees of humidity and are very adaptable to many soils, although overly wet or dry soil is not good. Purchase plants with clean, healthy, medium

Below: Crotons, cordylines, colocasia–some of the best foliage plants of the tropics.

green foliage. Propagate by seed or layering. Plant out near strong support with lots of space to spread. Water well to establish; thereafter, irrigate regularly but not excessively. Granular fertilizer applied at the beginning of the growing season is beneficial, particularly an acid-reacting fertilizer with micronutrients, which is especially helpful in limestone soils. Prune heavily immediately after flowering to control size; never prune in the winter—you will remove the flowering stems. Mulch regularly, which keeps nematode damage to a minimum. Reduce iron deficiency in alkaline soils by a foliar application of chelated iron.

CORDYLINE FRUTICOSA CABBAGE TREE, TI PLANT *Agavaceae*

This plant has been grown by man for so long that some green forms have lost the capacity to produce seeds and reproduce sexually; only the colored-leaf forms produce seeds. These shrubby plants range from 5 inches to 20 feet tall and produce leaves with remarkably striking patterns and colors, usually in combination of pink, green, purple, and red. They are often used as hedges. Though they make wonderful accent plants within a border and combine well with other foliage and flowering plants, a grouping of cordylines shows off their coloration best.

CULTURE Grow cordylines in partial shade in well-drained soil rich in organic matter. Temperatures should be warm and humidity should be high. When buying plants, look for healthy, insect-free specimens with good coloration. Soil should be kept moist and fertilizing every 3-4 months with 10-10-10 fertilizer (or annually with 10-30-10) is beneficial. Prune selectively to desired height; every cultivar has its own best height and shape, so watch your plant to see how it looks best. Though usually pest-free, cordylines sometimes are affected by mealybugs, grasshoppers, and leaf hoppers.

OUTSIDE THE TROPICS Cordylines are excellent houseplants if given medium light and average temperature; they will not tolerate low humidity and cool temperatures. They can be brought outdoors in summer in pots or planted in the ground.

SELECTIONS Many cultivars are available; Robert Hirano of Lyons Arboretum recommends **'Fire Fountain'**, **'Peter Buck'** and **'Kauai Beauty'**

COSTUS SPIRAL GINGER *Costaceae*

Spiral gingers are very ornamental, clumping, herbaceous, flowering plants with spirally arranged leaves. Some are low and spreading, making good groundcovers. Others are tall. Many have colorful foliage or are covered in hair. The flowers, which usually appear during warm weather, are produced in conelike structures that may appear on independent stalks arising directly from the ground; the "cones" are sometimes very ornamental and long-lasting. Botanists sometimes include this group of spiral gingers in the Zingiberaceae family.

CULTURE Many spiral gingers tolerate full sun, but light shade—especially in the hottest part of the day—is ideal. Soil should be fertile, moist, and well drained. These natives of tropical America, Africa, and Australia want a warm climate, with temperatures over 70° F; they do not tolerate freezing or even long periods of cold, dry weather without damage. Propagate by clump division; cut the canelike stems into sections or leave them whole, and lay them horizontally in a warm, moist bed. Deep planting with very slow-release fertilizer tablets in the planting hole promotes stronger growth. These are spreading plants; give them plenty of room.

Congea tomentosa.

CORDYLINE TERMINALIS (TI PLANT) Shrubby plant, 3-5 feet tall with pink-tinged green leaves forming loose rosettes. Partial shade, well-drained rich soil. Zone 10.

COSTUS CURVIBRACTEAUS (SPIRAL GINGER) Clumping herbaceous plants with spirally arranged leaves and conelike erect flowers. Light shade is best; fertile, moist, well-drained soil. Zone 10.

CRESCENTIA CUJETE (CALABASH) Small, open tree, to 20 feet, with spongy bark, sparse foliage, interesting flowers, and huge fleshy fruits. Full sun to light shade, moist, rich soil. Zone 10.

CRINUM ASIATICUM (SWAMP LILY) Large clumping plants to 5 feet tall and across with long stiff leaves and showy flowers borne in umbels. Full sun, deep, well-drained soil. Zones 9-10.

Heavy mulching is a good practice. Some species, such as *C. speciosus,* may be cut down in the cool, dry months; for all, cut flowering stalks to the ground once blooms are spent. Plants appreciate regular watering during periods of drought. Regular applications of palm fertilizer, plus extra potassium, are beneficial.

OUTSIDE THE TROPICS Costus needs more humidity than can be provided in most living rooms, but it thrives in pots in greenhouses and conservatories.

SELECTIONS *C. barbatus* grows to 7 feet tall, with dark green foliage and crimson red, elongated flower "cones"; tolerant of a wide range of cultural conditions and one of the best plants in the herbaceous landscape. *C. speciosus*, crepe ginger, grows to 9 feet tall, with dark green foliage and large white flowers produced from terminal red cones; blooms annually. *C. s.* **'Variegata'** is similar, with striking white-striped foliage; very sensitive to cold weather. *C. malortieanus* grows to 2½ feet, with large, bright green and delightfully fuzzy foliage. *C. pictus* grows to 6 feet, with dark foliage and red-spotted stems.

CRESCENTIA CUJETE CALABASH *Bignoniaceae*

This small tree seldom grows to be taller than 20 feet, with an open and rather sculptural shape, sparse foliage, and a soft, somewhat spongy bark. All these characteristics make this native of tropical America an excellent host for epiphytes such as orchids and bromeliads. The bell-shaped grayish flowers are borne along the length of the trunk and branches. Spherical, hard, gourdlike fruits are produced sporadically throughout the year. These hollow fruits are put to use as domestic utensils such as cups and bowls and as musical instruments and rattles.

CULTURE Grow in full sun to light shade, in moist, organically rich soil. Very warm and humid conditions are best. Propagate from seeds sown just below the soil surface and keep soil moist; cutting root easily as well. Plants will respond to applications of a granular fertilizer two to three times per year. Regular mulching is beneficial. Prune only to shape the basic skeleton.

SELECTIONS A related species is **Parmentiera cereifera**, Panama candle tree, which has similar growing requirements and habit except that the fruits are elongated, looking rather like yellowish candles.

CRINUM SWAMP LILY, CRINUM LILY, SPIDER LILY *Amaryllidaceae*

Crinums are robust plants with multiple linear leaves, some with reddish or purple coloration, arising from bulbs or thick, trunklike, fleshy stems (which are not apparent when plants are grown in pots in temperate climates). They range in height from 10 inches to 8 feet. Flowers are borne in umbels of up to 30 or more at the end of thick stalks, in white, purple, pink, red, or striped forms, often followed by huge fleshy fruits. Crinums are grand feature plants, making a strong statement with a tropical accent; flowers are usually abundant. The juice of some African species of this tropical native has antiseptic properties and is used on open sores.

Crinum flowerbud (above) and fruit (top).

CULTURE Most crinums require full sun or part shade, and most like deep, well-drained soil. Some, like *C. americanum,* are bog plants but are tolerant of a well-drained site. Warm temperatures in the 80-90° F range suit the majority of crinums, with humidity in the 50-60 percent range. When purchasing, look for firm bulbs or stems; avoid specimens with any sunken, rotten areas or spider mite damage. Propagate by division; seeds may germinate very slowly and take a long time to reach flowering stage. Plant at same depth as the original or, if original depth is not clear, leave upper half of bulb above ground. Do not bury leaf bases. Bulbs will later adjust themselves to a suitable depth. Keep moist, but if plants show signs of dormancy, withhold or reduce water until new growth starts. If this is not possible, plants will adjust to the conditions themselves. A root-promoting phosphate fertilizer like bone meal is beneficial at planting, or apply a general-purpose fertilizer like 10-30-10 at planting and to the surface. Mulch and dead-head plants, and lift and divide every few years or when plants become congested and/or no longer flower well. Slugs and spider mites may be problems.

OUTSIDE THE TROPICS Crinums are hardy through most of coastal California and southern Texas. *C. americanum* is often used as a container plant in water gardens. Some of the smaller species, such as *C.* x *powellii* and *C. bulbispermum,* can be grown indoors; they flower for four to five weeks, after which they need to rest in a cool room; give them bright light and water liberally from spring until they stop flowering.

SELECTIONS Many species and cultivars are available. *C. americanum* spreads by underground stems; it will grow in water and can be used in ponds with waterlilies. *C. asiaticum* forms large clumps, with stiff leaves 3-5 feet long and 3-5 inches wide atop a trunklike 15-inch stem; white flowers in huge heads of more than 30, 3-5 feet tall, produced frequently. *C.* **'Ellen Bosanquet'** has leaves 20-30 inches long; flowers are very colorful, broadly tubular, wine red in heads of 8-10, produced spring-summer. *C. asiaticum* var. *procerum* is similar to *C. asiaticum*, with wine red leaves; flower petals wine red outside and white inside; shiny, wine red fruit; striking, and flowers frequently. *C. xanthophyllum* is striking, similar to *C. asiaticum*, 4-5 feet tall; leaves pale to golden yellow, with excellent color in full sun or part shade; grows well in sandy soil. *C. rattrayii* is a very desirable crinum, with a strong erect habit, wide dark green leaves, and white flowers similar to those of *C. asiaticum*. *C.* **'Mrs. James Hendry'** is recommended by gardeners at Mercer Botanic Garden for its lemony fragrance and blush pink trumpet flowers.

CUPHEA HYSSOPIFOLIA [C. CARTHAGENESIS] FALSE HEATHER
Lythraceae

A useful and attractive garden plant with a heatherlike appearance, false heather grows 6-20 inches tall, with many reddish stems and an abundance of tiny purple-mauve or white flowers produced continuously during the summer. This South American native is a valuable landscape plant because it is easy to grow and naturally regenerates. Use it as a color feature, for interest on moderate slopes, or as a groundcover. It looks good planted among stones or in gravel, where it seeds freely. It may also be used a flowering houseplant or as an annual.

CULTURE Grows best in a hot, sunny location. Will grow in even poor, stony soil with added fertilizer, and tolerates a wide range of temperatures and humidity. Although tolerant of dry conditions once established, plants do best in moist (not wet), well-drained areas, where they will spread rapidly by self-sowing. Purchase pest-free plants with dark green leaves and tough stems. Set out 9-12 inches apart. Any general fertilizer is suitable. A thin mulch to control weeds is useful. Plants can be clipped for shape and form if desired; they will soon regrow. Even a

After its magnificent show of flaming flowers, royal poinciana's flat-topped shape is still attractive.

CRINUM AMABILE CV. (SWAMP LILY) Large clumping plants to 5 feet tall and across with long stiff leaves and showy flowers borne in umbels. Full sun, deep, well-drained soil. Zones 9-10.

CUPHEA HYSSOPIFOLIA (FALSE HEATHER) Low-growing heather-like groundcover, 6-20 inches tall with abundant purple or white flowers. Full sun, wide range of soil, temperature, humidity levels. Zones 9-10.

DELONIX REGIA (ROYAL POINCIANA) Small, fast-growing tree to 35 feet in some sites. Profusion of brilliant orange to red flowers over a long period, lacy foliage. Best in areas with wet and dry seasons, moderately fertile well-drained soil. Zones 9-10.

DICHORISANDRA THYRSIFLORA (BLUE GINGER) Erect, herbaceous plant to 6 feet tall or more, shiny green spirally arranged leaves, striking purple flower spike. Light shade, warm, humid conditions, rich soil. Zone 10.

DOMBEYA HYBRID (DOMBEYA) Large shrub or small tree with spreading habit, up to 30 feet tall, very ornamental pink to red flowers in pendant clusters. Full sun or light shade, warm humid conditions, well-drained, moderately fertile, neutral soil. Zone 10.

DRACAENA DRACO (DRAGON TREE) Small tree with interesting, horizontally spreading branches forming a tight, rounded crown. Full sun to partial shade; grows quickly with moist, rich soil, more slowly in drier, poor soil. Zones 9-10.

DURANTA REPENS (GOLDEN DEWDROP) Large shrub or small tree with drooping branches, small blue flowers, abundant clusters of round golden-orange berries. Full sun, adapts to a wide range of soils and temperatures. Zones 8-10.

EPIPREMNUM AUREUM (POTHOS) Vigorous vining plant with large (up to 18-inch) green leaves marked with white and gold. Partial shade is best, but full sun produces largest leaves; well-drained, rich, friable soil. Zone 10.

periodic high mowing will not daunt this adaptable plant. Generally pest- and disease-free.

OUTSIDE THE TROPICS Grown indoors, false heather requires high light and cool house temperatures and soil kept evenly moist. It does well in hanging baskets that can be brought outdoors in summer; it can also be planted in the ground as an annual then allowed to die back (take cuttings in later summer) or brought back indoors. It is hardy in coastal California, north to the San Francisco Bay area.

DELONIX REGIA ROYAL POINCIANA *Fabaceae*

Among the most flamboyant of trees, the royal poinciana is the quintessential tropical plant. Although common, it remains startling for its exuberant production of brilliant red-orange flowers that virtually cover the tree for up to four months of the summer; the tree seems almost to be on fire. When its magnificent blooms are gone, the flat-topped shape and lacy foliage of the royal poinciana are still attractive. Royal poinciana is an excellent specimen in areas where it has room to grow; its large, aggressive roots make it difficult to use as a street tree (though it often is seen on streets).

CULTURE The best location for a royal poinciana is a tropical site where two distinct seasons—wet and dry—exist. In very humid regions, the tree will bloom for a longer period, but with less concentration and thus less effect (though Hawaiian specimens bloom abundantly). In cooler areas—Zone 9—the tree will grow to only 20-30 feet tall. Choose a spot where the tree can be seen from a distance, and where its roots can spread and its brittle branches do not endanger buildings—at least 30 feet from the home. The tree grows very quickly in full sun in any moderately fertile, moist, well-drained soil—it can grow to 25 feet in only four years. Propagate by seed. Royal poinciana is sometimes bothered by termites and fungi, particularly if branches or trunk are injured; prune and clean breaks as necessary.

DICHORISANDRA THYRSIFLORA BLUE GINGER *Commelinaceae*

In spite of its common name, this striking plant is not a member of the ginger family, although it resembles some ginger species; blue ginger is actually a close relative of the wandering Jew plant. Blue ginger is erect and herbaceous, with leafy, jointed stems and shiny green, spirally arranged leaves, which may be attractively colored silver, green, and purple-red when young, with a striking purple underside. Plant in groupings where the 6-foot-plus stems will best display the beautiful china blue flowers, borne in terminal clusters in autumn. Native to tropical America.

CULTURE Blue ginger prefers filtered light, warm and humid growing conditions with maximum temperatures in upper 70° F to low 80° F, and moist, well-drained, organically rich soil; in Hawaii, the plant thrives in cooler areas. When purchasing plants, look for deep green foliage, several stems, and signs of vigorous growth. Propagate from division or from tip cuttings kept shaded and humid. Plants need regular watering; they must not dry out. Feed lightly but frequently (about once a month) with 20-20-20 fertilizer (this plant is fertilized only occasionally at Waimea Falls Park, with 10-30-10). Mulch to conserve needed moisture and add nutrients. Cut back straggly stems and stems that have flowered; they will usually branch, and you can use the cuttings to increase the number of plants. Periodically cut back all or part of the clump to the ground to encourage renewal of healthy new growth. In ideal, moist conditions, blue ginger tends to spread rapidly. Planting in poorer, drier soil in a hot site (mid-80° F to 90° F) will limit its spread somewhat. Spider mites occasionally attack if the environment is too dry.

DOMBEYA *Sterculiaceae*

The most interesting of the 200-odd *Dombeya* species are medium to large shrubs, usually with large, palmate, medium green leaves and clusters of showy flowers somewhat reminiscent of some *Hydrangea* species in autumn and winter. Leaves are broad and up to 12 inches long, and the small coral pink to red flowers form attractive 3-inch clusters; unfortunately, they remain on the plant when spent. These natives of Madagascar and Africa make fine accent shrubs; large tree specimens can be showy.

CULTURE Grow in full sun or light shade in warm, humid conditions, in well-drained, neutral soil with some organic matter. Propagate from seed or hardwood cuttings over heat (heat isn't needed in Hawaii), or buy full plants with medium green foliage. Water to establish and during very dry periods, although plants will tolerate some dryness. A complete granular fertilizer applied at the beginning of the growing period encourages the development of fuller plants and more flowers. Mulch heavily to suppress weeds and maintain a moist root environment. Mealybugs may be a problem.

SELECTIONS *D. wallichii* can be a spreading tree to 30 feet tall, with pink to red flowers in pendant clusters, very ornamental. *D. x cayeuxii* (*D. burgessiae* x *D. wallichii*) is variable, with pink flower clusters.

DRACAENA CORN PLANT *Agavaceae*

The large and small shrubs of this genus native to tropical areas around the world are widely grown both as tropical landscape plants and as indoor pot plants in cooler climates, valued for their ornamental, often brightly variegated foliage. The various species range from slender- to thick-stemmed; most tolerate shade well and so are very useful for thoroughly shaded areas of the yard.

CULTURE For most species, grow in shade in a spot protected from wind; low humidity is poorly tolerated. Other species, such as *D. draco,* are very drought-tolerant. Plants propagate easily from stem cuttings. Fertilize only infrequently; while plants tolerate pruning quite well, it is usually needed only for grooming. Spider mites, scale, and mealybugs may be a problem.

OUTSIDE THE TROPICS As houseplants, they are easy to grow in average soil and low light, although good light is necessary during winter months to maintain the brightest variegated foliage color; pots should be small in relation to the plant size.

SELECTIONS *D. fragrans* grows to 20 feet tall outdoors, with long, broad, strap-shaped leaves that arch over; the cultivar **'Massangeana'** has a broad yellow stripe down the center of the green leaves, while **'Lindenii'** has greenish yellow leaf margins. *D. marginata* has twisted, irregularly growing stems that produce an eye-catching landscape (to 12 feet tall) or house (to 8 feet tall) plant that changes appearance as the meandering stems grow; available varieties offer numerous variegated leaf color possibilities. *D. deremensis* has broad, glossy, gracefully curved, dark green leaves and is excellent grown in a pot or outdoors in heavy shade in the tropical garden; varieties with variegated foliage are available. **D. draco**, dragon tree, grows to about 70 feet and has leaves up to 2 feet long.

DURANTA REPENS GOLDEN DEWDROP, PIGEON BERRY
Verbenaceae

This native of tropical America is a highly decorative shrub or small tree with many drooping, sometimes spiny, branches. Small blue or white flowers are produced periodically throughout the year in clusters at the ends of branches, followed by abundant clusters of round, golden-orange berries that persist for many weeks. Both flowers and fruits attract butterflies and birds. This is a fine, tough, colorful feature plant for shrubberies and lawn specimens, and it also makes a good hedge.

CULTURE Grow in full sun, in a wide range of soil types and temperature and humidity conditions. Propagate from seed or cuttings. No special watering is required once plants are established. Fertilizer is needed only if plants show deficiency or poor growth. Mulch is beneficial. Prune for shape; plants can get large with age. You can cut plants back hard; they will regrow quickly, forming more flowering branches.

OUTSIDE THE TROPICS Duranta is hardy through much of coastal California and in the warmer regions of the southern states, particularly if grown in a protected area and covered with a protective mulch in fall.

SELECTIONS 'Alba' has white flowers; **'Variegata'** has blue flowers, white and green leaves.

EPIPREMNUM AUREUM POTHOS, VARIEGATED PHILODEN-
DRON *Araceae*

This vining aroid native to the Solomon Islands is familiar in a juvenile form as a potted plant in many a home and office. In tropical conditions where it can climb, the olive green and yellow foliage may be around 18 inches across and somewhat pinnate and perforated, especially as it reaches higher on its support. If growing horizontally or hanging, the plant branches often and produces small leaves; when the plant finds a support, the leaves grow larger. The vine will grow to 30 feet or even to 50 feet, holding to supports by roots. As a groundcover, pothos becomes dense enough to suppress many weeds. As it grows up to festoon a large tree or palm, it lends a particularly lush, tropical look to the landscape.

CULTURE Dappled shade is best; the large leaves are produced only in full sun or light shade (and may revert to green) and on an ascending vine; epipremnum will adapt to almost all light situations. Soil should be well drained, friable, with some organic matter, and it should retain some moisture. Ideal temperatures range from above 65° F to 90° F, with humidity over 50 percent, but plants will tolerate dry interior conditions very well. Choose specimens with a color form that appeals to you. Propagate from stem cuttings with leaves, in a moist but not sodden medium. Set out well-rooted plants near the intended support, which may be any upright, columnar object, live or inanimate; royal palms are an excellent support—pothos luxuriates in trees. Water to establish and thereafter only during drought periods. Monthly applications of liquid fertilizer are beneficial but not usually necessary. Organic mulch applied near the base of the support will allow for good terrestrial rooting. Pruning is needed only to control errant growth.

Dracaena reflexa

ERYTHRINA CRISTA-GALLI (CORAL TREE, CRY-BABY TREE) Large or medium-sized tree to 75 feet tall, with showy red flowers with reflexed petals. Full sun, moist rich soil, best in regions with distinct seasons. Zones 9-10.

ETLINGERA ELATIOR (TORCH GINGER) Very tall herbaceous rhizomatous plant, 10-20 feet tall with large leaves and club-like red flower on green stalk. Full sun or light shade, warm and humid conditions, moist, rich, well-drained soil. Zone 10.

EUCALYPTUS DEGLUPTA (RAINBOW BARK GUM) Tall tree to 100 feet with small gray-green leaves and extraordinary bark mottled in pink, blue, and light green. Full sun, light but rich soil. Zone 10.

EUGENIA UNIFLORA (SURINAM CHERRY) Large shrub or small tree to 25 feet tall with leaves that turn from red to pink to green as they mature, fragrant white flowers, and bright red edible fruits. Full sun, moist, well-drained soil. Zone 10.

Pests are seldom a problem outdoors; indoors, spider mites may be a nuisance in low humidity.

OUTSIDE THE TROPICS Pothos is one of the most commonly grown plants for indoor conditions, where it endures gross neglect for long periods with little ill effect.

ERYTHRINA CORAL TREE *Fabaceae*

Erythrina is a genus of thorny trees and shrubs native to tropics around the world, valued in the garden for its showy pink, white, or red flowers that attract hummingbirds. Plants are deciduous, often producing their display of bloom when they are bare of leaves. Larger types are useful as shade trees.

CULTURE Grow in full sun. soil must be well-drained and not too moist. Propagates easily from seed and from cuttings of growing wood. Most types are hardy only to Zone 10. Tip borers that eat the soft, flower-producing tips, can be a problem in Florida; spraying can sometimes help.

SELECTIONS *E. caffra*, native to South Africa, is a spreading, 60-foot tree with clusters of scarlet flowers produced in early spring during the plant's brief leafless period. *E. crista-galli*, native to Brazil, is the most hardy species, surviving to Zone 8; its long spikes of brilliant red flowers resemble sweet peas and appear from spring through fall; grows 10-20 feet tall and is drought-tolerant. It is easily trained into a small tree and is useful as an accent or specimen. *E. herbacea,* native to Florida and Texas, grows to 10-15 feet tall, with its scarlet flowers appearing in the spring. *E. variegata* (*E. indica*), native to East Africa and Southern Polynesia, has green leaves that drop during the dry season and are followed by a profusion of scarlet flowers; grows to 60 feet tall. Some cultivars have variegated leaves.

ETLINGERA ELATIOR TORCH GINGER *Zingiberaceae*

Torch ginger is a giant, herbaceous, rhizomatous border plant, growing 10-20 feet tall; it makes a showy specimen for a small bed. Produced on a separate stalk, the clublike inflorescence is a spectacular construction of red or pink bracts and many small flowers; numerous flowers and flower clusters bloom simultaneously. Arching, leafy stalks resemble palm fronds. The unopened "flowers" are used in Asian cuisine, thinly sliced, in salads. Native to tropical Asia and the South Pacific, torch ginger is a classic tropical plant because of its spectacular appearance and ease of care. Flowers appear during long periods of warm weather; in some areas of the tropics, torch gingers are everblooming. In order to fully appreciate the magnificent flowers, the bases of the plants should not be obscured.

CULTURE Grow in full sun or light shade, with warm and humid conditions, in organically rich, well-drained, and moist soil. If you are buying a division, be sure there is a sturdy young shoot attached to the rhizome. Propagate by clump division or dividing off single stems attached to a piece of rhizome; also, fresh seeds germinate easily and grow quickly. Plant as deeply as previously, and mulch heavily to keep the fleshy surface roots cool and moist. Because of their size and vigor, these plants use plenty of water, so irrigate regularly when rain fails to keep the ground moist. Application of palm fertilizer three to four times a year is beneficial; at Lyons Arboretum, 10-30-10 is used once a year. Remove spent flower stalks to the ground. Torch ginger is seldom bothered by pests, though mealybugs occasionally infest them.

SELECTIONS *E. elatior* is usually red; a smaller pink form is also available. *E. hemis-*

This *Erythrina variegata* 'Tropic Coral', located at Foster Botanical Garden on Oahu, is claimed to be the original upright coral tree from which many on the islands have been propagated.

phaerica, black tulip torch ginger, is a large plant with narrow purple leaves, also spectacular, but the tulip-shaped "flowers" are produced on much shorter stalks.

EUCALYPTUS EUCALYPTUS *Myrtaceae*

A genus of over 500 species of largely evergreen trees, *Eucalyptus* includes the gum tree that grows to a height of 100-300 feet and is distinguished by its smooth blue-green bark that peels as the tree matures as well as many other species with different habits and bark types.Often juvenile foliage is very different from adult foliage; juvenile foliage is often round, adult long. Originally native to Australia (where it is the favorite food of the koala) and Tasmania, it is cultivated in the warmer parts of the United States, including California and the Southwest, since it does not tolerate frost. Eucalyptus oil, which is derived from the roots leaves, and bark, contains an active germicide and thus has antibacterial uses; it should, however, always be diluted since it is toxic in large doses. Eucalyptus oil is also used for air fresheners. Dried eucalyptus leaves can be a lovely addition to a potpourri.

CULTURE Eucalyptus needs full sun and light loamy soil. Transplant young trees, making sure not to plant them close to other plants. If grown in a greenhouse, underwater eucalyptus since its leaves blister if overwatered. Eucalyptus are heavy feeders; unless soil is naturally rich, apply fertilizer annually. Eucalyptus has no serious pests or diseases, since the tree's own aroma repels insects.

OUTSIDE THE TROPICS Eucalyptus can be grown as an annual from seed in colder climates. Sow seed in early summer in part shade. When seedlings are 2-3 inches high, transplant to a pot. Plant outside the following year or when 6-12 inches high. Do not permit plant to be become rootbound. Some species (**E. camaldulensis,** river red gum; **E. microtheca,** coolibah; **E. pauciflora ssp. niphophila,** snow gum) are hardy to Zones 7 or 8.

SELECTIONS *E. citriodora*, lemon gum, a tree that grows 125-150 feet and has lemon-scented leaves can also be used as a pot plant.

E. sideroxylon, red ironbark, a 50- to 60-foot tree, has blue-green leaves that turn copper in the winter.

E. polyanthemos, red box gum, a 70- to 80-foot tree, tolerates drought and heat, is a fine landscaping tree, and makes good cut foliage.

E. ficifolia, red-flowering gum, a heat-tolerant tree, has red to white flowers in summer.

E. viminalis, white or ribbon gum, a 50- to 100-foot fast-growing tree, thrives in poor soils.

E. cinerea, silver dollar gum, has shining, round silvery leaves that are extremely popular as cut foliage, grows 20-50 feet, and withstands wind and drought.

E. deglupta, rainbow gum, is very large, but one of the best species for the tropics; it has magnificent multicolored peeling bark.

EUGENIA [SYZYGIUM] *Myrtaceae (Myrtle family)*

Eugenia is a genus of evergreen trees and shrubs native to tropics around the world that is often grown for its fruit (eaten out of hand or made into jelly) and as ornamental specimens or hedges, sometimes with strikingly showy flowers. Most have dense, attractive foliage, often very colorful before maturity. Fruits may be quite

Sygyzium paniculatum, dwarf bush cherry.

ornamental, resembling pink or red wax pears (even though the common name may include the word "apple"). The genus now includes *Syzygium*.

CULTURE Grow in full sun, in moist, well-drained soil. A warm, humid climate suits most types; some tolerate minimal frost, but others, such as cloves, are very cold-sensitive. When purchasing, look for a thriving plant with vigorous growth and clean foliage. Propagate by seeds, or cuttings using rooting hormone and bottom heat. Planting out at the beginning of warm, wet weather works best. Water to establish. Fertilize spring and midsummer. Mulching the root zone is beneficial. Prune to show the tree to best advantage. Pests are seldom a problem.

SELECTIONS *S. jambos*, rose apple, is a bushy, spreading tree growing to 30 feet, with long, narrow leaves blushed with rose when young, and large, greenish white, fragrant flowers followed by pale, fragrant fruits. *E. uniflora*, Surinam cherry, is a large shrub or small tree, to 25 feet tall, often pruned back as a small hedge; leaves change from bright red to pink to dark green as they mature; fragrant white flowers are followed (even on hedge-clipped plants) by spicy, edible, bright red fruits loved by birds; grow in full sun. *E. malaccensis* {*S. malaccense*}, Malay apple, is a beautiful tropical tree for truly hot climates, with long, dark green, distinctive leaves, showy magenta flowers produced several times a year, and red to pink fruits. The dried flower buds of *S. aromaticum* provide the cloves of commerce.

FICUS FIG *Moraceae (Mulberry family)*

Ficus is a very large genus, encompassing excellent large shade trees for the tropics, small trees grown for their delicious fruit, and some popular houseplants. Some species, particularly the fascinating banyan tree, have hanging roots that twist and intertwine: some specimens take up half an acre. Ficus trees are useful in the South. They are grown along highways and as street trees in many parts of Florida. In the tropics, some extraordinarily large with age and are often covered with their own epiphytic roots.

CULTURE Most fig trees are hardy only in Zones 9-10, though some small fig trees are grown for fruit with protection in the North. The trees need full sun, but will adapt to any soil, heavy to sandy. Plant in spring or fall; water well. Although fig trees adapt to dry soil, a generous watering during dry periods will keep them looking healthy. Fertilize lightly but regularly. Prune to maintain an open shape, cutting out crossed branches and dead wood. Propagate by seeds or cuttings. Ficus is not susceptible to any serious pests or diseases.

SELECTIONS *F. benjamina*, grown as a houseplant in the North, reaches 80 feet tall or more in Zones 9-10, where it is an important shade tree. It needs more light than most species and does not tolerate overwatering.

F. carica, common fig, can be grown with protection as far north as New York and Chicago (Zone 5), where dedicated gardeners regularly bring it to fruiting; it needs to be wrapped and covered for winter, or grown in a pot and brought indoors. In Zones 7-10, it is perfectly hardy and reaches 30 feet tall, providing shade as well as fruit. Excessive fertilizer will reduce fruiting but improve foliage. Root pruning and application of superphosphate aid in fruit production.

F. elastica, rubber plant, another popular houseplant, has long, almost black oval leaves and needs very little light and even less water; it does need a very large site. With protection in cooler areas, it can be grown outdoors in Zones 9-10.

Ficuses used as foliage plants, from top to bottom: *Ficus pumila* 'Snowflake', *Ficus trianglularis* 'Variegata', *Ficus montana*, *Ficus petiolaris*

FICUS BENGHALENSIS (BANYAN TREE) Very large, spreading tree (specimens have been known to take up almost an acre) with multiple trunks and hanging epiphytic roots; 8-inch long leathery oval leaves. Full sun, any soil, prefers generous water but will tolerate dry conditions. Zone 10.

FREYCINETIA CUMINGIANA (FLOWERING PANDANUS) Spreading herbaceous plant to 15 feet tall with showy orange to pink flowers consisting of fleshy bracts surrounding conelike flowers. Partial shade, warm to very warm, very humid conditions, moist, well-drained fertile soil. Zones 9-10.

GALPHIMIA (GALPHIMIA) Shrub to 10 feet tall, gray-green leaves, showy yellow flowers. Partial shade, any soil; tolerates drought and wind. Zones 9-10.

GMELINA PHILIPPENSIS (PARROT'S BEAK) Woody climber with small dark green leaves, showy yellow flowers hanging from hoplike chains through much of the year. Full sun, warm temperatures, high humidity, any soil. Zones 9-10.

F. macrophylla, Moreton Bay fig, has a spreading shape that makes it useful as a backyard shade tree. Zones 9-10.

F. religiosa, peepul, bo-tree, has an open habit that reveals its graceful structure. It is deciduous in some areas, but loses its pale green leaves for only a few weeks in spring.

FREYCINETIA CUMINGIANA FLOWERING PANDANUS
Pandanaceae

Freycinetia includes 175 species, usually lianas, with males and females on separate plants. Inflorescences are a strikingly showy combination of conelike structures surrounded by fleshy bracts. Flowering pandanus, which grows 15-20 feet tall, is a beautiful plant for a semishaded nook where a high canopy protects it from scorching. Against a shaded wall or as a specimen, it never fails to attract attention when it flowers in the late winter and early spring. This Philippine native has sometimes been misidentified as *F. multiflora*. Some *Freycinetia* species are exploited for their leaf fibers, which are used for weaving baskets and mats.

CULTURE Plants seem to prefer partial shade, although bright morning sun is acceptable. Climate should range from warm (over 65° F) to very warm (95° F), with high humidity; plants will tolerate only short periods of near-freezing weather. Purchase full, strong plants with some sign of vigorous, upright growth. Propagate from semihardwood cuttings under mist, using rooting hormone, or from layering of lowest branches. Plant out into moist, well-drained, fertile soil in a partially shaded location. A nearby supporting tree is useful if you want your flowering pandanus to climb; otherwise, you may grow it as a sprawling mound. Regular watering is required if rains do not keep the soil moist. Organic mulch helps maintain the needed soil moisture. Regular applications of a balanced fertilizer are beneficial. Pruning is unnecessary except to control unwanted stems. Disease and pest problems are minimal.

SELECTIONS *F. cumingiana* is only sometimes available from specialty nurseries, but it is worth the search.

GALPHIMIA *Malpighiaceae*

The name *Galphimia* is an anagram of malphigia, Singapore holly, to which this shrub is closely related. Both have glossy gray green leaves, but galphimia's yellow flowers are showier, and its habit is more refined and compact. The shrub grows to 10 feet, but can be pruned smaller, making it useful as part of a border, or since it does well in shade, under taller shrubs and trees. It blooms after only one or two years. It is also known as thryallis.

CULTURE Galphimia thrives in partial shade (full sun in Hawaii) in any soil; it tolerates drought and wind very well. It is usually necessary to prune annually to keep the plant in shape, removing crowded and crossing branches, and to remove seedheads to promote abundant blossoming. Prune when flowering is finished. Propagation from seeds or cuttings is remarkably easy.

OUTSIDE THE TROPICS Galphimia does well as a pot plant in any ordinary potting soil; provide water generously, fertilize with a liquid fertilizer every two weeks in spring and fall, and repot every two or three years.

The *Ficus benjamina* that grows as a potted plant in so many homes may reach a heigh of 80 feet in the tropics. *Top: Ficus benjamina. Above: Ficus religiosa,* a similar species.

Several forms of graptophyllum, combined with sanchezia, at Waimea Falls Park on Oahu.

GMELINA PHILIPPENSIS PARROT'S BEAK *Verbenaceae*

Parrot's beak is a spiny, woody climber with small, dark green leaves. It produces showy, golden yellow flowers from drooping, hoplike chains of greenish maroon bracts through much of the year, especially during the warmer months. It forms a strongly twining mound or shrub about 8-10 feet tall. Parrot's beak makes a beautiful espalier; it is readily trained as a specimen "standard," and it is also useful as a topiary subject. Native to Asia.

CULTURE Grow in full sun; warm temperatures and high humidity are beneficial, while cold weather will cause defoliation. Plants seem to thrive in most soils. Propagation is from seed or semihardwood cuttings. Plant against support to train as an espalier. Grown as a specimen, parrot's beak needs to be staked until the trunk is thick enough to support the head. Apply balanced fertilizer three or four times a year. Flowers are produced at the tips of new branches, so pruning to encourage new branches results in heavier flowering, while clipping back of new growth removes potential flowers. It may be necessary to remove excessively vigorous new growth to maintain control of the plant's shape. Pests and diseases are not a problem.

GOETHEA STRICTIFLORA *Malvaceae*

A member of a rarely seen genus, *G. strictiflora* is one of two ornamental Brazilian species, very unlike its hibiscus relatives. Plants can grow to 6-7 feet tall, but are usually much shorter and frequently have single or few stems with narrow, 8-inch-long leaves at the top. Tubular, reddish brown flowers are borne on the bare stems and among the leaves, with petallike rosy pink bracts mottled white. This remarkable and attractive plant adds unusual color and form to woodland settings and the shady border and combines nicely with rocks and moss.

CULTURE Give plants plenty of shade and moisture, and a good, rich soil with manure or mulch/compost added. High humidity and temperatures to the upper 70° F to mid-80° F are best. Plants will tolerate cool nights down to the lower 50° F. Purchase sturdy plants with healthy leaves; even young plants will have some flowers, but this is not as important as an actively growing plant with healthy terminal growth. If possible, select plants with multiple stems or more than one stem in a pot. Propagate from stem cuttings. Set out 10 inches apart, in clumps for best effect. Plant about ½ inch deeper than originally, to make sure each plant is well supported. Keep moist at all times, and keep mulched to maintain moisture and humidity. Apply a balanced or liquid fertilizer if plants show signs of lack of vigor. Normally, do not cut back except to get material for propagation. Pests and disease do not seem to be a problem, although mealybugs might become a nuisance.

GRAPTOPHYLLUM PICTUM CARICATURE PLANT *Acanthaceae*

This evergreen shrub, growing to 9 feet tall, is very useful both indoors and out for its colorful foliage and its versatility, being both a sun- and shade-lover. Its name is probably derived from the word *character*, used because the irregular markings on the plant resemble characters or letters. Many foliage variations are available–purple, pale green with cream edges and dark blotches, purple with maroon blotches, green with yellow edges, and on and on. The showy foliage ranges from 3-10 inches long and is sometimes twisted. Native to New Guinea,

GOETHEA STRICTIFLORA (GOETHIA) Plant 6-7 feet tall, usually shorter, usually a single stem with 8-inch leaves on top and tubular reddish brown flowers borne on the stem. Partial to deep shade, generous moisture, rich soil. Zone 10.

GRAPTOPHYLLUM PICTUM (CARICATURE PLANT) Evergreen shrub, to 9 feet tall; foliage with many color and pattern variations. Sun or shade, moist or dry soil, warm climates. Zone 10.

GUAIACUM SANCTUM (LIGNUM VITAE) Evergreen small trees or large shrubs, to 30 feet tall but usually smaller; fine, deep green leathery foliage, bright blue flowers with yellow stamens in warm season. Full sun (light shade tolerated), well-drained moist to dryish soil, hot, humid weather. Zone 10.

HEDYCHIUM GARDNERANUM (KAHILI GINGER) Rhizomatous, herbaceous plants with showy clusters of flowers, often very fragrant; 2-8 feet tall. Full sun to semishade, warm and humid conditions promote vigorous growth; dry, cool periods are tolerated. Zones 8-10.

V I E W P O I N T

HELICONIA IN THE LANDSCAPE

Heliconia rostrata has the most exotic pendulous flowers, but the plants are slow to increase here on the Gulf Coast. *H. lathispatha* has distichous flowers which are not as exotic but it is very quick to spread. *H. sharonii* is a very good dwarf heliconia with distichous flowers, and it increases quickly.
LINDA GAY, MERCER ARBORETUM AND BOTANIC GARDEN, HUMBLE, TEXAS

Very few heliconias are *not* good in the landscape. Location must be taken into consideration; obviously very tall species and those with running stems are only suited to large landscapes or smaller places with adequate skilled staff. Smaller kinds look good anywhere, singly or in clumps.
KEITH WOOLLIAMS, WAIMEA FALLS PARK, OAHU, HAWAII

Despite my admiration of heliconias, I feel that certain ones are terrible landscape plants. Some, like *H. lathispatha* are downright weedy and hard to control. They grow quickly and rampantly. Others, like *H. psittacorum* are unattractive after they've flowered. There are excellent landscape heliconias as well, including H. caribea and *H. orthotica*.
DAVID BAR-ZVI, FAIRCHILD TROPICAL GARDEN

the plant is used medicinally among the Pacific islands.

CULTURE Caricature plant tolerates low light levels as well as full sun and adapts to drier organic soils as well as soils with ample moisture. It is best grown in temperatures from 65-85° F. Propagates easily from seed and cuttings. Plants can be set out any time, but the wet season is best. Space 5 feet or more apart. Fertilize plants when young; mature plants do not need much feeding. For best results, keep soil moist. Promote colorful new growth by pruning branches back to half their length once a year or as needed; this healthy new growth also keeps plants free of pests and disease.

SELECTIONS *G. pictum* 'Tricolor' has attractive 10-inch-long leaves, greenish purple with an irregular creamy rose area along the midrib, which–along with the petioles–is brilliant red.

GUAIACUM LIGNUM VITAE *Zygophyllaceae*

These natives of South Florida, the Florida Keys, and the West Indies are small to medium trees or shrubs, commonly grown in the landscape as shrubs, with deep green, fine, evergreen leathery foliage. They bear bright blue flowers with yellow stamens two to three times during the warm months. The extremely dense, resinous wood is in such commercial demand–it is used in food-handling machines, supplies the medicinal substance guaiacum, and provides hardwood for pulleys and neck bearings that need self-lubrication–that the plants are considered endangered.

CULTURE Full sun is best, but plants tolerate some light shade. Well-drained, even dryish soil is good, and hot, humid weather is best. Freezing will cause defoliation. Propagation is from seed but is very slow; remove red fleshy coat from seed, scarify, soak at least overnight, and sow just below soil surface, keeping warm. When purchasing, look for a full shrub; however, plants are difficult to find commercially. Once plants are established, extra irrigation is not necessary or even desirable, nor is special fertilization. Minor pruning to shape may be done if absolutely necessary. Light mulching is beneficial if it's not too deep.

SELECTIONS *G. sanctum* is denser than **G. officinale**, which grows somewhat faster and is more commonly seen in the West Indies.

HEDYCHIUM BUTTERFLY GINGER *Zingiberaceae*

Most of the 50 species of *Hedychium* originated in India and Malaysia. They have been transported to all parts of the tropical world, where some have become completely naturalized. In summer, these rhizomatous, herbaceous plants bear showy clusters of often deliciously fragrant flowers (used for perfumes and leis) from the tips of leafy stalks that arch from the soil to heights ranging from 2 to more than 8 feet. Any moist woodland edge or waterside site benefits from hedychium planting. As they are tough and tolerant once established, they are often planted in sunny, periodically dry areas–even in sandy soil–with success. Great favorites for siting just outside home windows because of their delightful colorful flowers and perfume.

CULTURE Hedychium will grow in full sun to semishade, preferably in warm and humid conditions. Some are tolerant of cool, dry periods when they may be deciduous. While some hedychiums are naturally epiphytic, most require deep, organic, always moist but well-drained soil. However, under these ideal conditions,

HEDYCHIUM CORONARIUM (WHITE GINGER) Rhizomatous, herbaceous plants with showy clusters of flowers, often very fragrant; 2-8 feet tall. Full sun to semishade, warm and humid conditions promote vigorous growth; dry, cool periods are tolerated. Zones 8-10.

HELICONIA ANGUSTA 'HOLIDAY' HELICONIA) Herbaceous plant, 2-10 feet tall, with upright showy red and white flowers. Deep shade with some strong sun, high humidity, warm to very warm temperatures, moist, well-drained soil. Zone 10.

HELICONIA HIRSUTA 'JAMAICA SPIKEY' (JAMAICA SPIKEY)
Herbaceous plant, 2-10 feet tall, with pendant showy yellow and red flowers. Deep shade with some strong sun, high humidity, warm to very warm temperatures, moist, well-drained soil. Zone 10.

HELICONIA INDICA 'SPECTABILIS' (HELICONIA) Large, paddle-shaped reddish leaves, to 8 feet tall; flowers are inconspicuous. Deep shade with some strong sun, high humidity, warm to very warm temperatures, moist, well-drained soil. Zone 10.

plants can become invasive—for more controlled growth, give less shade, nutrition, and moisture. When purchasing, look for vigorous, healthy foliage or plump, fresh rhizomes. Propagate by rhizome or clump division; choose pieces with several old leaves and a piece of rhizome with two or more healthy, young, new growths, about 12 inches long. When planting during dormancy, cover the rhizome with soil to a depth about twice the rhizome's thickness, but no deeper than previously. Add slow-release fertilizer to the planting hole, and apply fertilizer lightly three to four times during the year while the plants are actively growing; beware of overfeeding, which will result in rampant growth. Water hedychium during very dry periods, and mulch heavily to maintain soil moisture. Remove spent flowering stems. Cut back deciduous types when they seem to be dying back; if evergreen, remove all or some leaves periodically (even annually) to encourage healthy new growth. Hedychium has no serious pests.

OUTSIDE THE TROPICS In colder climates, hedychium is grown in the greenhouse or indoors, although it is a large plant.

SELECTIONS *H. coronarium*, white ginger, has heavily scented, white flowers with a lime green center to the lip. It can grow at water's edge or in water. *H. flavum*, yellow ginger, has very fragrant yellow blooms with an orange center to the lip. *H. gardnerianum*, Kahili ginger, with fragrant red-stamened and golden yellow flowers, is used in hybridizing. *H. coccineum* var. *angustifolium* has nonfragrant orange flowers; plants are very striking in a shaded area, but have a short blooming period. All grow 3-6 feet tall.

HELICONIA LOBSTER CLAW, PARROT BEAK *Heliconiaceae*

Heliconias are bananalike plants with long, broad leaves; the hundreds of species range from heights of under 2 feet to over 18 feet. The flowering stalks of the New World species are large, showy, either erect or hanging, carrying large bracts in colors dominated by vivid reds, yellows, and oranges, with a kaleidoscope of other tints also available. The Pacific Island species often have colorful foliage; several have green flower bracts and red seeds. Heliconias can be landscape prima donnas, with dramatic, attention-getting flair if used as specimens. They may also be used as lush screening, and some make very attractive border plantings. With proper grooming, they can easily cause a sensation. Certain species (such as *H. psittacorum* and *H. densiflora*) are well suited to large containers, which prevents them from taking over the garden and produces a more concentrated flower display. Flowers appear throughout the year but are more abundant during warm weather. Low-growing types combine well with other plants and are attractive near rocks.

CULTURE In the wild, most heliconias grow in breaks in the forest; cultivated, most prefer at least some strong sun, but several perform beautifully in deep shade. All heliconias love high humidity, and most thrive in warm to very warm temperatures. High winds or dry, cold conditions will make the plants look very stressed. They recover quickly when favorable conditions prevail again. Heliconias want moist, well-drained soil; some even grow as semiaquatics. Since the plant parts are sometimes easily torn, this is not a reason to reject a plant when buying. Do check for signs of insect infestation; if rhizomes show any signs of borers, do not purchase. Look for plants with several strong new shoots or rhizomes with a clean, turgid stalk. Propagate by clump division or by dividing off a single mature

Above: Heliconia rostrata.
Top: Heliconia chartaceae **'Sexy Pink'**.

Heliconia caribaea.

Heliconia indica 'Spectabilis'.

Heliconia psittacorum.

Heliconia spissa.

Heliconia zebrina.

Heliconia 'Golden Torch'.

Heliconia caribaea x *Heliconia bihai*
'Richmond Red'.

(pseudo)stem with an intact piece of rhizome. Set the latter vertically in an open
soil mix, and keep warm and moist but not wet. When planting out, the top of
the rhizome should be about twice the depth of the leaf width. A slow-release fertilizer in the planting hole is very beneficial; 13-5-13 slow-release planting
tablets–originally developed for use with rice plantings under very wet conditions–have proven useful. Regular watering is required when weather is dry.
Heliconias are heavy feeders; regular feeding with, especially, palm fertilizer is
good practice. Keep plants heavily mulched with organic materials. Prune off
unsightly foliage or as needed to reveal flowers. Cut spent flowering stalks to the
ground. Every few years it is worthwhile to dig, divide, and replant into reworked
and amended soil; between flowering cycles, is best. Heliconias have few disease
problems except where the soil is too wet.

SELECTIONS LARGE *H. caribaea* grows 10-20 feet tall and is sturdy and erect. Its very
large, dramatic "flowers," often produced year-round, come in a wide range of
colors. It thrives in semishade to full sun. *H. bihai* is a medium to large plant, 7-12
feet tall, with huge leaves. Generous and dramatic, its flowers come in many vivid
colors. *H. x jacquinii* is very sturdy, hardy, and drought-tolerant; its orange and yellow "flowers" appear all year. *H. collinsiana* has pendant red "flowers" that hang
dramatically beneath waxy foliage; it blooms July through November.

MEDIUM *H. stricta* has erect, dramatic "flowers," often in brilliant reds. *H. s. 'Sharonii'*
has particularly attractive foliage and red and cream "flowers." *H. subulata* is hardy,

HEMIGRAPHIS ALTERNATA (RED IVY) Low-growing herbaceous perennial up to 18 inches tall; grayish purple leaves with red undersides. Full sun or partial shade, moist or dryish soils. Zone 10.

HIBISCUS ROSA-SINENSIS 'NAGAUZO' (HIBISCUS) 3- to 4-foot-tall shrub with 3-inch red flowers with yellow stamens. Full sun to very light shade, rich, well-drained, constantly moist soil. Zones 8-10.

HIBISCUS SCHIZOPETALUS (CORAL HIBISCUS) Tall, vigorous shrub or small tree with arching branches and pendulous flowers. Full sun to very light shade, rich, well-drained, constantly moist soil. Zones 9-10.

HIBISCUS TILIACEUS (HAU, FAU, VAU) Vigorous, much-branched tree or shrub to 20 feet; 3-inch yellow flowers with dark purple eyes turn orange by evening. Full sun to very light shade, rich, well-drained, constantly moist soil. Zones 9-10.

Hybrid hibiscus, from top to bottom: 'Norman Lee', 'Peewee Herman', 'Lady Bird'.

with good foliage and long, erect, red and yellow "flowers." **H. psittacorum** grows 3-6 feet tall and is available in dozens of colors. It is fast-growing, loves full sun, and tends to spread quickly but is good in confined, bright areas. **H. pendula**, 4-6 feet tall, produces pendant, showy, red or pink "flowers." **H. rostrata**, which grows to 3-10 (or more) feet tall, is called "hanging heliconia": its spectacular, pendant, red and yellow flower clusters several feet long are borne over a long period; a very fine garden plant.

SMALL H. stricta 'Dwarf Jamaican' flowers at a height of 15 inches to 3½ feet and has a long period of bloom. **H. nutans** grows to a height of 3-7 feet and has pendant "flowers." **H. angusta** grows 2-10 feet tall and is called "Christmas Heliconia"; **'Holiday'** is 2-4 feet tall, with red bracts and distinct white flowers in winter. **H. psittacorum x spathocircinata 'Golden Torch'** grows 6-9 feet tall and bears golden and yellow flowers and bracts.

HEMIGRAPHIS ALTERNATA HEMIGRAPHIS, RED IVY *Acanthaceae*

Hemigraphis is a low-growing perennial, reaching only 18 inches in height and spreading freely. Leaves are metallic grayish purple above and deep purple below. Inconspicuous white-with-purple flowers appear on terminal spikes. This native of Java is an attractive and tolerant groundcover and a good subject for hanging baskets.

CULTURE Hemigraphis likes filtered as well as full sun and adapts to drier soils with humus as well as soils with ample moisture. Good drainage is advantageous. Optimum temperatures are 65-85° F. Propagate from terminal cuttings or from division of rooted stems. Cuttings can be rooted directly into the ground during the wet season; otherwise, root cuttings in pots and plant out after they are established. Apply granular fertilizer to young plants and after established groundcover has been cut back. For best results, keep soil moist but not wet. Can be cut back to desired height or size at almost any time, which rejuvenates it and keeps it under control. Hemigraphis has few pest or disease problems, although it has a tendency to develop root rot if too wet. Scale insects are occasionally a nuisance.

OUTSIDE THE TROPICS Indoors, hemigraphis performs best in medium light and average to high temperatures.

SELECTIONS H. alternata 'Exotica' has glossy, deep purple leaves curved inward at the edges and puckered; creamy white flowers are ¼ inch across.

HIBISCUS HIBISCUS *Malvaceae*

Hibiscus is a very variable genus of about 200 species, native to temperate and tropical areas around the world. A few are herbaceous; nearly all are woody. Hibiscus are prostrate to erect shrubs (some viny) or trees, usually smooth-stemmed, although some are very spiny. Leaves are oval to deeply lobed, entire to toothed, smooth or hairy. Flowers part into fives, with a collar of bracts below the calyx, followed by a capsulated fruit. Cultivars in the *H. rosa-sinensis* group are widely popular in the tropics and are the national or local emblem in many countries. Some species have religious, medicinal, timber, fiber, and food uses. Hibiscus has many uses in the landscape—as feature trees, shrubs, or shade trees, for arbor growing, or just for masses of color. In the ornamental or edible garden, species that can be eaten add an extra dimension. Hibiscus of various kinds can be planted to produce interest all year round.

CULTURE Grow in full sun to very light shade, in rich, well-drained soil that is constantly moist (a few hibiscus are swamp plants). All species do best in warm summers, with temperatures of 75° F or more, but many (if not all) can tolerate short periods in the low 50° F. Some species are adapted to periodic drought conditions, but horticulturally fare much better with even moisture. Purchase bushy plants with strong, healthy growths. Tree types should have firm, stout stems and healthy terminal growths and growth-buds present. If possible, check for strong, healthy roots that are not potpound. Species hibiscus are frequently grown from seeds; hybrids of the modern *H. rosa-sinensis* group need grafting, but older forms root easily from cuttings. All will air-layer with moderate ease. When setting out, plants can be buried ½-1 inch deeper than the soil level of the container. Water well and–this is very important–do not allow the soil to dry out for the next two to three weeks. Incorporate a general fertilizer with the soil in the planting hole, or add after planting as a surface dressing. Most hibiscus do not tolerate dry conditions and wilt easily; keep plants moist for best results. Promote healthy and active root and shoot growth by periodic applications of a balanced fertilizer such as 10-30-10. Flowers are usually borne on young wood. Mulching is advantageous, 3-4 inches deep but ½-1 inch deep where in contact with trunk or stem. Many hibiscus need little pruning other than periodic shaping. Others, like the *H. rosa-sinensis* group that flower heavily on young growths, benefit from a periodic heavy pruning, removing about one-third of the growth, which encourages root and shoot vigor, every two to five years. White fly, scale on leaves and stems, mealybugs on leaves, stems, and roots, and bud weevil (which causes bud drop) are all periodic pests. Mites can cause leaves to become stunted and produce swollen gall-like growths. When nematodes attack, this is usually a sign that plants are old and need replacing or that you have serious soil problems.

OUTSIDE THE TROPICS Hibiscus is a much-used plant in temperate climates, as an annual, as a difficult but rewarding houseplant, as a shrub, and as a tropical-looking perennial. *H. rosa-sinensis* is the species used in annual plantings and as an indoor potted plant. *H. moscheutus,* rose mallow, with huge flowers (often up to 2 feet across), is used as an accent in perennial gardens; and *H. syriacus* is a shrub hardy to Zone 5.

SELECTIONS *H. acetosella,* red-leaved hibiscus, is a striking 4- to 6-foot-tall shrub; leaves and flowers most commonly red-purple, but green forms are also available. It is short-lived, behaving as an annual or lasting for two to three years, but it comes true from propagated seeds. Red-leaved hibiscus is an excellent feature plant in groups of three or more, very striking if used in a combination of red-purple- and green-leaved forms.

H. arnottianus **ssp.** *arnottianus*, Oahu white hibiscus, is endemic to moist, upland mountain areas of Oahu. Its form varies from large shrubs to small trees, 10-15 feet tall, with scented white flowers and leaves with a purplish tint. It tolerates full sun but does best in overcast or lightly shaded sites. Fine for shrubbery or as feature plants, Oahu white hibiscus is very floriferous, blooming in spurts from spring to early winter.

H. brackenridgei, ma'o-hau-hele, is an endangered species found only in the Hawaiian Islands; it is the Hawaiian state flower. This shrub or small tree bears 4-

Hybrid hibiscus, from top to bottom: 'Blue Bayou', 'The Path', 'El Capitolio'.

Hibiscus evolution garden at Waimea Falls Park.

inch bright yellow flowers with a basal maroon eye; spreading petals make the plant spectacular in full flower. It is easily propagated from seed or cuttings and is a dryland plant, so do not overwater. Roots are weak and shallow, so do not give too much nitrogen fertilizer. This plant lives only about five years in cultivation; susceptible to nematodes, soil-borne fungi, and fusarium diseases.

H. 'Brilliant', common red hibiscus, hedge hibiscus, a very old form of the *H. rosa-sinensis* complex, is a bushy shrub 6-8 feet tall. Its 3- to 4-inch red flowers have darker eyes at the base of its petals. Popular for hedges (space 30-36 inches apart in a single row or 15-18 inches apart in double rows), it flowers well and responds well to cutting back; also a fine individual specimen plant.

H. calyphyllus, an erect, spreading shrub 4-8 feet tall, bears 4- to 5-inch yellow flowers with maroon eyes. It tolerates considerable shade (but then produces few flowers) and grows well in any soil that is not too heavy, including poor, sandy soil. It propagates easily from seeds or cuttings; plants propagated from nonerect terminal shoots and horizontal branches are spreading, 2-3 feet tall, suitable for groundcovers. Healthy, actively growing plants are striking and very floriferous, grown singly or in groups of three or more.

H. hamabo is a branching shrub, to 15 feet tall, with 3-inch light yellow flowers. It likes well-drained fertile soil and full sun and is recommended for central Florida.

H. mutabilis, cotton rose or Confederate rose, is a large, vigorous, bushy shrub, 8-12 feet tall. The most commonly cultivated form has 2- to 4-inch double flowers that open white and slowly turn to bright pink by evening; other forms are white or pink, single or double. It propagates easily from seed. Allow it to grow to full size with pruning only for shape, or cut back annually just after flowering to about a foot from the ground, which produces a good flush of flowers and enables you to grow this type in a modest space.

H. sabdariffa, roselle or Jamaica sorrel, is an annual or very short-lived subshrub to 6 feet tall. It bears 1- to 2-inch yellow flowers with maroon eyes and calyces that become fleshy and juicy; when ripe, they are used for making jams, jellies, pies, and acid drinks, and when unripe they are used as a vegetable. Its small, rather upright habit and yellow flowers make this a useful addition to the garden as long as you keep in mind its short life.

H. schizopetalus, coral hibiscus, is unique because of arching branches with pendulous flowers on long, slender stalks and deeply laciniate petals. The tall (15 feet and more), vigorous shrub or tree is usually multistemmed. Innumerable hybrids exist; in the wild, plants have all-red flowers and fruit readily. The plant commonly in cultivation is apparently sterile, and its flowers have some white coloring. A fine feature plant, especially good when allowed to spread naturally and especially lovely viewed from the side and below, it is also valuable in shrubberies. Keep its vigor and arching habit in mind when siting.

H. tiliaceus, called hau, fau, or vau in the Pacific, is a very variable, vigorous, much-branched shrub or tree to 20 or more feet tall. Its leaves are light green to purple, usually with white feltlike hairs below, and its abundant flowers are 3 inches long, yellow with dark purple eyes, and produced frequently throughout the year. During the afternoon, flowers turn to orange and to reddish orange by evening. A common sight along rivers and streams where it grows to dense thickets, it tolerates drier conditions, including sandy and windy coastal areas. Specimens are very attractive, but need a large landscape for best effects; good for hedges, barriers, oceanfront sites, and arbors. Throughout the Pacific, local forms have arisen: purple-leaved forms with deeply lobed leaves are especially attractive, as are forms with cream or pink variegated leaves. **H. t. var. potteri** is a huge tree with a single trunk; a variant from Fiji forms a round 6-foot ball.

H. 'Variegata' (often 'El Capitolio' in nurseries); a small shrub, 4-6 feet tall, of the *H. rosa-sinensis* group, this plant has very unusual flowers–stamens at the end of the staminal column have reverted to petals, resulting in a basal flower with a terminal tuft of petals, all light red, some with white edging. It works well in front of shrubbery and in a prominent position where something very unusual is required. **'Variegata Sport'** ('El Capitolio Sport') has peach-colored flowers, and **'Sport of Sport'** is yellow-flowered.

H. waimeae, Kauai white hibiscus, a tough, strong plant, ranges from a shrub to a 30-foot tree in cooler climates. Its 4- to 5-inch flowers are white, usually fading to pale pink. Only Hawaiian white-flowered hibiscus like this one have scented blooms. It becomes a large shrub in lowlands and full sun or very light shade, but rapidly becomes a large tree in overcast, cool, moist conditions of higher elevations. It is fine for shrubberies, near the house for scent, and as specimen plants.

HIPPEASTRUM AMARYLLIS *Amaryllidaceae*

Amaryllis are herbaceous, bulbous plants native to tropical America with straplike leaves and produce large, showy, trumpet-shaped flowers on the end of a long, hollow stem at least once a year. A range of colors is available, including pink, orange, red, purple, white, and variegated. Several species are deciduous for part of the year. Amaryllis make fine houseplants. Large containers can make very attractive groupings, and small to large beds of seasonal color can be produced using just hippeastrum. Most flower in late winter or early spring. There is also a genus *Amaryllis* with one species, *A. belladona,* native to South Africa.

CULTURE Outdoors, grow in full sun to partial shade; make sure air circulates well. Conditions should be warm and humid while plants are growing, with a period of cool dryness in winter. Soil should be organically rich and well draining; sandy loam is best. Buy large, firm bulbs with no sign of injury or decay. Purchased plants should have clear, dark green foliage with no reddish, irregular marks or spots. Bulb offsets may be removed and grown separately. Plant out as a dormant bulb or as a plant rooted in a container. The neck of the bulb should be just emerging from the soil. You may water in a leafless bulb and then hold it on the dry side until new growth emerges. Often the flowers appear first; when the new leaves do appear, water plants regularly. At the end of the growing season when leaves naturally begin to die, withhold water, and keep plants drier throughout the dormant season; If leaves don't die back, remove them. An application of bonemeal to the planting hole helps to develop strong roots and bulbs; balanced fertilizer during the growing season and light mulching are beneficial.

OUTSIDE THE TROPICS Indoors, grow in bright light but not direct sun, and average to cool temperatures. Amaryllis bulbs can be forced indoors easily; keep the bulbs in a warm dark place until you want them to flower, then move to a fairly bright spot with good humidity; water every few days and fertilize every two weeks.

SELECTIONS While many of the Dutch hybrids are fine garden plants, some of the

Hybrid amaryllis is attractive when planted in masses; it tolerates crowding. Though it blooms for only a short time, it provides bright color in its season. Planting stored bulbs at biweekly intervals from November to February produces a succession of spring bloom.

HIPPEASTRUM PUNICEUM (AMARYLLIS) Herbaceous, bulbous plants with straplike leaves and showy trumpetlike flowers in late winter or early spring. Full sun to partial shade, warm temperatures in growing season, cooler at other times, rich, well-drained soil. Zones 9-10.

HYMENOCALLIS PEDALIS (SPIDER LILY) Clump-forming herbaceous plant with sword-shaped leaves and clusters of lilylike, fragrant white flowers. Full sun; adapts to a range of soils and temperatures. Zones 7-10.

IRESINE HERBSTII (BLOOD LEAF, BEEFSTEAK PLANT, CHICKEN GIZZARD) Shrub to 6 feet tall, with quilted pink-striped dark red foliage. Full sun, warm during day and cooler at night; evenly moist soil in summer; drought tolerant. Zones 9-10.

IXORA COCCINEA CV. (JUNGLE GERANIUM) Bushy evergreen shrub with showy, intensely colored clusters of small flowers. Full sun, rich moist soil. Zone 10.

old-fashioned hybrids and even the species are just as spectacular. ***H. reticulatum*** has mauve-red flowers, and ***H. r. var. striatifolium*** has additionally a white midrib stripe along the length of the leaf.

H. puniceum has red flowers in many forms, including double-flowered. **'Apple Blossom'**, **'Red Lion'**, and **'Picotee'** are popular hybrids. ***H. papilio*** is a rather expensive evergreen species, interesting in the garden but not as showy as the hybrids.

HYMENOCALLIS PEDALIS SPIDER LILY *Amaryllidaceae*

Spider lily is a popular garden plant, with clusters of thick, tapering, sword-shaped leaves. The sweetly scented, lilylike white flowers are borne in clusters; each flower is a long, slender, greenish tube topped by a cuplike structure to which the stamens are joined; below the cup hang the long, narrow petals, each about 4 inches long and reminiscent of spiders or ribbons. With age, spider lily forms large clumps that produce an abundance of flowers in spring and summer. This is a tough plant for hot, dry, coastal areas; it is not much affected by salty winds. It is also very suitable for more inland areas. Native to eastern South America.

CULTURE Grow in full sun or light shade. Spider lily will grow in a variety of well-drained soils; deep, sandy soil is especially suitable. It is also very adaptable to a variety of temperature and humidity conditions, but it thrives in warm to hot coastal situations. It appears to do best when allowed plenty of air circulation and when not crowded by other plants. Propagate from seed, or by division at any time when the plant is not flowering, especially when new shoots are growing. When setting out, take care not to bury the base of the leaves. Space 10-12 inches apart, and water in well. If weather is hot and dry, provide light shade for a few days after planting. Keep plants moist when growing and flowering, and apply a general fertilizer in the spring. Remove old flower stems and leaves as needed. Pests and diseases are not much of a problem, although mealybugs may become a nuisance in the outer leaf bases.

SELECTIONS The very attractive cultivar ***H. pedalis* 'Variegata'** has a broad white stripe down the midrib. ***H. caribaea*** and ***H. speciosa*** are similar, robust species. ***H. latifolia*** will grow as a pool plant. ***H. crassifolia,*** a Florida native, grows in stream banks.

IRESINE HERBSTII BLOOD LEAF *Amaranthaceae*

When bright foliage is needed to set off a shrub or provide color when flowers have faded, iresine is an excellent choice. Though its flowers are insignificant, the quilted pink-striped dark red foliage of this plant make it attractive in all seasons.

CULTURE Iresines do best in full sun and in climates where temperatures are warm during the day and cooler at night. In summer, keep soil evenly moist, but allow it to dry slightly in winter (not necessary in Hawaii); the plant is drought tolerant. If desired, shear to whatever height is best. Pinch out the tips of new shoots to encourage bushy growth. Propagate by root cuttings taken in late summer. For cooler climates, plant outdoors when the weather is warm from cuttings in 3- to 4-inch pots.

OUTSIDE THE TROPICS Iresine also does well in containers, baskets, windowboxes, and as houseplants. Bring indoors before frost; keep in high light and reduce watering in winter.

Ixora will grow to 6 feet, but can also be sheared for use as an edging plant.

IXORA *Rubiaceae (Madder family)*

These evergreen shrubs are among the showiest plants of the tropics, with a bushy growth habit and often spectacular clusters of showy, intensely colored flowers produced almost continuously. They are grown as specimens, as informal hedges, and, in cooler climates, as houseplants. Dwarf forms provide a continuous and brilliant display of color in the rock garden. Native to tropics around the world.

CULTURE Ixora is easy to grow and needs little pruning except to keep a hedge at the desired height. Ixoras luxuriate and flower best in full sun in acidic soil that is moist but well drained; it may become chlorotic in high-pH soil. It tolerates light shade. It is not very tolerant of frost, but will recover if only lightly frosted. Light shade is beneficial during the hottest months. Propagate from cuttings. Caterpillars may attack flower buds and must be controlled; scale and sooty mold sometimes appear and can be controlled with soap water sprays.

OUTSIDE THE TROPICS Grown as a houseplant, ixora needs warm temperatures and high humidity; it prefers high light but will tolerate medium light; keep soil evenly moist and reduce watering during the winter months.

SELECTIONS *I. coccinea*, jungle geranium, is often used as a 4-foot hedge or foundation planting; it blooms virtually constantly, with clusters of coral-red flowers 3 inches across; slow-growing; needs full sun; native to India. *I. casei [duffii]* is similar but grows to 10 feet with flowers twice the size of *I. coccinea*. *I. javanica* grows as well in semishade as in sun and more quickly than other ixoras, with very large heads of orange-red flowers.

JACARANDA MIMOSIFOLIA GREEN EBONY *Bignoniaceae*

Jacaranda is a deciduous to semi-evergreen tree or shrub native to tropical America, growing 25-40 feet tall, with lacy, fernlike leaves and tubular blue flowers produced in showy clusters, followed by decorative seed capsules. Trees are often used as street trees or lawn specimens. They are especially appealing when planted on the top of a hillside or on a second-story patio so that they can be viewed from below. Purple bougainvillea climbing up a jacaranda tree is an extraordinary sight.

CULTURE Jacaranda grows quickly, adapts to a wide variety of soils (though it prefers sandy soil), and is fairly tolerant of occasional cold snaps and drought. Several fifty-year-old trees, which had withstood 26° F cold froze and died at 17° F at Bok Tower Gardens. Jacaranda rarely needs watering or fertilizing and does not suffer from any serious pest problems. Provide full sun. Propagates easily from seed or cuttings. Pruning is needed only if you want to control the size or shape of the tree, but staking is often necessary to achieve a single trunk.

OUTSIDE THE TROPICS Mature trees are hardy to 32° F (Zone 8); young trees are not frost-hardy. Jacarandas can be grown indoors in warm, sunny rooms; they will not bloom, but make elegant foliage plants about 3 feet tall.

SELECTIONS A white flowered form, **'Alba'**, is also available; its bloom is sparser but lasts longer, and its foliage is denser.

JASMINUM JASMINE *Oleaceae*

Although they are highly ornamental and long-blooming, jasmines are loved more for their potent fragrance than for any other quality. Used in leis in Hawaii,

in tea in China, in perfume in France, the scent of jasmine is unmistakably tropical. Most are evergreen shrubs or vines with small white or yellow flowers; the
shrubby varieties can be used as hedges, the vines are beautiful when draped over
terraces or gates.

CULTURE Jasmines need full sun or partial shade and grow in any ordinary, moist
soil; large-leaved varieties need the most water. Most are frost-tender, but *J. nudiflorum* (winter jasmine) is hardy as far north as Boston in a protected site. Provide
a trellis or support for vining types. Most jasmines need pinching and pruning to
remain in bounds. Propagate by seed or cuttings.

OUTSIDE THE TROPICS Jasmines make wonderful houseplants, imparting a strong
tropical scent to whatever room they grace. They should be grown in bright light
and given some support for their vining growth; planting them outdoors in summer, or taking pots outside, is very beneficial. They need a cool period in winter,
and rich, always moist soil. The best species for indoor growers are *J. polyanthum,*
pink jasmine, (which grows well outdoors as well) which is easy to grow and
sometimes requires pruning, and *J. officinale,* white jasmine, which produces white
flowers in summer through autumn.

SELECTIONS *J. floridum,* a sprawling shrub has yellow flowers in spring and summer.
J. grandiflorum, Spanish jasmine, poet's jasmine, is the species used in perfumes. A
semievergreen vine, it produces loose clusters of 1- to 2-inch white flowers all
summer.

J. nitidum, star jasmine, angelwing jasmine, an evergreen vine, produces very ornamental white flowers with pointed petals. It does well in containers and can be
pruned as a groundcover.

J. multiflorum, downy jasmine, is a profuse bloomer, cold hardy in central Florida.

J. nudiflorum, winter jasmine, is the hardiest species, but it is not fragrant. A deciduous shrub or vine, it does best in cooler climates. Flowers are yellow.

J. sambac, Arabian jasmine is a climber with very fragrant double or single white
flowers; particularly recommended for the Gulf Coast, where it blooms through
the worst summer heat and often all through a mild winter.

JATROPHA PEREGRINA *Euphorbiaceae*

Jatrophas respond well to the gardener's touch; they can be trained to bushiness
or to climb up trellises. The leaves usually remain small and sparse, allowing the
architecture of the plant itself to be seen through the foliage. Although jatrophas
are not as lush as many other tropical plants, they have an exotic nature that
blends and contrasts well in a tropical setting. Jatropha is a splendid specimen
plant for a small—or a tiny—garden. It can be kept small to reach windowbox
height and blend with plants in the windowbox. It does well in containers.

CULTURE Jatrophas need hot climates, but are adapted to most types of well-
drained soil, even sandy types. They do best in partial shade. Fertilizer is rarely
needed, except in the very poorest soils. Water to keep soil moist, but do not
allow jatropha's roots to stand in water. Prune to desired shape; for a bushier
plant, retain lateral branches. Jatropha can be trained to climb up trellises and
onto porch railings. Propagate by seeds or cuttings. Leave cuttings outside to dry
for a day before placing them in potting medium. No serious pests or diseases.

OUTSIDE THE TROPICS *J. podagrica* can be grown as a moderately large houseplant; it
produces flowers for only a short time in summer, but its bulbous base is an inter-

Jatropha can be trained as a single-
stemmed, open tree. Shown below, it
just reaches baskets of impatiens
hanging from a second story window.

Above: Pachystachys lutea, also called shrimp plant (or golden shrimp plant), is similar to justicia in culture; it produces showy and unusual waxy golden candles from spring to late summer.

Top: Justicia carnea, pink Brazilian plume, is a fairly hardy evergreen shrub that has large, showy pink "flowers"; a white form is also available. It is often seen as a tidy, sheared hedge in southern California.

esting shape. Provide bright light and plenty of water. Though hardy only in Zone 10, jatropha can be grown in tubs moved indoors in winter and outdoors during the summer. Allow the plant time to acclimate to the new environment. **SELECTIONS** *J. integerrima*, the most common type, reaches 3-10 feet tall; flowers in many shades of red. *J. podagrica,* gout plant, tartogo, has a knobby, swollen base.

JUSTICIA SHRIMP PLANT, BRAZILIAN PLUME *Acanthaceae*

Justicia and *Pachystachys,* pantropical in origin, include over 300 species of flowering shrubs, many of which are very showy and bloom much of the year. The "flowers" are terminal and usually consist of a spike of bracts from which flowers protrude. Use justicia and pachystachys in the landscape as informal hedges or grouped for larger areas of color.

CULTURE Grow in full sun (for best flower production) to semishade. Warm, humid conditions are best for most species, which can be damaged when temperatures drop below 50° F. Most justicia and pachystachys prefer moist, organically rich, slightly acid soil. When buying, look for full, bushy plants with healthy, green foliage. Plants are very easy to propagate from tip cuttings. Water established plants if the weather or soil is dry. Regular light applications of a balanced fertilizer are beneficial. Heavy mulching with organic matter enhances root growth and keeps nematodes—which can be a problem—in check. Prune back after flowering to encourage branching and new growth that will terminate in flowers.

OUTSIDE THE TROPICS Grown indoors, justicia requires a lot of light in order to flower well. *P. lutea* will flower for a long period if provided bright lighting and plenty of water and humidity from spring to autumn; water sparingly in winter.

SELECTIONS *J. brandegeana*, shrimp plant, has bronzy or orange "flowers" with a chartreuse color phase; its water requirements are moderate. *J. aurea*, golden plume, produces large, showy yellow "flowers," particularly in winter months. *J. californica,* chuparosa, is native to desert areas of Colorado and Arizona, and is quite drought tolerant; it produces small leaves and ornamental tubular flowers.

KAEMPFERIA PEACOCK GINGER *Zingiberaceae*

These shade-loving groundcover gingers have 3- to 10-inch-wide leaves with many different colored markings and feathered zoning; they resemble calathea and prayer plants. They are available in heights from 4-10 inches tall and grow from underground tubers that are hardy in the Gulf Coast area to Zone 8b.

CULTURE Grow kaempferias in filtered, dappled, or full shade in well-drained, organic soil. They are heat-loving plants, so don't expect sprouting until May on some of them. Keep the soil evenly moist; a mulch is beneficial. Propagation is by division of tubers.

SELECTIONS *K. rotunda*, Asian crocus, resurrection lily, is the first kaempferia to bloom. Fragrant purple and white orchidlike flowers, which rest on the ground, usually appear before foliage in late winter; foliage is swordlike and 20-24 inches tall with zoning on top and purple undersides.

K. pulchra, peacock ginger, has rounded quilted leaves and flowers all summer. **'Bronze Peacock'** is 5 inches tall with chocolate-colored leaves and beautiful silver zoning. Iridescent purple flowers last from summer to frost. **'Silverspot'** has large blue-green leaves with silver markings in a feather pattern; flowers dot the top of the foliage.

JACARANDA MIMOSIFOLIA (GREEN EBONY) Deciduous tree to 50 feet tall with ferny foliage and showy clusters of lilac flowers. Full sun, adapts to a wide variety of soils, tolerates occasional cold. Zones 8-10.

JASMINUM NITIDUM (STAR JASMINE, ANGELWING JASMINE) Vining plant with shiny green leaves and purple buds opening to very fragrant white flowers with pointed petals. Full sun to partial shade, light, rich well-drained soil. Zones 9-10.

JATROPHA INTEGERRIMA (PEREGRINA) Small shrub can be trained to vining, single-trunk, open, or bushy habit. Small leaves, small intensely red flowers with yellow stamens in clusters. Partial shade is best, adapted to many soil types including dry soil. Zone 10.

JUSTICIA BRANDEGEANA (SHRIMP PLANT) Shrub 3-6 feet tall produces shrimp-shaped orange or bronze flowers. Full sun is best, partial shade is tolerated; moist soil is best, but this species requires less water than other. Zone 10.

KAEMPFERIA PULCHRA (PEACOCK GINGER) Groundcover to 6 inches tall with quilted rounded leaves and flowers all summer. Partial to deep shade, well-drained organic soil. Zones 8-10.

LITCHI CHINENSIS (LYCHEE) Tree 25-50 feet tall with dense rounded crown, very ornamental, fragrant, edible fruit. Warm moist summers followed by cool but frost-free, dry winters are best for fruit production; full sun; moist, rich soil. Zone 10.

MALVAVISCUS ARBOREUS (SLEEPY HIBISCUS) Much-branched shrub with softly hairy leaves and bright red (sometimes white) flowers that usually stay closed. Full sun, moderate humidity, any moist soil; somewhat drought tolerant. Zone 10.

MANGIFERA INDICA (MANGO) Large tree, to 50 feet tall, with broad, rounded crown, long leathery leaves, huge panicles of flowers, large single-seeded fruit. Full sun for fruit production, partial shade for ornamental use; any fertile moist soil with good drainage. Zone 10.

LITCHI CHINENSIS LYCHEE *Sapindaceae*

Lychee is a highly ornamental fruit tree, growing 25-50 feet tall with a dense, rounded crown. The fruit, an inch or so in diameter, is dusty to bright red (sometimes yellow), usually borne in the spring, in clusters near the end of the branches. Its black central seed is surrounded by a translucent, white, crisp flesh, sweet or sweet-acidic and often fragrant and delicious. The outer skin is thin, brittle, and easily popped off. Lychee has been cultivated in its native China for centuries, and the fruit is a staple of Chinese cuisine. This large, rounded, and spreading tree makes a fine shade specimen.

CULTURE For good fruit production, lychee prefers very warm and moist summers followed by drier, cool, but frost-free winters. Grow in full sun and organically rich, moist, well-drained soil. Both waterlogging and severe drought are harmful. When purchasing, be sure roots have not grown around the container's walls and thus twisted around one another. Mature foliage should be deep green. Propagate by air layering. Transplant into a hole enriched with organic matter. Water well to establish and if necessary during the summer months. Do not apply manufactured fertilizer until the tree is well established; then, apply a granular, slow-release fertilizer at fruit set and after fruit is harvested. Maintain a layer of organic mulch over the root zone. After initial shaping, little or no pruning is needed. Stem borers and stink bugs can be problems; introducing parasitic wasps and keeping the surrounding area clean of debris will help in control.

SELECTIONS Each area has its own particular success story; check in your growing area to see what variety will give the results you want—many are available. **'Mauritius'** and **'Brewster'** seem well adapted to southern Florida, being fairly reliable, although some years are considerably more productive than others. **'Sweet Cliff'** seems better suited for the west coast of Florida. **'Peerless'** is reported to be a superior variety chosen from a 'Brewster' seedling. **'Groff'**, **'Kwai mi'** and **'Kaimana'** are popular in Hawaii.

Mango trees are prolific fruit bearers; gathering fruit can become a problem.

MALVAVISCUS ARBOREUS SLEEPY HIBISCUS, MEXICAN TURK'S CAP *Malvaceae*

This much-branched shrub, native to tropical America, is very similar to hibiscus. The softly hairy, toothed leaves may be narrow or broadly oval, lobed or unlobed. Flowers, usually bright red, stay more or less closed, with the stamens protruding, resembling a hibiscus about to open. Sleepy hibiscus is a valuable, if sometimes invasive, plant for full-sun conditions in a shrubbery. It flowers well and often, grows rapidly in moist soil, and is quite trouble-free. The blooms attract hummingbirds and other nectar-seeking birds.

CULTURE Grow in full sun, in a warm climate with temperatures ranging from 65-85° F and moderate humidity. On the Gulf Coast, it does well in partial shade and blooms in winter (it is widely naturalized in the area). Any moist soil suits it well. When purchasing, make sure plants have sturdy roots and are free of mealybugs. Plants are easily propagated from basal self-rooted branches, which are frequently present or can be induced by mound layering, or from firm terminal branches. Even large branches will root where they are to grow if inserted during cool, moist weather. Some 10-30-10 fertilizer is beneficial at planting time; once established, plants require little feeding. Mulch is useful to maintain moisture.

MANGO

Akbar, Mugal emperor of India from 1556 to 1605, planted an orchard of 100,000 mango trees; when the English horticulturalist Charles Maries located the orchard 300 years later, some of the trees were still vigorous. The mango has been cultivated for 6,000 years and is of the same importance in Asia as the apple in Europe and North America. Its standing in the East is indicated by its name, which in Sanskrit means also "provisions" or "victuals." Portuguese colonists are credited with bringing the mango to Brazil, from where it spread to the rest of the Americas.

Pruning consists of keeping the plant under control and removing diseased or crossing branches. Flowers are produced on young wood. Usually pest- and disease-free.

SELECTIONS *M. arboreus* has red flowers; attractive and little-grown pink- and white-flowered forms are also available. A very downy form with smaller, often heart-shaped leaves and red flowers about 1 inch long is often given the name *M. mollis,* but usually considered to be included within *M. arboreus.*

MANGIFERA INDICA MANGO *Anacardiaceae*

Mango develops into a very large tree, growing to at least 60 feet tall, widely planted for shade as well as fruit. Leaves are long and leathery; when young, they hang down and are red or russet in color, giving the tree a vibrant look as if it were in full bloom. Flowers are borne in huge panicles early in the year, providing another display. Blooms are followed in the summer and fall by the well-known, usually oval fruit with a fibrous peachlike pulp surrounding a single, very large seed. Some people who are sensitive to poison ivy are also allergic to the sap and skin of mangos; in extreme cases, even walking near a tree can cause hives and swollen eyes and face. While this can be a find specimen or shade tree, before adding a mango to your landscape, consider possible allergic reactions and the question of who will rake up the abundant fruit that will fall from a huge mature tree. Native to India and Malaysia.

CULTURE Plant in full sun for fruit production or, for ornamental purposes, plant as understory and allow to grow through the lower canopy. Any fertile, moist soil suits mango, but good drainage is advantageous. Temperatures of 65-85° F are best. Purchase strong, healthy, vigorous plants. Easily grown from seed; cultivars are grafted. Mango has no special requirements if planted during the wet season. It will not tolerate dry conditions when young, but it grows rapidly and soon no longer needs special care; when older, it adapts to extended dry periods but may not fruit well. Applications of a balanced fertilizer twice a year will ensure rapid and healthy growth of young plants; mature trees need little or no feeding. Mulching is beneficial for young trees. Little or no pruning is required other than to remove diseased and crossing branches and to maintain shape. Mango has few pest or disease problems.

SELECTIONS Seedlings of the common mango will provide excellent shade and a superb show of new foliage color in spring. For fruit, consider some of the fine cultivars, such as **'Pope'** and **'Haden'**. **'Julie'** and **'NeeLum'** are dwarf cultivars; **'Keit'** produces fruit later than most others. Mangos range in quality; the best are considered by some to the most delicious of all fruits.

MANIHOT ESCULENTA CASSAVA, TAPIOCA *Euphorbiaceae*

Manihot is an excellent, easy-to-grow, virtually maintenance-free tropical ornamental. With their long, narrow lobes divided almost to the base, the leaves impart an open feeling to a landscape, and their coloring—green above, whitish below—adds extra interest. Below ground, many tubers form, rather like dahlias or sweet potatoes; when boiled, they are an important staple of the diet in many parts of the world. Often sold in vegetables stores under the name yuca, this species produces tubers that contain prussic acid; the acid is mostly neutralized by cooking, but the plant should *never* be eaten raw. Native to Brazil.

MANIHOT ESCULENTA 'VARIEGATA' (VARIEGATED TAPIOCA) Long lobed leaves with underground tubers (edible if properly cooked). Full sun for food production, sun or shade for ornamental leaves; moist, deep, organic soil, moderate humidity, generous water. Zones 9-10.

MANILKARA ZAPOTA (SAPODILA) Upright tree to 50 feet tall with dense dark green foliage and 2- to 4-inch edible fruits. Full sun, well-drained slightly alkaline soil is best but adapts to other conditions. Zones 9-10.

MEGASKEPASMA ERYTHROCHLAMYS (BRAZILIAN RED CLOAK) Large, semiwoody shrub to 15 feet tall with showy spikes of magenta bracts enclosing small white flowers. Full sun to partial shade, rich, slightly acidic moist but well-drained; high humidity is best. Zones 9-10.

MONSTERA DELICIOSA (SWISS CHEESE PLANT) Climbing epiphytic plant with very large, deep green perforated leaves; can climb 30 feet or more. Light to deep shade, moist but perfectly drained soil, high humidity. Zone 10.

RAINFORESTS

All rainforests have a large quantity of annual rain–usually 70 inches–but there are many kinds of rainforest, and even in a single forest the vegetation varies according to several factors, primarily elevation. Most of the world's rainforests are in South and Central America, eastern Africa, and southeast Asia, and they are divided into types according to environment, such as equatorial, tropical (or selva), subtropical, and monsoon. Seen from a track or riverbank, a rainforest presents a tangled mass of seemingly impenetrable vegetation, but this is only because the sunlight available along waterways and tracks leads to rich growth. Rainforests are actually fairly easy to travel in because the dense crowns of the largest trees cut out so much light that few low-growing plants can exist on the forest floor–rainforests are darkly shaded, allowing little groundcover (where light does penetrate to the ground, the vegetation is thick). Rainforests are dominated by hundreds of different species of trees and woody-stemmed vines (lianas). Although the crowns of the trees appear to join to form a solid canopy, the trees do not interlock and instead stand slightly apart, a characteristic known as crown shyness. Many animals have learned to glide or fly across such gaps. The leaves of many species are regular in form but have "drip tips," pointed ends to allow them to shed rainwater quickly. Rainforest vines climb trees in different ways: scramblers use barbs or hooks; clingers send out aerial roots; twiners coil themselves around trunks; and tendril climbers send out coiled tendrils that can take advantage of any support. The forest floor is usually quite hard because the constant heat quickly recycles humus. The world's rainforests count for a significant portion of the oxygen produced on our planet and are an ongoing scientific laboratory: new species of plants--and insects--are discovered each year. Most have not yet been named

CULTURE When grown for food, place in full sun; for ornamentation, grows well in sun or shade. Moist, deep, organic soil is best, as are temperatures of 55-85° F, with moderate humidity. When purchasing, select plants with a strong root system and stems. This is very easy to grow from terminal stem cuttings, 8-24 inches long, with lower leaves removed. Simply push stems into the moist ground where they are to grow, and keep moist. Even though the leaves may wither and fall, the cuttings usually root rapidly. For tuber production, planting on raised mounds or growing like potatoes is advisable; for ornamentation, no special planting techniques are required. Manihot is a water-loving plant; water as needed, and add mulch to maintain a healthy, moist soil. This is a fast-growing, leafy plant; it benefits from an annual application of general fertilizer or an abundance of organic matter in the soil. Virtually pest- and disease-free.

SELECTIONS *M. esculenta* '**Variegata**', variegated tapioca, is an underused plant that adds greatly to the landscape, with beautifully variegated green and yellowish white leaves; especially lovely in shady locations.

MANILKARA ZAPOTA SAPODILLA, NASEBERRY, NISPERO, CHIKO *Sapindaceae*

Sapodilla is a wind-tolerant, upright tree growing 50 or more feet tall, with shiny, deep green and dense foliage. The fruits, which develop from small, seemingly insignificant flowers, are brown, round or oval, and scurfy, measuring 2-4 inches in diameter. They are very hard until perfectly ripe. Ripe fruit is soft to the touch and separates easily from the stem without bleeding latex, and a light scratch to the skin reveals a slightly yellowish rather than green color. Once ripe, fruits can be eaten out of hand. The texture is slightly granular (like some pears), and the flavor is very like brown sugar. The latex that permeates the entire plant is chicle, the original substance used in the manufacture of chewing gum. Grown for shade or as a large screen, sapodilla is very attractive, with its dark, glossy foliage and very dark and distinctive, deeply fissured bark. Native to tropical America from Mexico to Venezuela.

CULTURE Grow in full sun. Best soil is well-drained and slightly alkaline, but sapodilla is tolerant of a wide range of soil conditions, from sandy to heavy. Trees prefer a warm and moist climate but are tolerant of cooler and dryer conditions, and mature specimens are slightly tolerant of freezing. Purchase plants with glossy, dark foliage that are not potbound. Propagate by seed; named varieties are grafted. Plant out in the warmer months at least 10-12 feet from buildings or other trees. In an exposed site, stake and tie. Water in well to settle soil and establish; thereafter, during extremely dry times, water deeply every 10 days. Apply granular 4-7-5-3 (the 3 being Mg) fertilizer in early spring, early summer, and early autumn. Maintain a good layer of mulch over the root zone. Pruning is rarely necessary. Sapodilla seems to have few pest or disease problems.

SELECTIONS '**Russell**' produces round, 4-inch fruits. '**Prolific**' has smaller fruit but is a heavy bearer. '**Brown Sugar**' is a very good variety.

MEGASKEPASMA ERYTHROCHLAMYS BRAZILIAN RED CLOAK *Acanthaceae*

Red cloak is a large, semiwoody shrub, native to Venezuela, very showy in bloom, with large terminal spikes of persistent, magenta red bracts enclosing white flowers. The only species in cultivation, it is fast-growing and gives a long period of color in the garden, generally blooming from autumn through spring and sometimes at other times as well. Leaves are large, quilted, and medium green; overall height can be up to 15 feet. Because of its size, red cloak is not easy to use in a small garden, but it is attractive as a specimen or in a large garden.

CULTURE Grow in full sun to partial shade in organically rich, slightly acid, moist but well-drained soil. Plants thrive in high humidity and are sensitive to actual freezing. When buying, choose clean, nonspotted foliage of a medium to dark green color; watch for scale or mealybugs. Red cloak is very easy to propagate from semihardwood cuttings. As plants can become quite large, set out 6-8 feet apart. Water regularly, especially when plants are establishing themselves. Red cloak responds well to regular, light applications of a balanced fertilizer. Regular, heavy mulching with a well-decomposed organic mulch is beneficial. To control plant size, remove flowered-out branches back to the main stem. Deadheading keeps the plant looking clean. Sucking insects like mealybugs sometimes infest the flower spikes; regular deadheading helps control this.

MONSTERA DELICIOSA SPLIT-LEAF PHILODENDRON, SWISS CHEESE PLANT, BREADFRUIT VINE *Araceae*

This native of Central America is a climbing epiphytic aroid with large, deep green, oval, perforated leaves. It can grow to a length of 30 or more feet, often starting out on the ground and eventually becoming completely an epiphyte as the older, terrestrial parts die of old age. The large white "flower" yields a corn-cob-size fruit that is edible only when fully ripe and is reminiscent in flower of pineapple and banana. The bold, leafy plants cover a breast-high area or thrive as a vine in a large tree.

CULTURE Grow in light to heavy shade, in moist, perfectly drained soil. Best temperatures are 70-95° F, but plants will tolerate ranges of 45-100° F and even higher; best humidity conditions are above 50 percent. Purchase plants with dark green foliage of heavy substance, with new leaf and root growth. Propagate from terminal cuttings in moist, shady conditions. Set out during warm, moist periods in a well-drained place, resting the growing tip on or very near the support. Water established plants whenever weather is dry. Fertilize lightly several times annually to encourage growth, especially with high-nitrogen liquid fertilizer. Mulch heavily. Do not prune off roots; instead, guide them to grow where they are not intrusive. Diseases or pests are very seldom a problem. Indoors, provide low to medium light and allow the plant to dry between soakings.

OUTSIDE THE TROPICS This tough species has also made its way into homes, offices, and apartments as a decorative potted plant; while it reaches its full potential only in outdoor tropical conditions, it functions perfectly well indoors with poor light and irregular watering.

SELECTIONS *M. d.* 'Albovariegata' is a striking plant with large splashes of white.

MUEHLENBECKIA PLATYCLADA (HOMALOCLADIUM PLATY-CLADUM) CENTIPEDE PLANT, RIBBON BUSH, TAPEWORM PLANT *Polygonaceae*

This Solomon Islands native is a most unusual, often tangled, freely branching shrub growing 8-10 feet tall. It bears slender, round main stems and flattened

EPIPHYTES

Rainforest trees grow so thickly that little sunlight reaches the forest floor, making survival on the ground nearly impossible for ferns and other plants. Some of these plants find refuge in the upper canopy, closer to the source of light, where they live as epiphytes–plants that grow without soil on other plants while producing their own food by photosynthesis. Epiphytes can grow on the trunk, branches, or leaves of the host plant (sometimes growing so thickly as to damage the plant by crowding out its leaves or by causing mechanical stress by their weight). Epiphytes are found in every group of the plant kingdom but are most abundant in the moist tropics. The best-known tropical epiphytes are orchids and bromeliads, both of which have special adaptations for storing supplies of rainwater–the pseudobulbs of orchids and the tanks or vases of bromeliads.

MUEHLENBECKIA PLATYCLADUS (TAPEWORM PLANT) Freely branching, tangled shrub to 8 feet tall with flattened, segmented leaflike branches. Full sun and deep, fertile, evenly mosit soil are best, but tolerates some shade and poor, sandy, stony soil. Zones 8-10.

MURRAYA PANICULATA (ORANGE JASMINE) Shrub or small tree, 10-12 feet tall with small, leathery dark green leaves, and abundant fragrant white flowers that appear several times each year. Full sun or part shade, rich moist soil. Zone 10.

MUSA ACUMINATA 'DWARF CAVENDISH' (EDIBLE BANANA) Treelike plant with very large paddle-shaped leaves and clusters of edible fruits. Full sun, moist, rich soil, warm to very warm humid conditions. Zones 8-10.

MUSA VELUTINA (RED FLOWERING BANANA) Upright evergreen plant, to 8 feet tall, with fuzzy, pink, seedy fruits. Full sun, moist, rich soil, warm to very warm humid conditions. Zone 10.

and segmented branches that look like leaves. Plants occasionally produce real leaves, which soon fall off, and frequently produce tiny white-pink flowers at the segment junctions, sometimes followed by small red berries. This odd plant, tough and reliable for an airy location, is sure to attract attention. It looks good used in conjunction with a groundcover of contrasting color, such as hemigraphis, and also near large boulders. It can be used to cover dry banks and fits in with both dry and more normal landscapes.

CULTURE This plant is adaptable, but full sun is best. Though tolerant of poor, sandy, or stony soils, it does best in deep, fertile soil with even moisture. Ideal temperatures are in the 80-90° F range, but it will tolerate short minimums in the low to mid-50° F. Once established, plants will withstand dry conditions, although they won't produce lush growth. When purchasing, watch for mealybugs. Propagation is easy from cuttings; frequently, branches at ground level root themselves. You can sever these stems and pot them, or even plant them out if showery weather prevails. Plants require only routine watering and fertilizing. Sometimes branches develop dead areas; remove these. Good pruning to thin, remove, and regulate the often tangled, multiple branches enhances the plant's attractiveness and makes management easier. Mealybugs may be a problem.

OUTSIDE THE TROPICS Grown indoors, medium light is preferable, although high light is tolerable; temperatures may be cool, average, or hot; keep soil evenly moist, and fertilize three times in summer.

SELECTIONS *Muehlenbeckia complexa,* wire plant, is a vigorous but delicate-looking slender, vining shrub native to New Zealand. The thin, branching stems are dark-colored and wirelike in appearance. Leaves are tiny and more or less round; flowers are inconspicuous and not always produced. The plant likes to grow on and over things and soon develops into a dense mat. It is excellent for covering rocky areas or boulders or for informally growing over tree stumps and the like.

MURRAYA PANICULATA ORANGE JASMINE *Rutaceae*

Murraya is a workhorse plant; it is unfussy in its requirements and serves many purposes, often acting as a screen or hedge up to 12 feet tall or as a patio plant or specimen. Native to India and a member of the citrus family, this plant has attractive glossy green leaves, very fragrant white flowers, and bright red fruit; the flowers appear several times a year, sometimes simultaneously with fruit.

CULTURE Murraya thrives in any ordinary garden soil of average fertility in full sun or partial shade. It can be pruned or sheared in late summer or early winter, and benefits from annual applications of fertilizer and regular moisture. It may die back after a cold or wet winter, but will recover, although slowly. Propagate from cuttings, which root easily.

OUTSIDE THE TROPICS Murraya thrives as a pot plant in greenhouses and sunrooms; it can be grown indoors if the humidity is high. Keep the soil moist and fertilize frequently; take the plant outdoors for the summer.

SELECTIONS Two other species are sometimes seen. ***M. stenocarpa*** is a smaller shrub, to 4 feet, native to China. ***M. koenigii,*** curry leaf, has aromatic leaves used in curries.

MUSA BANANA *Musaceae*

The origin of the banana is obscured by time; most edible types are sterile varieties that have been propagated and used by humans for millennia as an important food. The family is thought to have originated in Asia, but it is commonly found

BANANAS
Alexander the Great's army encountered banana trees in India, but the usually bold conqueror looked askance at the strange fruit and refused to allow his soldiers to eat it. Nearly two thousand years later, bananas were still relatively unknown in Europe: the shop of apothecary John Parkinson became famous in the 1640s for displaying the first bunch of bananas ever seen in Britain. Bananas came from far away, and until the invention of banana boats, specially equipped with air-conditioned holds, they were a popular rarity on European markets, giving us the Edwardian music-hall ditty "Yes! We have no bananas!" Of course, the cultivation of bananas was spread throughout the tropics; during his last days on St. Helena Napoleon developed a fondness for banana fritters with honey.

A banana plant growing in the perennial garden at Callaway Gardens, Pine Mountain, Georgia. The plant shown is two years old; it survived its first winter with its trunk wrapped in burlap. Although the plant froze and died back over winter, its shoots returned vigorously.

wild in South America. Bananas are small to large herbaceous, treelike plants with leaves held at the top of what appears to be a trunk but is actually a tightly packed whorl of leaf sheaths and leaf stalks that emerge from an underground stem. After all the leaves expand, a flowering stem emerges as the final structure. In the common fruiting varieties, this structure hangs downward. Flowers give way to fruits, which develop in groups on the stem; each group is called a hand, and individual bananas in the hand are called fingers. Many ornamental bananas have erect and colorful flowering stems. Some species have colorful foliage. Banana plants in the landscape can provide bold accents and tropical lushness.

CULTURE Grow bananas in full sun in moist, organically rich soil, and in warm to very warm and very humid conditions. Protect from strong wind. Bananas shriveled to the ground by cold will resprout from the underground stem. Purchase plants with firm, strong growth. If digging plants, be alert for signs of insect penetration, especially near the base. Propagate by clump division, then plant a single pseudostem with its roots where it is to grow. Plant the base deeply, from 18 inches to 2 feet deep even if it was growing at the soil surface. Keep the soil constantly moist but not saturated. Setting out with a slow-release planting fertilizer (13-5-13) works well. Fertilize established plants regularly, and provide extra potassium, which is abundant in the fruits themselves. Mulch heavily. Remove dead or tattered foliage as needed. Once the pseudostem has fruits, you may cut it back to soil level; new suckers will successively appear from the base, fruit, and die back. Mealybugs and spider mites are the main pests of bananas; pruning out affected portions of the plant helps to control them. Panama disease, a rot spread by water, is devastating to commercial plantations; it is best to remove affected plants.

OUTSIDE THE TROPICS Smaller varieties of banana are sometimes grown in pots for their ornamental foliage; provide bright light and some direct sunlight if possible. Some species can be grown outdoors in Zone 8; if not actually frozen below soil level, the plant will die back in frost, but roots will remain hardy and shoots will spring up quickly. In cooler areas, they are grown for foliage only.

SELECTIONS *M. acuminanta* 'Dwarf Cavendish' is perhaps the most popular edible ornamental banana variety. Among the more ornamental bananas are *M. uranoscopus* [*M. coccinea*], red flowering banana, strictly tropical; *M. ornata*, a hardier type with lavender to purple, showy, erect flowering stalks; *M. velutina*, smaller, with maroon bracts and fuzzy pink fruits that open up like flowers; *M. sumatrana*, with beautiful red-spotted foliage that is red-maroon underneath; and *M. x paradisiaca* 'Koa'e', an old Hawaiian cultivar, with white variegations, even on its edible fruit.

MUSSAENDA *Rubiaceae*

Mussaendas are small to large (up to 30 feet tall) shrubs with very large and colorful sepals surrounding small flowers. Native to tropical Asia and Africa, the plants generally resemble poinsettias with showy red, pink, or white flower clusters. These are fine flowering shrubs for the warm months of the year, and the flowers are useful for attracting butterflies.

CULTURE Grow in full sun to partial shade in moist, well-drained soil rich in organic material. Warm and humid conditions make the plants thrive. Purchase well-rooted plants with a full branching habit in as large a container as you can afford. Propagate from semihardwood cuttings as the growing season begins, using rooting hormone. Irrigate to establish and later in the absence of regular rainfall.

Apply a granular fertilizer recommended for gardenias once each in spring, summer, and fall. Apply mulch regularly to the root zone. Mussaendas bloom on new growth, so encourage this by pruning, cutting back to just above a joint. Occasional hard pruning will result in more compact, fuller plants. Prune only after all cold weather has passed. Mussaendas have few pest problems.

OUTSIDE THE TROPICS Mussaenda can be used in Zone 9; it will die to the ground in frost, but will regrow if protected with mulch; it does well at Bok Tower Garden.
SELECTIONS *M. erythrophylla* is a very showy, sprawling shrub with blood red sepals aptly called Ashanti blood. *M. e.* '**Queen Sirikit**' has light pink sepals with a pencil-thin darker border. *M. philippica* '**Dona Aurora**' is a denser shrub with white sepals, while *M. x* '**Dona Luz**' and *M. x* '**Dona Paciencia**' have pink sepals.

NERIUM OLEANDER OLEANDER *Apocynaceae*

Sometimes also called rosebay, this bushy evergreen–a native of the Mediterranean region–was a favorite in Victorian-era English hothouse gardens and remains a popular garden and coastal plant in the South and Pacific West. Its narrow, lance-shaped leathery leaves are reminiscent of bamboo or willow foliage, and provide a fine backdrop for oleander's colorful summer floral display. Single- and double-flowered varieties yield clusters of white, red, lilac, pink, or yellow blooms. Note: All parts of the plant are poisonous. Keep children and pets away from plantings. Foliage causes skin rash in some individuals. Do not burn clippings.

CULTURE Oleander thrives in a hot, sunny location (though it will tolerate some shade) with fertile, well-drained soil. It is notably impervious to salt air, wind, and drought. Most oleanders are container-grown and should be planted in the spring. Fortify the soil with peat moss or compost and water generously. Once established this is a tough shrub tolerant of poor conditions. Oleander tolerates drought very well. It should be watered only during extreme drought. Oleander benefits from an early-spring feeding for maximum bloom. Monitor plants regularly for aphids, mealybugs, scale, and oleander caterpillar. Prune in the spring to control shape. Root-prune or remove old stems at the soil line every few years to keep mature plants from becoming overgrown. Oleander propagates easily from seed, from soft-wood cuttings, and from hardwood cuttings treated with rooting hormone. This is a versatile shrub, especially useful in coastal areas or urban settings, where it stands up well in foundation plantings or borders to wind, salt spray, dry soil, and pollution. It is also an excellent container plant.

OUTSIDE THE TROPICS In northern regions oleander is grown as a tub plant and moved to a sunny but cool indoor location for the winter.

SELECTIONS Numerous commercial cultivars offer gardeners a wide variety of flower types and colors. *N. oleander* '**Petite Pink**' is a compact form with lovely light pink single flowers. '**Isle of Capri**' displays pale yellow blooms. Popular red-flowering types include '**Algiers**', '**Cardinal**', and '**Calypso**'. '**Ruby Lace**' is noted for its wonderful large, dark red, fringed blossoms. '**Casablanca**' and '**Sister Agnes**' are among white-flowering cultivars. Double-flowered types include '**Compte Barthelemy**' (red) and '**Mrs. Roeding**' (pink).

ODONTONEMA STRICTUM FIRESTICK *Acanthaceae*

Firestick is a dark green shrub native to Central America that grows 6 or more feet tall. From late winter to the end of summer, the shrub is covered with spikes of 1-inch-long, tubular, crimson flowers. During the warmest part of the year, some

SACRED TROPICAL PLANTS

Many tropical trees and plants have acquired spiritual significance. In tropical Asia the most important are various species of *Ficus*, particularly *Ficus religiosa,* known as the bo, peepul, or Bodhi tree, under which the Buddha is said to have attained enlightenment. One such tree at Anuradhapura in Sri Lanka is considered the world's oldest historical tree, having been brought there from India as a seedling in 288 B.C. and its life recorded ever since. Buddha himself was presented with a mango grove so that he might find repose beneath its shade

Because the banana bears fruit only once, it became a Buddhist symbol of the futility of earthly possessions, and in classic Chinese iconography the Buddha is shown meditating on this key to wisdom at the foot of a banana tree. Many believe that the banana, not the apple, was the fruit of Eden, in accordance with which early botanists named it *Musa paradisiaca.*

Frangipani, a tropical American shrub of the genus *Plumeria,* has been cultivated in Asia for at least two centuries. It is known as the temple tree in India and is planted in Muslim cemeteries and the gardens of Buddhist monasteries. Scented shrubs like jasmine have long been popular near temples not just for their fragrance but because they provide flowers for garlands to be used as offerings.

Camellia japonica is known in Japan as tsubaki, "the tree with shining leaves." It was worshiped in the Shinto religion as the residence inhabited by gods during their earthly trans-figuration.

MUSSAENDA PHILIPPICA x M. ERYTHROPHYLLA CV (MUSSAENDA)
Small to large shrub (to 30 feet tall) with large colorful sepals surrounding small flowers. Full sun to partial shade, moist, well-drained soil; warm, humid conditions are ideal. Zones 9-10.

NERIUM OLEANDER (COMMON OLEANDER, ROSEBAY) Medium- to fast-growing shrub, to 20 feet tall, with narrow 4- to 12-inch-long leathery leaves and single or double red, pink, yellow, or white flowers; can be trained to a single trunk. Full sun; tolerates any soil and drought. Zones 8-10.

ODONTONEMA STRICTUM (FIRESTICK) Shrub to 6 feet tall or more, covered with spikes of 1-inch tubular flowers from late winter through summer. Partial shade, moist, well-drained soil, warm, humid conditions. Zone 10.

PANDANUS ODORATISSIMUS (SCREW PINE) Much-branched shrub or small tree, to 20 feet tall, with 3- to 5-foot-long leaves hanging from the apex. Best in hot, dry areas, but does not tolerate drought; full sun, deep, well-drained rich soil. Zone 10.

flower clusters tend to compress into bundles, and the plant becomes covered in peculiar cockscombs. Whether this is caused by environmental factors or by annual invasions of mites is not clear. However, the condition is interesting and does not need to be treated. This colorful shrub makes a dense screening hedge, and the flowers attract hummingbirds and nectar-seeking butterflies.

CULTURE Firestick is best grown partially shaded from the hottest sun, in moist and well-drained soil and warm, humid conditions. Purchase plants with dark green foliage. Propagation from stem cuttings is very easy. Plants may be set out slightly deeper than they are growing in the nursery container. Water well to establish and during dry weather. Apply a slow-release granular fertilizer three to four times annually, or more often in sandy, easily leached soil. Maintain a layer of mulch over the root zone. Cutting back after blooming promotes dense growth. Mealybugs may be a problem in the flower clusters; prune off or spray.

PANDANUS SCREW PINE *Pandanaceae*

A South Polynesian native, the screw pine lends a tropical feel wherever it is planted. It is less demanding than most palm trees but can be used to similar effect. It grows slowly, and, as an added benefit it transplants easily. Screw pines are small enough to be used as specimen plants in medium-sized gardens; they can also be planted in groves on large sites.

CULTURE Although it does best in hot, dry areas—it does particularly well near seashores—screw pine will grow almost anywhere. It does not tolerate extended drought. Dig soil deeply before planting. Provide protection from wind until the plant is established. Water only during times of extreme drought. Fertilizer is unnecessary. Cut branches will not regrow; therefore badly damaged branches should be cut where their stumps will be least noticeable. A large branch can be planted directly into the garden; it will root easily. Seeds removed from the fruit clusters and placed face-up in a potting medium (do not cover them) will germinate in eight to twelve weeks. Monitor for mealybugs.

OUTSIDE THE TROPICS Pandanus will not do well outdoors outside of Zone 10. It is a good specimen plant for a warm greenhouse. A potted plant can be brought outdoors in its container for the summer. Screw pines will grow slowly indoors, but will eventually become a showy, stately addition to any room if given good light (direct sunlight is best) and plenty of water; mist frequently.

SELECTIONS *P. veitchii*, the variegated screw pine, has well-shaped, green-and-white striped leaves.

P. odoratissimus, native to the Pacific (Australia to East Asia), produces less ornamental leaves that have many economic uses.

PEPEROMIA *Piperaceae*

Best known as a potted plant, peperomia is available in many species and cultivars, and several are very suitable for planting out in tropical and subtropical gardens. Plants are low-growing, fleshy, and branching; most love deep shade. Leaves are roundish or somewhat pointed; minute flowers appear on erect spikes, often referred to as rat's tails. Plants are mound-forming, erect, or vining. In the wild they are frequently found in cooler, moist conditions, often growing in moss on branches or rocks. Ideal for mass planting as a groundcover, for growing up or over rocks or boulders, or as smaller feature plantings; especially good when

Pandanus fruit.

P. magnoliifolia 'Jellie'.

grown with moss or on rotten logs. Native to the tropics.

CULTURE Most species are shade lovers and can tolerate only passing sun at best; types with thick, fleshy, or silvery leaves will tolerate more light than others. Good drainage and high organic matter are essential to peperomia cultivation. A mix of garden soil, compost, leaf mold, fine cinder, and gravel is advantageous. Although selections noted here will tolerate wider conditions than many others, peperomia does exceptionally well in high humidity and cooler temperatures, from the upper 50° F to the low 80° F. Purchase plants with a strong root system, firm crown, and no signs of rot. Propagate in a very well-drained medium; by division is best, but terminal stem cuttings also work. Set out 4-8 inches apart at the same level or higher than originally grown, in open, well-drained soil. Some do well planted in moss or with moss added after planting. Most peperomias do not tolerate drying out; on the other hand, the crowns of many can rot if too wet. Choose a garden location where these moisture requirements can be met. Organic liquid fertilizer is best. Mulching is very important, with either organic matter or layers of cinder or stones. The ideal is to provide a cool, moist soil surface and also nutrients. Slugs and snails can be a problem, but fungal/bacterial stem rots are more serious. At first signs, destroy rot-infected parts or whole plants, remove the nearby soil, and replant.

OUTSIDE THE TROPICS Peperomias are among the most popular of houseplants; grow in medium to low light and repot as needed in average, well-drained soil mix. They perform best if kept evenly moist, but tolerate drought and resist rot if kept dry. Fertilize three times in summer. **P. argyreia,** watermelon peperomia, **P. caperata** 'Red Ripple', **P. magnoliifolia** 'Jellie', and **P. pereskiifolia** are among the best species for indoors.

SELECTIONS **P. glabella** is an easy-to-grow, vigorous, trailing plant with pointed, ovate leaves; it will climb over moist rocks and other objects. **P. glabella** 'Variegata' is an exceptionally fine cultivar with yellow and green variegated leaves. **P. leptostachya** is an erect, branching plant, 12-15 inches tall and more; light green, velvety foliage; grows in ground and on rocks and branches. **P. obtusifolia**, jade plant, is a vigorous, erect or trailing plant with thick, fleshy leaves; several variegated cultivars offer green and cream or yellow foliage; a good groundcover that will also grow over moist rocks. **P. magnoliifolia**, also called jade plant, is similar. **P. pellucida** is very different; it is an erect annual, 1-8 inches high, with round, almost transparent leaves and short, very light green flower spikes; reseeds itself freely. **P. argyreia,** watermelon peperomia, is a popular potted plant; stemless with ornate, nearly heart-shaped leaves striped like a watermelon; healthy, well-established plants make an unusual and attractive groundcover.

PERSEA AMERICANA AVOCADO *Lauraceae*

Depending on the type of avocado, the tree may be erect or spreading to 30 or more feet tall, useful for shade as well as fruit production. It is evergreen or almost so, sometimes losing leaves in a cool, dry period. The foliage is dark green and glossy. The flowers, although produced abundantly, are small, yellowish green, and not showy. Although male and female components are present in the same flower, they are functional at alternate times of day, necessitating cross-pollination. The fruits, sometimes called alligator pears, are generally pear-shaped, and the skin of mature fruit may be rough and almost black to smooth and green. The flesh, which surrounds one large seed, is buttery rich and not sweet. Avocado

PEPEROMIA CAPERATA 'RED RIPPLE' (PEPEROMIA) Low-growing, free-branching groundcover plant, to 10 inches high, with bright red stems (usually covered by foliage) and quilted, crinkly, dark red leaves. Partial to full shade and rich, moist well-drained soil is best, tolerates drought. Zone 10.

PERSEA AMERICANA (AVOCADO) Erect or spreading evergreen tree, to 30 feet tall, with dark green glossy foliage and pear-shaped fruits. Full sun; adapts to many soil types including alkaline soil; some types need hot humid conditions, others tolerate light frost. Zones 9-10.

PETREA VOLUBILIS (QUEEN'S WREATH, SANDPAPER VINE) High-climbing vine with rough-surfaced dark green leaves and clusters of lavender-blue or white flowers. Full sun or very light shade, warm, humid conditions; free-draining neutral or slightly acid soil. Zones 9-10.

PHILODENDRON BIPINNATIFIDUM (PHILODENDRON) Climbing herbaceous plant with epiphytic roots and huge (up to 4 feet long) deeply lobed glossy dark green leaves. Partial to deep shade, rich, well-drained soil, high moisture, high humidity is best, but adapts to lower humidity. Zones 9-10.

AVOCADOS

The avocado is native to tropical America. The name itself comes from an Aztec word meaning "testicle" (a reference to the fruit's shape), and the Aztecs used avocados to make guacamole (also an Aztec word, meaning simply "avocado sauce"). When the Spanish arrived in Mexico, they found the Aztecs eating their guacamole with agave worm, also known as maguey slug. The Spaniards brought the avocado to Florida, although the cultivation of avocados there really dates to 1833, when Henry Perrine sent trees from Mexico to his land below Miami. In 1871 R. B. Ord brought three trees from Mexico to Santa Barbara, but the variety destined to become most important in California was imported from Mexico in 1926 by a Pasadena postman named Rudolph Hass. There are three recognized varieties of avocado—Mexican, Guatemalan, and West Indian—but hybrids among the species are common and commercially important. In the United States avocados are divided in two main groups, those from California, such as the Hass, and the larger Florida avocado.

fruits cannot ripen on the tree; they must either fall or be taken off and allowed to ripen so that the skin has a slight give. Never store avocado fruit in the refrigerator. The avocado might well have originated in Mexico, but it has been grown since antiquity all over the American tropics.

CULTURE Full sun is best. Trees are adaptable to varying soil conditions; a pH of 6-7 is ideal, but avocados will grow in alkaline soil. They cannot tolerate waterlogged conditions. West Indian avocados require hot, humid, tropical conditions. Guatemalan avocados are hardier, while Mexican types can tolerate light freezing without harm. When buying, avoid rootbound containerized plants. Plants propagated from seed take only four to five years to fruit, but since trees are hybrids, seedlings may not resemble their parents. Choose a site where other avocado trees exist to promote pollination. Select varieties are grafted. Plant out at any time from containers, being very careful not to disturb roots during planting. Water well to establish and during excessively dry seasons, being sure soil drains well. Established trees benefit from applications of fertilizer at a rate of 3-4 pounds three times per year, starting after fruit set; season of fruiting varies with type. Young plants need a very light application of fertilizer every eight to ten weeks. Maintain a layer of mulch over the root zone. Occasional pruning to control size and shape may be needed; avocados have brittle wood, so overgrown, unpruned trees are particularly susceptible to storm damage. Root rot is the most serious disease of avocados; you can avoid it where drainage is good. A range of chewing and sucking insects attacks avocados, but they are generally easy to control and don't do a lot of damage.

SELECTIONS Many commercial varieties are available, but a good commercial variety usually bears too abundantly for the average household. Sometimes a local nurseryman can recommend a type that is a good size and quality for a family garden. Often the shy bearers produce superior fruits. Fairchild Tropical Garden suggests the following varieties: West Indian **'Fuchs'**, **'Maoz'**, **'Pollock'**; Guatemalan **'Edranol'**, **'Hazzard'**, **'Taft'**; Mexican **'Gottfried'**, **'Mexicola'**, **'Puebla'**; 'Guatemalan x Mexican **'Choquette'**, **'Fuchs-20'**, **'Hall'**.

PETREA VOLUBILIS QUEEN'S WREATH, SANDPAPER VINE
Verbenaceae

This high-climbing woody vine produces graceful clusters of short-lived purple or white flowers enclosed by much longer-lived purple or violet calyces, all produced from the youngest leaf axils. The dark green leaves have a sandpaperlike surface texture. Can be grown as a self-supporting shrub. As a vine, it makes a wonderful display on a pergola or on a support against a wall; it will easily help to disguise an ugly structure or fence. In flower, in early summer, the plant is reminiscent of wisteria. Native to the West Indies, Mexico, and Central America.

CULTURE Grow in full sun or very light shade, in warm and humid conditions. Soil should be free-draining with some organic matter present; neutral or slightly acid is best. Purchase plants with dark green leaves and vigorous growth. Propagate by layering, or from semihardwood cuttings with rooting hormone and bottom heat. In alkaline soil, prepare the planting hole with extra organic matter. Set out near support. Water well to establish; irrigate regularly during the growing season and as needed during periods of less active growth. Application of an acid-reaction fertilizer in slow-release form is beneficial. Prune after flowering in early summer to maintain size. Keep a layer of mulch over the root zone. Scale and mealybugs can be a nuisance; regular hosing with a strong jet will help to keep infestations to a minimum.

SELECTIONS *P. volubilis* is the blue-purple form. *P. volubilis* '**Albiflora**' is the white-flowered form. The two can be mixed in one planting with very nice effect.

PHILODENDRON *Araceae*

As its name suggests, philodendron are tree lovers, climbing trees by attaching aerial roots or running along the ground in their shade. Often vining, the genus includes many leaf forms, ranging from small (particularly when young) to huge and bold. Philodendrons are pollinated by the scarab beetle and contain calcium oxalate crystals, making them toxic if ingested or rubbed on skin.

CULTURE Philodendrons thrive in low light—from semishade to even deeper shade—and in moist, fertile soil under warm and humid conditions. Buy plants with clean, healthy leaves. Philodendron is easily propagated by stem cuttings or layering. Keep soil evenly moist and fertilize with a balanced fertilizer annually to keep it lush. Philodendron grows rapidly and needs to be cut back frequently, or it will get out of control. It suffers from few insect and disease problems; occasional mealybugs are easily controlled by hosing it off or soap.

OUTSIDE THE TROPICS Philodendrons are classic houseplants for low-light areas. Keep them evenly moist and repot as needed.

SELECTIONS *P. bipinnatifidum* is a good choice as a specimen, especially the frilly-leaved types. *P. gloriosum* is a lovely groundcover. *P. scandens,* the most common type, is the tropical equivalent of *Hedera helix* (ivy) with small dark green heart-shaped leaves; juvenile leaves are velvety and tinged with purple on undersides. It is an excellent groundcover for dense shade. *P. selloum* is self-heading, producing a large crown of leaves 6-8 feet long and becoming woody with age. It is hardy in Zone 8.

PITTOSPORUM TOBIRA JAPANESE PITTOSPORUM *Pittosporaceae*

This handsome flowering evergreen, a native of the Far East, is a favored hedge plant in Florida, southern California, and along the Gulf Coast. Its tidy, spreading but compact growth habit and shiny green foliage create an exceptionally dense mass perfect for borders or screening. In spring it bears 2- to 3-inch-wide clusters of small creamy white to yellowish flowers. Though not particularly showy, the blooms give off a delightful orange-blossom fragrance. Pittosporum is widely used in foundation or mass plantings as well as in hedges and screens. It is also an attractive container plant for the patio.

CULTURE Pittosporum is a remarkably adaptable shrub that will do well in almost any well-drained soil, whether light or heavy, acid or alkaline. It prefers a hot, dry, sunny location but is also tolerant of shade. Most nursery-grown pittosporums are sold in containers. Transplant in early spring. Although pittosporum tolerates drought very well, it performs best when watered regularly. For established plants, a yearly spring application of a general-purpose fertilizer with a 1-3-2 or similar ratio is generally adequate. It suffers from no serious insect or disease problems, though leaf spot can sometimes be troublesome. This rugged shrub will withstand heavy pruning or clipping but seldom

Petrea covers an arbor, providing shade for a bench. For much of the summer, the vine is covered with blue flowers. In spring, before the flowers appear on the petrea vine, a group of amaryllis provides color.

PHILODENDRON GLORIOSUM (SATIN LEAF PHILODENDRON) Low-growing herbaceous plant with large (up to 2 feet long) medium green leaves. Partial to deep shade, rich, well-drained soil, high moisture, high humidity is best, but adapts to lower humidity. Zones 9-10.

PITTOSPORUM TOBIRA 'VARIEGATA' (JAPANESE PITTOSPORUM) Broad, dense, shrub or small tree, usually 6-15 feet tall, with gray-green leaves edged in cream, clusters of small white flowers, round green fruit. Full sun to partial shade, best in moist, rich soil, tolerates some dryness. Zones 8-10.

PLUMBAGO AURICULATA [P. CAPENSIS] (CAPE PLUMBAGO) Sprawling shrub to 6 feet tall, 8-10 feet wide, with attractive light to medium green foliage and clusters of blue flowers over a long season. Full sun, tolerates well-drained dryish soil, tolerates drought well. Zones 9-10.

PLUMERIA OBTUSA (SINGAPORE PLUMERIA) Evergreen shrub or small tree with glossy dark green leaves and very fragrant white flowers. Full sun, moist, rich soil, very warm climates. Zone 10.

needs it, due to a naturally compact and dense growth habit. Propagate from seed, from semi-hardwood cuttings taken in summer, or from hardwood cuttings. Avoid overly moist rooting medium.

SELECTIONS The leaves of *P. japonica* **'Variegata'** have a pleasant lemon scent and are streaked with white along their margins. **'Wheeler's Dwarf'** is similar to the species, but smaller in both form and foliage. Both cultivars can be grown as house plants in the North. *P. eugenoides* is one of the tallest varieties, and can be trained to tree form. It grows to 40 feet tall and has dark green leaves edged in white. *P. undulatum,* sometimes called Victorian box or mock orange, bears clusters of bright orange berries after flowering.

PLUMBAGO AURICULATA [P. CAPENSIS] CAPE PLUMBAGO

Plumbaginaceae

Prized for its blue-petalled flowers with pink tubes, growing in multi-flowered clusters, which bloom from spring to winter (and all year round in warm climates), plumbago is a colorful addition to any landscape. Cape plumbago grows 6 feet tall with an equal spread; with support, it can reach 12 feet tall. Plant plumbago for the richness of its color and its exquisite sky blue flowers, and for its late-flowering season, from midsummer to midfall.

CULTURE Plumbago does best in full sun; it will grow in any type of soil (in fact, it likes rather poor, dry soil.) Plumbago is hardy to Zone 8, and needs protection from wind so plant in a sheltered spot. Plant in early spring from root cuttings or start with young plants. Plumbago thrives in drought and poor soil; do not overwater or overfertilize. It has no serious pest or disease problems. Plumbago will grow best if it is cut back to the ground each year. (It will die back to the ground in northern areas.) Cut back all stems, old and new, each spring to 1-3 inches off the ground. In frost areas, plumbago will drop its leaves after frost; once the plant has died back, its rootstock needs to be protected. Divide the roots of plumbago in mid-spring or take semi-hardwood cuttings in summer.

SELECTIONS The genus *Ceratostigma* also contains several plants known as plumbago. *Ceratostigma willmottianum,* Chinese plumbago, has similar but medium blue flowers, and grows only to 2-4 feet. It blooms from midsummer to midfall, and will tolerate some shade. *C. minus* is a shorter version.

C. griffithii grows to 3 feet tall with an equal spread; it has evergreen leaves with purple edges and flowers in late summer.

PLUMERIA FRANGIPANI *Apocynaceae*

A common sight in Hawaii, where its flowers are often strung onto leis, frangipani provides valuable shade, lovely, long-lasting blossoms, and a sweet scent that typifies the tropics. Dwarf forms as well as 25-foot trees exist; the species' flowers are yellow, red, or white, but numerous cultivars come in every permutation of these colors, including "rainbow" mixed versions. Plumeria, which has deep green oval leaves, is usually evergreen, but sometime sheds its leaves. Plumerias are excellent specimen or shade trees, useful near seating areas. Some types, such as the Singapore variety, can be used as hedges. Dwarf types are often incorporated into perennial borders, where their well-shaped flowers and dark-green foliage are equally useful.

CULTURE Plumerias thrive in full sun, in dry to moist soil; they do not like wet feet.

Dwarf plumeria.

Harden off transplants in the shade for a few days before planting in a sunny location. Leave adequate space between plants; remember that crowns may grow to 10-12 feet across. Water cautiously until established–water thoroughly then allow soil to become fairly dry before another deep watering; wet feet promotes rot. Once established, they tolerate drought quite well. Fertilize young plants to speed growth. Plumerias require little care. Prune occasionally to remove dead wood and maintain shape of plant. Propagate by cuttings of stems and branches. Allow the cut end of the branch to heal before planting it in a well-drained potting medium. Humidity is beneficial, but wetness is not. Transplant when leaves appear on the branches. Plumerias can also be propagated by seeds. Rust is a serious problem in Florida; control with oxycarboxin.

OUTSIDE THE TROPICS Some new varieties are hardy to Zone 8. In cooler regions, they can be taken indoors before frost and make a spectacular flowering houseplant. Cuttings of plumeria will grow well indoors in full sun; avoid overwatering and fertilize frequently.

SELECTIONS *P. rubra,* the most common type, produces white flowers. *P. rubra* var. *acuminata,* pagoda tree, has white or yellow flowers; is a fast grower, usually growing to 20 feet in several years. It has a broad crown and dense foliage. *P. obtusa,* Singapore plumeria, is often used as a hedge.

PROTEA *Proteaceae*

The protea family includes several genera that produce unusual, showy flowers, including *Banksia* and *Leucospermum* (pincushion flower). Though grown mostly for the cut-flower market, they are attractive, though very fussy, garden plants. Most species are shrubby, though several grow to tree size and develop thick trunks. They are used as accent plants or hedges.

Pincushion flower, closely related to protea, planted with agaves; though these plants have different requirements for water, both adapt to the same site.

PROTEA CYNAROIDES (KING PROTEA) Tall upright plants (to 3-5 feet) with showy 8- to 12-inch flowers consisting of pointed petals around a chokelike center. Need warm temperatures, low humidity, perfect drainage, constant water. Zones 9-10.

PROTEA 'PINK MINK' (HYBRID PROTEA) Tall upright plants (to 6-8 feet) with showy 12- to 15-inch flowers consisting of closed pointed petals around a chokelike center. Need warm temperatures, low humidity, perfect drainage, constant water. Zones 9-10.

BANKSIA ERiCIFOLIA (HEATH BANKSIA) 4- to 6-foot-tall shrub with 12- to 14-inch conelike flowers, covered with fuzz. Need warm temperatures, low humidity, perfect drainage, constant water. Zones 9-10.

LEUCOSPERMUM REFLEXUM (ROCKET PINCUSHION) Large, sprawling shrub to 12 feet tall and 6 feet wide, with many narrow flowers surrounding a thistlelike head. Need warm temperatures, low humidity, perfect drainage, constant water. Zones 9-10.

Pyrostegia, used as a groundcover.

CULTURE Grow proteas in full sun. They require perfect drainage and should not be attempted unless that can be provided; a deep raised bed or slope site is ideal. Provide good air circulation and protection from drying winds; keep soil evenly moist—but not wet—in summer; after summer, cut back watering to only when soil is dry. Proteas do best in acid soil that is not too rich. A light annual application of nitrogen fertilizer is beneficial, but avoid phosphorus, which can kill plants because they overdose on it. Once established, most proteas will survive occasional frost. Chlorosis is sometimes a problem and can be controlled by addition of a limited amount of iron.

SELECTIONS *P. cynaroides,* king protea, grows 3-5 feet tall and needs watering throughout the year. *P. mellifera,* sugarbush, is a 5- to 8-foot tall shrub with 5-inch white or red flowers. *P. nerifolia,* oleander-leaved protea, does well in alkaline soil and is hardy to Zone 8 once established. *Banksia integrifolia,* tree banksia, grows to 30 feet tall, and tolerates sandy soil and wind. *Leucospermum nutans,* nodding pinchusion, grows to 4 feet tall and wide and produces excellent flowers for cutting. *L. reflexum,* rocket pinchusion, grows to 12 feet tall and sometimes as wide; its flower petals curl downward.

PYROSTEGIA VENUSTA (IGNEA) FIRECRACKER VINE, ORANGE TRUMPET VINE, FLAME VINE *Bignoniaceae*

This very vigorous vine, native to Brazil, uses branched tendrils to attach itself securely to its support. The beautiful, tubular flowers are 3-4 inches long and brilliant orange, produced abundantly in spring. Excellent for a spectacular show of splendid color from January to May and as a cover for fences and archways.

CULTURE Grow in full sun. While good, deep soil is best and fertile soil produces rapidly growing plants, good drainage is most important, and the best plants are often found growing in stony soil. This vine is adaptable to various temperatures, from lows in the 30° F to highs in the mid-90° F, and to both low- and high-humidity conditions. Purchase pest-free plants with actively growing stems and vigorous roots. Propagates easily from cuttings of mature—but not old—stems. Terminal cuttings are too soft and usually will not root. If planted to provide a screen, space every 4-6 feet for rapid covering, or up to every 10-20 feet or more if you're not in a hurry for the screen. Keep moist when young; later on, plants are able to survive dry periods. Fertilize at planting time with a general granular fertilizer; apply this or a liquid feed later if you notice loss of vigor or leaf color. (Gardeners at Bok Tower Gardens find fertilizing is unnecessary, even in sandy soils.) Mulching is valuable, especially when plants are young. Vines grow rapidly and may need directing or twining over and through a support fence. For vines that are to grow up a tree, train up wires or thin strips of chicken wire; once vines reach the smaller branches, they will grow and spread rapidly on their own. This has very few pest or disease problems. It may be damaged by a hard freeze, but will come back quickly.

RAVENALA MADAGASCARIENSIS TRAVELER'S PALM *Strelitziaceae*

This is a very striking, large, ornamental plant native to Madagascar, with large, bananalike leaves atop a robust trunk. The leaves are presented in a single plane, like a fan. Large but not showy, the inflorescence is a series of boatlike bracts

PYROSTEGIA VENUSTA (FIRECRACKER VINE) Vigorous vine with showy, 3- to 4-inch tubular flowers over a long period. Full sun; deep rich soil is best, stony soil is tolerated, good drainage is important. Zones 9-10.

RAVENALA MADAGASCARIENSIS (TRAVELER'S PALM) Treelike plant, to 40 feet tall, with large, bananalike leaves on thick trunk. Full sun is best, partial shade is tolerated; warm, humid conditions; rich moist soil (dry soil is tolerated). Zone 10.

RHOEO SPATHACEA (OYSTER PLANT, MOSES-IN-A-BOAT) Succulent groundcover to 12 inches tall with rosettes of bright green leaves with purple undersides and boat-shaped bracts covering small white flowers. Full sun or very light shade, any well-drained soil. Zones 9-10.

RUELLIA COLORATA (MONKEY PLANT) Spreading shrub to 4 feet tall with vivid orange and yellow tubular flowers. Filtered to full sun, moist, fertile soil, warm conditions. Zones 9-10.

In this sophisticated planting, low-growing rhoeo is mixed with spikey *Sansevieria trifasciata* 'Laurentii' and flowering *Lobularia maritimia* (sweet alyssum).

arranged in a vertical zigzag pattern very like bird of paradise. The plant earned its common name because water collects in the hollow base of the leaves, providing liquid refreshment for travelers. In spite of the common name, this plant is more closely related to the banana family, and usually, like the banana, it produces suckers from the base. When the suckers are left in place, the plant eventually forms a clump. For a single-trunked solitary specimen, all suckers may be removed, or the naturally single-trunked forest-dwelling ecotype of the species may be planted. This is a large, dominating plant, best for a large garden space. Single trunks are a more manageable size for a smaller, private garden. In larger areas, they may be planted in avenues, with the crowns aligned.

CULTURE Grow in warm, humid conditions. Full sun is best, but plants will tolerate partial shade. Moist, rich soil is ideal, but plants often tolerate much drier soil. Propagate from seed or clump division. Purchase plants with dark sea green leaves. Set out during the warm, wet season, and irrigate to establish. Palm fertilizer, especially with additional potassium, is beneficial, as is regular mulching. Tired-looking ripped foliage may be removed, starting from the outside, but never remove more than few layers at a time, giving new foliage time to grow in before removing more. Do not tear off leaf bases, as this may cause trunk injury. Mealybugs sometimes colonize several parts of the plant.

SELECTIONS There is only one species, ***R. madagascariensis.*** A similar species, *Phenakospermum guyannense,* from tropical America, is not in general cultivation.

RHOEO SPATHACEA (R. DISCOLOR) OYSTER PLANT, MOSES-IN-A-BOAT, BOAT LILY *Commelinaceae*

This popular genus provides feature and groundcover plants that require little care, plus easily grown houseplants. Rhoeo is rather succulent, with a very short, stocky stem and rosettes of narrow leaves, bright reddish purple beneath contrasting nicely with the purplish green above. Several white flowers are borne within large, purplish, boat-shaped bracts in leaf axils. Some people are allergic to the juice of this and other Commelinaceae, which can cause itchy welts on the skin. Valuable as an almost maintenance-free groundcover and as an unusually colored feature plant; it enhances the form and color of many plants it is set underneath. Native to Mexico and the West Indies.

CULTURE Grow in full sun or light (not too much) shade in any well-drained soil; high fertility is not important. Rhoeo does best in warm temperatures, 60-85° F. Purchase plants with strong root systems and actively growing leaves. Propagate by division at any time of year other than summer, when conditions are too hot and dry. Encourage strong root formation by an application of bone meal or a general fertilizer high in phosphate, such as 10-30-10, to the soil at planting time. As these plants are quite succulent, once established they do not require much watering; overwatering can induce root rot. Apply 10-30-10 fertilizer only when vigor wanes. A very thin mulch at planting time could be useful, but a deep mulch around the stems can induce disease. Later, the plants will meet and form a solid cover, so no care will be needed other than replanting every five years or so. Rhoeo is virtually pest-free. Occasionally, fungal or bacterial rots attack, usually because of poor drainage and resulting loss of plant vigor; remove and burn infected plants, rework the soil, and then replant.

OUTSIDE THE TROPICS Indoors, rhoeo tolerates low to medium light and average to warm temperatures; keep evenly moist and apply a balanced fertilizer once a month.

SELECTIONS *R. spathacea* has a dwarf form about half the size of the species; even more desirable because of its low, compact nature. *R. spathacea* 'Concolor' is a pale green version.

Rhoeo's flowers are borne within small bracts almost hiding the flowers—hence the common names Moses-in-a-boat and boat lily.

RUELLIA *Acanthaceae*

Ruellias are evergreen ornamentals, diverse in size and appearance, from spreading perennials to bushy subshrubs. Flowers range in color from rose and scarlet to lavender and violet-blue. The beautiful foliage and flowers make ruellia excellent in the informal garden, and some species also make fine groundcovers. This is an easy, low-maintenance plant native to tropics around the world.

CULTURE Grow in filtered to full sun in fertile, moist soil. Tolerates temperatures of 65-85° F. Propagate from cuttings, seeds, and division. Give young plants ample water until they are established. Fertilize plants when young or when signs of nutrient deficiency are apparent. Prune back branches to half the length after flowering to encourage new growth, which will be pest- and disease-free, or prune spreading groundcover types to the desired height.

OUTSIDE THE TROPICS Ruellia will grow indoors if given a warm, moist site and bright light (but no direct sunlight). *R. brittoniana,* a shrubby perennial is hardy to northern California; it produces funnel-shaped blue flowers.

SELECTIONS *R. makoyana,* monkey plant, is a 2-foot-tall, spreading evergreen; its

RUSSELIA EQUISETIFORMIS (CORAL PLANT) Low-growing shrub with slender, drooping stems and arching clusters of short, tubular red flowers. Full sun, any very moist soil; can be grown at water's edge. Zones 9-10.

SAMANEA SAMAN (MONKEY POD, RAIN TREE) Very large tree, to 60 feet tall and wide, with umbrella-shaped crown, produces petalless flowers with pink stamens and 9-inch-long fruit. Full sun, deep, fertile, moist soil. Zone 10.

SANCHEZIA SPECIOSA (SANCHEZIA) 6-foot-tall shrub with large, medium to dark green leaves with striking yellow or white veins and golden yellow flowers. Full sun, warm temperatures, moist soil. Zones 9-10.

SARACA THAIPINGENSIS (ASOKA) Compact tree, to 30 feet tall, with long leaves that emerge purple and turn green and very showy yellow-orange flowers to 6 inches across. Very warm temperatures, rich, moist soil, full sun. Zone 10.

leaves are maroon-red mingled with green above, purple beneath, with silvery veins; flowers are 2 inches across, solitary, rosy red. **R. devosiana** grows to a 1½-foot-tall, compact, spreading groundcover with maroon-red leaves mingled with green above, purple beneath; flowers are 1½ inches across, solitary, and white with lavender streaks. **R. californica,** an evergreen shrub, is drought tolerant once established; it bears 2- to 3-inch purple flowers; it is hardy in the Arizona desert, but will sometimes drop leaves during cold snaps.

RUSSELIA EQUISETIFORMIS (R. JUNCEA) CORAL PLANT
Scrophulariaceae

Coral plant is a remarkable low-growing shrub native to Mexico with long, slender, four-angled stems, usually completely leafless and drooping. The much-branched plant abundantly produces arching clusters of short, tubular red flowers at the ends of branches, borne continuously. This colorful, tough plant is very valuable for mass feature plantings, for the rock garden or around boulders, and for hanging over walls or drooping from a pot. It grows exceptionally well near ponds or streams.

CULTURE Full sun is best. Any soil, including poor and stony, will do, provided it is moist. Plants are very tolerant of a wide range of temperature and humidity conditions. Purchase strong plants with plenty of shoots. Propagate from division or from branches that have rooted where they touch the ground. Provide a balanced granular fertilizer at planting time; feeding is not otherwise required unless plants lose vigor. In moist conditions, russelia will be vigorous, almost invasive; nevertheless, it is also very drought-tolerant and, while not attractive under stress, rebounds very rapidly from adverse conditions. Mulch is very advantageous to conserve the preferred moisture. Occasionally, the older branches need removing, and the plant will need pruning for shape and control. Every few years, you may cut the whole plant, or part of it, to the ground to induce vigorous fresh, new growth. Mealybugs may occasionally be a problem.

SELECTIONS **R. sarmentosa** is an arching, 6-foot-tall shrub that continuously blooms with red flower clusters, attracting butterflies. Tolerates drought.

SAMANEA SAMAN MONKEY POD, RAIN TREE *Fabaceae*

One of the most characteristic trees of Hawaii and other tropical places. The huge tree, growing to well over 60 feet high and wide in mature specimens, is well known from its enormous umbrella-shaped crown. From spring to summer, trees may be covered with petalless flowers consisting of masses of pink stamens. Pods are about 8 inches long and bear several seeds embedded in a sticky pulp. An extremely popular tree in the islands, and not only for its shade: gardeners love its compound leaflets, which make excellent compost and mulch. The leaves close at night–causing condensed dew to drop like rain–or when it is raining, hence the popular name. Wood is used for bowls and construction, and seedpods are fed to cattle. Trees are frequently more or less evergreen. However, trees in Hawaii erratically go dormant in winter; not all trees do this every year, and a tree that drops its leaves one year may go several years before losing its leaves again. Native to tropical America. The older name, *Pithecellobium saman*, is sometimes used, as is *Albizia saman*.

Ruellia flowers differ markedly.
Above: Ruellia colorata.
Top: Ruellia squarrosa.

Saraca thaipingensis displays its spectacular flowers and pink juvenile foliage. *Wayside Trees of Malaysia,* by Corner, describes the tree "In the forest, saracas always grow in stream valleys, mostly at the very edge of the stream, and their dark, fibrous roots, beset with nodules, trail out in bundles in the running water. Indeed, in this country, whatever river we ascend, we will find eventually that it is bordered with saraca trees . . ."

CULTURE Monkey pod requires full sun, but young plants can be started in quite deep shade. Deep, fertile, moist soil is best for healthy, rapid growth of young plants. Tolerant of temperatures from the low 50° F to the 90° F range. Purchase a plant with a healthy root system and firm terminal growth buds. Propagation is from seed. Provide a granular fertilizer at planting time; older trees growing in good, moist soil do not need feeding. Water to establish young plants; mature trees are extremely drought-tolerant due to their huge root system. Mulching is beneficial for young plants. Pruning is needed only to maintain the shape of the tree, especially when young. Caterpillars can defoliate the tree, but Bt spray will control this. As trees get older, fungal rots can occur in branch crotches or at the site of previous damage; treat this early. Keep a close watch for dead branches high up in the tree, which frequently result from damage–often years previously–to far-ranging roots cramped in confined spaces.

SANCHEZIA *Acanthaceae*

Sanchezia is a shrub up to 9 feet tall grown especially for its striking yellow-striped foliage. Excellent for color variation in the informal landscape.
CULTURE Full sun to light shade and temperatures of 65-85° F are best. Buy actively growing, healthy plants. Propagate from cuttings. Keep soil moist. Cut back to half the length after each flowering season to encourage new growth, and then apply fertilizer; after this cutting back, plants will be relatively pest- and disease-free.
OUTSIDE THE TROPICS Sanchezia needs more humidity than can be provided in most homes, but it does well in greenhouses and conservatories.
SELECTIONS *S. speciosa* is a 6-foot-tall shrub with medium to dark green leaves with yellow or white veins and golden yellow flowers.

SARACA ASOKA *Fabaceae*

Saraca, a small tree that grows to about 30 feet tall, is considered by some to be the most beautiful of all flowering trees; it is also tough, surviving many adverse conditions, which is why it is so common. Saracas put on a long-lasting and impressive show. Showy flowers open yellow, change to apricot-yellow and then to deep yellow with a blood red eye; new leaves grow as dangling pink tassels which turn green in a few days; and fruits, which do not appear in Hawaii, are a vivid purple. The tree is sacred to Hindus and Buddhists, who believe that Buddha was born under it.
CULTURE Grow in partial shade, in deep, well-drained but moist soil, under warm and humid conditions. Propagate by seeds or layering; layering is best because it consistently produces the expected results. Site where the tree can be seen from all sides and where flowers can be viewed from beneath the canopy; allow room for spread. Soil should be kept moist; water daily if necessary in dry areas. Fertilize annually with 10-30-10 fertilizer or several times per season with 14-14-14. Mulching helps retain moisture. Prune to expose branches on which flowers will be borne. Problems with insects or diseases are rare.
SELECTIONS *S. thaipingensis* is the showiest and hardiest species, to Zone 9. *S. indica* is also lovely. *S. cauliflora* has been introduced in Florida.

SCAEVOLA SERICEA BEACH PLUM, NAUPAKA *Goodeniaceae*

This coastal shrub, native to the Pacific and Indian Ocean region, is found growing at the edge of the vegetation line in warm climates. Freely branching plants

SCAEVOLA SERICEA (BEACH PLUM) Freely branching shrub with glossy dark green leaves, white flowers, shiny red fruits. Full sun, light sandy soils; thrives in beach conditions. Zones 9-10.

SCHAUERIA FLAVICOMA (SCHAUERIA) Subshrub, to 4 feet tall, produces unusual yellow flowers with long bracts. Filtered to full sun, fertile moist soil. Zones 9-10.

SCHISMATOGLOTTIS x 'SILVER LIGHT'(DROP-TONGUE) Herbaceous plant with erect or rhizomatous stems, to 1 foot tall, with 12- to 15-inch long silver-gray leaves. Partial shade, well-drained, moist, rich soil, warm, humid conditions. Zone 10.

SOLANDRA MAXIMA (CHALICE VINE) Woody vine with 4- to 6-inch-wide yellow flowers with purple markings. Full sun to partial shade, moderately fertile soil, warm conditions. Zone 10.

Carissa grandiflora, natal plum, is similar to scaevola, and has also naturalized along beachfronts.

vary in leaf size (3-12 inches long, 2-4 inches wide) and texture and in height (2-8 feet tall or more). The blooms are distinct, with each resembling a half flower, white with purple streaks and borne in clusters in leaf axils. Seeds are round, white berries. This plant is used medicinally in many countries. A Hawaiian legend tells of two lovers who quarreled; the young woman refused to make up with the young man until he brought her a naupaka with a perfect, whole flower–an impossibility. This shrub is a boon to coastal gardeners and those living in exposed, windy areas; it can be grown right on the beach, where it is valuable as a soil stabilizer and windbreak. Its light green leaves and constant flowering are a cheerful and reliable sight.

CULTURE Grow in full sun; passing light shade during the day is acceptable. Light, sandy soils suit it well, but plants are very adaptable. Fertility is not as important as good drainage, although plants do respond to good nutrition. Tolerates high pH; poor, sandy soils; and salt spray and high winds. Adaptable to a variety of hot and humid lowland conditions, but is not very suitable for cooler upland areas. Purchase strong plants with healthy roots and shoots. Propagate from seeds (two per fruit are produced) or from terminal cuttings about 8-12 inches long. Do not set out more deeply than previously grown. Adding fertilizer to the planting hole is beneficial; once established, feed plants only if they lose vigor. Keep moist while plants are establishing themselves; later, plants are adaptable to dry conditions. Mulching is useful. Pruning is needed only to shape shrubs and keep them under control. Mealybugs may occasionally be a problem.

SCHAUERIA *Acanthaceae*

Schaueria is a small genus of ornamental evergreen subshrubs, native to tropical Brazil, distinguished by an unusual flower cluster consisting of blooms with long, hair- or bristlelike bracts, giving a bottlebrush appearance. Attractive and pleasing in the natural landscape setting.

CULTURE Grow in filtered to full sun, in fertile and moist soil. Schaueria tolerates temperatures from 65-85° F. Purchase healthy, pest-free plants, or propagate from cuttings. Fertilize young plants until established and after pruning back. Keep soil moist. Prune back branches to half their length after flowering to encourage bushiness and healthy new growth, which will keep plants relatively pest- and disease-free.

SELECTIONS *S. flavicoma* grows 4 feet tall; has 4-inch-long flower clusters with long, light, yellow bracts and pale yellow flowers.

SCHISMATOGLOTTIS DROP-TONGUE *Araceae*

Schismatoglottis is an herbaceous plant with erect or rhizomatous stems, grown for its ornamental foliage or as groundcover.

CULTURE Grow in semi-shade, in well-drained, moist soil with high organic content, under warm and humid conditions. Buy plants with healthy root systems, or propagate by suckers. Keep soil moist but not wet and fertilize annually with a balanced fertilizer. Mulching helps to keeps soil moist. Slugs are sometimes a problem, but the plant is usually trouble-free.

SELECTIONS *S. concinna* and *S. emarginanata* are attractive and available species. *S. x* **'Silver Light'** is a lovely, low-growing cultivar with silvery blue-gray foliage.

SPATHIPHYLLUM FLORIBUNDUM (SNOWFLOWER) Herbaceous perennial, 1-2 feet tall, with dark-green leaves with white markings and white spathe flowers. Partial shade, very rich, moist soil. Zone 10.

SPATHODEA CAMPANULATA (AFRICAN TULIP TREE) Tall, narrow tree, to 50 feet tall, with long, light green leaves and clusters (usually in rings of five) of golden to orange tuliplike flowers. Full sun or light shade, deep fertile soil is best, drier soil is tolerated. Zones 9-10.

STEPHANOTIS FLORIBUNDA (MADAGASCAR JASMINE) Small to medium-sized vine, to 15 feet long, with dark green fleshy leaves and fragrant white flowers. Full sun, but some protection in hot weather, moist, loamy soil, humid conditions. Zones 9-10.

STIGMAPHYLLON CILIATUM (GOLDEN CREEPER) Twining, woody vine with foliage that emerges deep red and turns deep green and clusters of golden flowers in long, stalked clusters in spring. Full sun to partial shade, moderately fertile soil, warm, humid conditions. Zones 9-10.

Solandra maxima.

SOLANDRA CHALICE VINE *Solanaceae*

Solandra comprises about 10 species of ornamental, woody vines or climbing shrubs. The leathery, glossy leaves and large, showy yellow or white flowers command attention. The striking flowers typically resemble a chalice, being in the shape of a large, open cup; they are fragrant at night and usually open cream-colored and then turn golden. They flower two or three times a year, during warm weather. Specimens trained against a hard-surfaced wall such as stone or stucco are often spectacular. Solandra is also wonderfully effective embellishing the eaves of a building, clambering over a pergola, or growing around a pillar.

CULTURE Grow in full sun to partial shade, in moderately fertile and well-drained soil and in warm and moderately humid conditions. Purchase plants that show signs of vigor and have glossy, clean foliage; look for distinct variegation in variegated types. Propagate from seed, or from cuttings of firm, young growth with a heel over bottom heat. You can set out container-grown plants at any time of year, but late autumn as the weather cools is ideal, as growth then becomes more rapid. Plant near support, and water well to establish. Irrigate in late autumn and winter while plants are growing quickly; drier conditions are preferable for the summer. A slow-release, low-analysis fertilizer applied in the autumn will enhance growth. Prune to control by removing weak shoots and shortening those that are too long. Light mulching, kept to a minimum, helps to protect the soil and reduce weeding. Sucking insects can be a problem at certain seasons.

SELECTIONS *S. maxima* and *S. guttata* both have large, yellow flowers marked with some purple. *S. longiflora* has narrower white flowers; it is no less showy, but it is a somewhat less vigorous grower.

SPATHIPHYLLUM SPATHE FLOWER *Araceae*

This attractive plant–popular indoors and as an outdoor groundcover–produces large white flowers consisting of a spathe and a spadix; in some cases, the flowers are fragrant. This genus is one of only two that occur in both the old and the new worlds (the other is *Homalomena*).

CULTURE Spathiphyllum thrives in partial or even deep shade; its pure white flowers light up dark areas. It prefers loamy, well-drained soil high in organic matter and warm, humid conditions. Purchase plants with healthy root systems or propagate by suckers or offshoots. Small species (see "Selections" below) should be closely planted, as they are slow to produce offshoots. Large species should be given room to spread. Don't allow the soil to dry; water as necessary. Fertilize occasionally with 10-30-10 fertilizer or regularly with 10-10-10. Spathiphyllum requires little care and rarely suffers from pests and diseases other than infrequent mealybugs.

OUTSIDE THE TROPICS Spathiphyllum is used frequently (perhaps even overused) in low-light situations such as malls and office interiors. They should be kept evenly moist and repotted rarely.

SELECTIONS *S. floribundum,* snowflower, is a small Columbian species that puts on a beautiful show of delicate flowers with tiny leaves. **'Silver Streak'** and **'Misty'** are recommended cultivars. *S. cannaefolium* is an excellent large plant with fragrant flowers. *S. wallisii* [*S.* **'Clevelandii'**], another large species, has rich, dark green leaves with undulating edges.

SPATHODEA CAMPANULATA AFRICAN TULIP TREE *Bignoniaceae*

This slender tree, more than 50 feet tall when mature, is a familiar sight in the tropics. The shiny, light green leaves can be up to 2 feet long and are pinnately divided, with many pairs of leaflets and a terminal one, each about 5 inches long, broadly ovate and characteristically coarsely veined. The large deep orange to golden flowers are 3-4 inches long and, in tropical climates, are borne on and off all year in large terminal clusters; in the subtropics, the bloom is seasonal. Blooms are followed by slender pods that split longitudinally into two boat-shaped halves, releasing the paperlike seeds to the wind. This fast-growing tree provides an abundance of color throughout the year; because of its height, it is not useful for shade—mature specimens have a long, clear trunk for many feet. Unfortunately, this is a potentially beautiful weed tree, for seeds germinate easily and in every niche, a factor that must be considered when landscape planning. Native to tropical Africa.

CULTURE Young plants do best in a moist place in full sun or light shade. Trees are adaptable to varied soil conditions: deep, fertile soils suit them well, but seedlings will grow in drier, stony places or in poorly drained, wetter areas. In Hawaii, most African tulip trees grow in the warm, humid lowlands, but more recently they are being found in greater abundance in cooler, wet upland areas. Purchase strong young plants with a strong terminal bud, or propagate from seed. Keep moist when newly planted; later, trees will adapt to wet or dry conditions and easily tolerate prolonged dry spells. Trees require little or no fertilizing, mulching, or pruning.

SELECTIONS A golden yellow-flowered form is equally as striking as the scarlet-blooming species and appears to seed less and be less likely to become weedy.

STEPHANOTIS FLORIBUNDA MADAGASCAR JASMINE, BRIDAL BOUQUET *Asclepiadaceae*

This is a small to medium vine, growing to 15 feet, with dark green, somewhat rubbery foliage and clusters of pure white, sweet-smelling flowers borne all summer and often used in bridal bouquets. Native to Madagascar, this is a popular flowering vine for patio or portico.

CULTURE Grow in sun, but provide shade during the hottest times of day. Plants thrive in moist, loamy soil and warm, humid conditions. Purchase plants with healthy, deep green foliage and uninjured stems. Propagate from seed or from cuttings of half-ripe wood rooted over bottom heat. Set out near a support, and water well to establish. Apply liquid 20-20-20 fertilizer on alternate weeks, except during cool weather. Soil should never dry out completely, but it must drain well. Regular mulching will maintain moisture levels, suppress weeds, and inhibit nematodes, which may be a problem.

OUTSIDE THE TROPICS Under the right conditions, stephanotis will flower freely indoors. It needs a stable atmosphere of warmth in summer and coolness in winter, moist compost (water only sparingly in winter), and high humidity.

STIGMAPHYLLON GOLDEN CREEPER, *Malpighiaceae*

Two species of this twining, woody vine (also known as butterfly vine and orchid vine) are commonly grown, **S. ciliatum** and **S. periplocifolium.** Both have beautiful

Spathiphyllum is a houseplant for people who say they can they can't grow houseplants. It thrives on neglect, even under adverse conditions.

STRELITZIA NICOLAI (BIRD OF PARADISE) Treelike plant to 20 feet with leaves that fan out, revealing blue and white flowers covered by boatlike bracts. Full sun to semishade, rich, moist soil (some seem better in dry soil). Zones 9-10, Zone 8 with protection.

STROBILANTHES DYERIANUS (PERSIAN SHIELD) Striking, iridescent blue-purple-green leaves, 12-18 inches long, less showy lavender flowers. Partial shade is best, fertile, moist soil. Zones 9-10.

STRONGYLODON MACROBOTRYS (JADE VINE) Vigorous vine, to 30 feet with spectacular hanging bluish green flowers in 3-foot-long clusters. Full sun or light shade, well-drained, rich, moist soil. Zone 10.

TABEBUIA CARAIBA (SILVER TRUMPET TREE) Tree to 25 feet tall or more with small crown that is covered with showy campanulate yellow flowers all through spring. Full sun, good air circulation, dry conditions acceptable. Zones 9-10.

displays of brilliant golden yellow flowers that appear in long, stalked clusters in the spring, completely clothing the vine. New foliage emerges as a deep red, chestnut color before turning a deep green. This makes a fine disguise for a fence or an enhancement for a pillar. Native to tropical America; the scientific name is sometimes wrongly spelled *Stigmatophyllon*.

CULTURE Grow in full sun to partial shade in warm, humid conditions. Vines are not particular, but moderately fertile soil promotes better growth. Propagate from semihardwood cuttings in a sandy mix with bottom heat. Plant out from containers any time, near a support. Water to establish, then during dry periods as needed. A slow-release granular fertilizer applied just before new growth begins is beneficial. Prune to maintain size and to control after flowering. Maintain mulch over the root zone. Vines have no particular pest or disease problems. Occasionally aphids congregate on new growth; a sharp spray with water usually controls this.

Birds of paradise provide bright color to this planting of dwarf plumeria, rhoeo, and *Cycas circanalis*.

STRELITZIA BIRD OF PARADISE *Strelitziaceae*

A relative of the banana family native to South Africa, the exotic-looking bird of paradise has two main species. **S. reginae** is herbaceous, widely grown in the tropics and also suitable as a houseplant; it grows 3-4 feet tall, with large, grayish, leath-

Strobilanthes' flowers are not the plant's best feature; they are usually grown for their unusual iridescent foliage.

ery leaves and showy orange and blue flowers—the "birds"—held on a smooth stalk emerging from between the leaves. The flowers are long-lasting when cut and are popular with florists. **S. nicolai** (named for Tsar Nicholas I) is clustering and tree-like, growing to 20 feet and holding its undivided leaves fanned out at the top of a straight or sinuous trunk. The white and blue flowers emerge from boatlike bracts that peep out from between the leaves. Birds of paradise are striking as an addition to the herbaceous border, as accent plants, or as a foundation planting.

CULTURE Grow in full sun to semishade, in well-drained soil in climates ranging from warm and moist to hot and dry. Some cultivars of *S. reginae* have very small leaf blades; these require full sun to bloom. Purchase full, clean plants, and check for signs of scale or mealybugs. Propagate from seed well-soaked before sowing or from clump division. Set out well-rooted plants as large as possible. Add slow-release fertilizer to the bottom of the planting hole, and take care not to injure fleshy roots. Water in well to establish; otherwise, do not irrigate. Mulch well. Feeding three to four times a year with palm fertilizer seems to work well. Pruning to four or five stalks makes the flowers more visible. Scale and mealybugs at the root zone can be a serious problem.

OUTSIDE THE TROPICS *S. reginae* can be grown as a houseplant in a large tub or container. It needs good light but not hot sun, so an east window is a suitable location. Keep soil evenly moist while plants are growing and blooming but fairly dry during the several months while plants are resting. It will also grow outdoors in protected areas in Zone 9.

STROBILANTHES DYERIANUS PERSIAN SHIELD *Acanthaceae*

This medium-sized evergreen shrub, native to Asia, is grown more for its foliage than for its bell-shaped lavender-blue flowers. The unusual iridescent purple foliage makes strobilanthes an interesting addition to the informal landscape. It is attractive for background or feature plantings, but some species can look weedy when out of flower and not pruned regularly. It likes areas protected from harsh, windy conditions, which will break off branches.

CULTURE Strobilanthes normally does not object to growing in bright sun (though they sometimes burn on the Gulf Coast), but foliage color will improve in partial shade or in a lath house. Soil should be fertile and moist. Tolerates temperatures of 65-85° F. Purchase healthy, pest-free plants, or propagate from cuttings. Fertilize young plants until established, and feed after pruning. Keep soil moist. Prune back branches to half their length at least once a year for an attractive appearance and to produce healthy new growth that will be relatively free from pests and diseases.

STRONGYLODON MACROBOTRYS JADE VINE *Fabaceae*

Jade vine is the gem of its genus, grown for its spectacularly presented and most unusually colored flowers. It is a strong-growing liana with foliage that starts out deep, almost black, wine-purple or very pale green, and then becomes dark green. The 3-foot-long hanging clusters of the showy, bluish green flowers are produced mainly in spring, occasionally at other times. This is a striking plant trained to a pergola or along the eaves of a building; it is also an interesting landscape feature grown into a tree with a crown that is not overly dense. No photograph can do this Philippine native justice. Seeing jade vine in bloom is one of the unique privileges of being in the tropics at the right time.

CULTURE Grow in full sun or light canopy shade, in freely draining, rich, moist soil. Conditions should be warm to very warm, and humid. When buying, look for a full plant showing signs of new growth. Jade vine does not thrive for long in a container, and after rooting it is sometimes very slow to grow at all. Propagate from seed, or from semihardwood cuttings taken in spring. Plant out near a strong support as soon as possible after purchase, preferably in warm, moist weather. Water well to establish, and provide regular irrigation thereafter if rainfall is not reliable. Application of a slow-release, citrus formula, granular fertilizer as a top dressing in late winter enhances growth. A layer of organic mulch helps to maintain a healthy root zone. During vigorous growth, it is imperative to train the new growth to its bounds; remove the excessively errant new sprouts rather than pruning out hardwood. Vines have been known to die from overly heavy pruning. Jade vine seems to have few pest or disease problems.

TABEBUIA GOLD TREE, PRIMA VERA *Bignoniaceae*

Tabebuia is one of the most beautiful early flowering trees, especially appreciated in Hawaii as a herald of spring. It grows to 50 feet or more, with distinctive gray bark and a small crown. During February, March, and April, this spectacular tree produces stunning displays of yellow, crinkly, tubular flowers in clusters at the ends of more or less deciduous branches. These are followed by new, palmate leaves, each with five to seven leaflets up to 10 inches long. Gold tree is exceptionally valuable as a seasonal focal feature.

CULTURE Grow in an open position in full sun. Trees are not particular about soil, but good drainage is important. In Hawaii, gold tree grows in the hotter, drier lowlands, where temperatures of 65-90° F are usual, but cooler temperatures would probably also be acceptable. Gardeners at Fairchild Tropical Gardens notice that individual plants seem to flower better when slightly stressed, as after a cold, dry period, or in a hot, dry location. Purchase a plant with a strong root system. Propagate from seed or from 8-inch-long cuttings of ripe wood. Add a granular general fertilizer when planting to give young trees a good start. Water until plants are established; later, trees are tolerant of moderate dry conditions periodically. Annual applications of a general fertilizer such as 10-30-10 are beneficial to encourage healthy annual growth; once the tree reaches maturity, feeding is no longer necessary. Mulch is advantageous to conserve moisture and add nutrients. Pruning is not needed other than occasional shaping. Trees have no particular pest or disease problems.

SELECTIONS *T. caraiba* (formerly *T. argentea*), silver trumpet tree, is an evergreen that grows to about 25 feet tall; it has pronounced grayish silver leaves and terminal heads of golden yellow tubular flowers produced in spring and periodically throughout the year. *T. heterophylla* is an adaptable, small, evergreen tree with shiny leaves and large terminal heads of pink flowers produced at intervals throughout the year. *T. donnell-smithii,* also known as *Cybistax donnell-smithii*, is native to Mexico and Guatemala, and is the species most often grown in Hawaii.

TACCA CHANTRIERI (BAT PLANT) Tuberous, clump-forming perennial to 2 feet tall with quilted dark green leaves and dark flowers surrounded by dark bracts. Filtered light, moist rich soil. Zone 10.

TAPEINOCHILUS ANANASSAE (PINEAPPLE GINGER) Vigorous branching plant to 10 feet tall with large leaves and stiff, oval, pineapplelike flowers. Moderate to half shade, deep, rich soil. Zones 10.

TECOMA CAPENSIS (CAPE HONEYSUCKLE) Loose, open shrub with pinnate leaves and tubular orange or yellow flowers through spring and summer. Full sun or light shade, any soil, moderate humidity. Zones 9-10.

TECOMANTHE DENDROPHILA (PINK TRUMPET VINE) Vigorous, twining, woody vine, to 30 feet long, produces abundant clusters of 5-inch trumpet-shaped flowers. Full sun for foliage (wood may be in deep shade), warm, humid conditions, moist, well-drained soil. Zone 10.

TACCA BAT PLANT, DEVIL FLOWER, CAT'S WHISKERS *Taccaceae*

Tacca is a tuberous-rooted herbaceous perennial native to Southeast Asia, growing to 2 feet tall, with dense clumps of large, dark green "quilted" leaves. The tall
flowering stems emerge often all summer topped by a cluster of nearly black,
cuplike flowers, below which are fairly large purplish or brownish black bracts
resembling bat's wings and long, filamentlike bracts reminiscent of cat's whiskers.
This very interesting plant is useful as a border or even as a mass planting and
makes a conversation specimen in a filtered light situation.

CULTURE True to its tropical forest origins, tacca thrives in filtered light beneath
trees and taller shrubs, in moist and organically rich soil and warm, humid conditions; somewhat drier conditions during the cool season suit it well. Propagate
from plant division or from fresh seed sown in a light soil mix kept moist and
shaded. Tacca is an excellent container plant, in rich soil with excellent drainage,
or it may be planted out in a shaded, moist location. Provide regular irrigation in
the warmest months; allow some drying in the cool months. Apply 20-20-20 fertilizer monthly. Maintain a light mulch around the plant, but be alert for snails
during the wet season. Remove damaged or dead leaves by pulling them off
rather than clipping them back.

SELECTIONS *T. chantrieri* is the species most likely to be available from specialty
sources. *T. integrifolia,* a similar species, is sometimes also available.

Tecomanthe with Spanish moss and orchids.

TAPEINOCHILUS ANANASSAE PINEAPPLE GINGER, INDONE-SIAN WAX GINGER *Costaceae*

This is a genus of vigorous, branching gingers, with stems arising from the
ground. The large leaves, 13 inches and more long and up to 3 inches wide, are
usually found near the ends of branches/branchlets. Flower clusters up to 12 inches or more long usually appear on separate stems arising from the ground but are
occasionally found on leaf and branch-bearing stems. These inflorescences are stiff,
oval, pineapplelike structures about 6 inches long that are actually comprised of
close, overlapping reddish bracts enclosing flowers that are orange outside and
whitish within. This very spectacular and exotic plant makes a fine accent for
areas where it grows well. Native to Indonesia and New Guinea.

CULTURE Grow in 30 to 50 percent shade. Deep, organic soil is best. Pineapple
ginger is a plant of forest floors and edges; it needs high humidity and temperatures in the 60-85° F range for best growth. Purchase multistemmed plants with
healthy new growths visible. Propagate by division, or by snapping off a short
branchlet with a swollen knob at the base and shallowly inserting this in a sandy
medium to root. Incorporate a general granular fertilizer at planting time, and
add a layer of mulch. Do not plant deeper than previously grown. Be sure to keep
soil moist at all times, for both young and established plants; maintain a layer of
mulch to provide the needed moisture and nutrients. If growth is poor, apply a
liquid organic-based fertilizer. Replanting every five years or so is advisable.
Pineapple ginger has no special pest or disease problems.

TECOMA CAPENSIS CAPE HONEYSUCKLE *Bignoniaceae*

Until recently referred to as *Tecomaria capensis*, this native of South Africa is a
straggly, almost viny shrub that produces abundant long, tubular orange flowers
at the growth ends periodically throughout spring and summer. Leaves are pin-

THUNBERGIA GRANDIFLORA (CLOCK VINE) Vigorous vine, to 30 feet long, produces heart-shaped dark green leaves and 5-inch sky blue, trumpet-shaped flowers. Full sun or light shade, moist, well-drained soil. Zones 9-10.

TULBAGHIA VIOLACEA (SOCIETY GARLIC) Tuberous plant with linear leaves and delicate lilace or pink flowers on slender stems, to 3 feet tall. Full sun, well-drained sandy soil; warm and humid in summer, cooler and drier in winter. Zones 9-10.

TURNERA ULMIFOLIA (YELLOW ALDER) Compact shrub, 2-5 feet tall with showy yellow flowers. Full sun, very warm, humid conditions, any soil (including rocky and dry). Zones 9-10.

ZINGIBER SPECTABILE (BEEHIVE GINGER) Tall plant, to 4-6 feet, with leafy, arching stems and yellow and orange cones covering black flowers that last nine months. Light shade, warm, moist, and humid in growing season, cool and dry when dormant; rich soil. Zone 10.

nate with 7- to 9-inch-long leaflets. Flowers are followed by 4- to 6-inch-long, narrow seedpods enclosing paperlike seeds spread by the wind. This plant sends up shoots from underground roots and can become quite invasive and hard to eradicate when growing in moist, rocky locations. Nevertheless, it is very valuable for covering a difficult bank or for an area with poor, stony soil. Very good, tough, and reliable where a periodically flowering vinelike plant is desired.

CULTURE Full sun is best, but light or passing shade is also suitable. Not particular about soil, this plant grows as well in well-drained stony soils as in deep, fertile soils. Floral display is best in full sun in cooler growing conditions, with temperatures of 55-85° F. Moderate humidity is ideal. Purchase healthy, pest-free plants with strong, active growths. Propagate from seed (unless from a cultivar), from cuttings of ripe wood, or from self-rooted branches. No watering, fertilizing, or mulching is required once plants are established. If you have only one or two plants, remove flowered stems once spent; otherwise, cut back to near ground level annually, or every few years, to rejuvenate. Occasional mealybugs or spider mite attacks may occur.

SELECTIONS *T. c.* **'Aurea'** is a yellow form. *T. stans,* yellow bells, yellow elder, will grow to tree-size in tropical areas, and will remain shrubby in areas where frost occurs regularly. It needs deep, rich soil and produces 2-inch bright yellow flowers from early summer to winter.

TECOMANTHE DENDROPHILA [T. VENUSTA] PINK TRUMPET VINE *Bignoniaceae*

This vigorous twining liana has a delightful habit of producing copious clusters of 5-inch trumpet-shaped flowers along the older, leafless portions of the vine. It's a wonderful woody vine to train along the eaves of a building, and it is beautiful if allowed to grow into a strong tree with the flowers visible at eye level. Native to Australasia. It grows to 30 feet tall and flowers most heavily in spring.

CULTURE The foliage needs full sun, but the old wood may be deeply shaded. Plants need warm, humid conditions and moist, well-drained soil. Even very young specimens will flower, so when purchasing plants, look for signs that the buds along the stem have produced flowers; they will continue to do so once the vine is established. Propagate from softwood cuttings, under mist. Plant near a strong support, such as a nearby tree. Regular watering is needed only during very dry periods. Feed two to three times a year with a granular 6-6-6 or a citrus fertilizer; superphosphate will encourage the stems to mature and thus to flower earlier. Mulching around the base helps to keep roots moist and cool. Train young, flexible growth to positions that will display the spectacular flowers to best advantage. This vine has no special insect or disease problems.

SELECTIONS *T. dendrophila [T. venusta]* and *T. hillii* are the only two species of this beautiful genus available; a third species has been reduced to a single specimen in the wild.

THUNBERGIA CLOCK VINE *Acanthaceae*

Thunbergia is a genus of 90-100 species of shrubby and vining plants, most of which are native to tropical Africa and India. They are grown as attractive flowering shrubs or dense, low hedges; as clambering vines covering trellises, arbors, and pergolas and dripping with long, hanging clusters of large flowers in a variety

Above: Thunbergia alata, often used as a quick-growing annual vine in temperate zones.
Top: Thunbergia mysorensis, an excellent vine for the tropics.

Any grove or wood is a fine thing to see. But the magic here, strangely is not apparent from the road. It is necessary to leave the impersonal highway, to step inside the rust gate and close it behind. By this, an act of faith is committed, through which one accepts blindly the communion cup of beauty. One is now inside the grove, out of one world and in the mysterious heart of another. Enchantment lies in different things for each of us. For me, it is this: to step out of the bright sunlight into the shade of orange trees; to walk under the arched canopy of their jadelike leaves; to see the long aisles of lichened trunks stretch ahead in a a geometric rhythm; to feel the mystery of a seclusion that yet has shafts of light striking through it. . . After long years of spiritual homelessness, of nostalgia, here is that mystic loveliness of childhood again. Here is home. An old thread, long tangled, comes straight again.

MARJORIE KINNAN RAWLINGS,
CROSS CREEK

of colors; and, in cooler climates, as trailing annuals in hanging baskets and windowboxes. Blooms in late summer and fall as an annual and at intervals all year in the tropics, although hedge-grown plants will flower less frequently because of trimming.

CULTURE Grow in full sun or light shade. Propagates easily from seed, cuttings, or layering. This plant adapts to a variety of soils, but does best in rich, well-drained moist soil, under warm and humid conditions. Buy plants with strong roots, or propagate by cuttings. One or two of the vine types are sufficient for a trellis 6-8 feet long. Shrubs can be kept small with heavy pruning. Keep soil moist but not wet, and apply 14-14-14 fertilizer two or three times per year or 10-30-10 annually. This plant rarely suffers from pests or diseases, but some species can be invasive, particularly in Hawaii where *T. grandiflora* has escaped and has become a pest.

OUTSIDE THE TROPICS *T. alata* is a popular annual vine or basket plant in temperate climates; it is often used to create a quick screen. It can be brought indoors for winter and kept in bright light, though it will rarely flower again.

SELECTIONS Shrub: **T. erecta,** king's mantle, has royal purple flowers with a deep yellow throat, borne profusely; this bushy, sprawling shrub grows to 8 feet; native to Africa, it is popular in Hawaii. Vines: **T. alata,** black-eyed susan vine, twines to 8 feet; it is widely naturalized in the tropics and is often grown as an annual in cooler areas; many cultivars offer a range of colors from whites to yellows to oranges. It has naturalized in central Florida. **T. coccinea** has scarlet flowers with a yellow throat. **T. grandiflora** features 8-inch-long heart-shaped leaves and clusters of big, trumpet-shaped blue flowers with a white throat; at Bok Tower Gardens it grows well but occasionally freeezes. **T. laurifolia** is similar. **T. mysorensis** is a beautiful choice for trellises with orange-red and mahogony-red flowers with canary yellow centers. In Hawaii, it flowers almost yearround with long, pendulous inflorescences and is recommended highly by Robert Hirano of Lyons Arboretum.

TULBAGHIA SOCIETY GARLIC *Alliaceae*

Tulbaghia is a genus of tuberous or cormous plants with thin, erect, linear leaves resembling in appearance and odor some species of garlic or onions; when used in place of garlic in cooking, the leaves of these plants are more subtle and leave no garlic breath–hence the common name. The bright lilac or pink flowers of this South African native are borne on slender stems above and among the leaves periodically throughout the warm months. Society garlic is lovely in the herbaceous border and also as a pot plant.

CULTURE Grow in full sun in well-drained sandy soil with some organic matter. Best conditions are warm and humid; however, winter weather can be drier and cool, but not freezing. Where society garlic can't overwinter outside, grow it as a pot plant, or cut it back to the base at the end of the growing season, pot it up, and bring it indoors; water sparingly during the winter. Propagate by seed or by dividing the growing mass. Plant out at any time in warm climates to a depth of 1-2 inches, watering well to establish. A bloom-booster fertilizer helps to produce heavier blooming. Deadhead plants occasionally. Mulch carefully so as not to bury plants. Mealybugs and caterpillars may be a problem.

OUTSIDE THE TROPICS Hardy to Zone 7 in protected areas; mulch heavily before winter. In cooler areas, bulbs can be dug up and brought indoors for winter.

SELECTIONS *T. fragrans* and *T. violacea* are similar, the former with bright, very fragrant mauve blooms and the latter with bright lilac flowers.

TURNERA ULMIFOLIA YELLOW ALDER *Turneraceae*

This tropical American native is a showy, yellow-flowered shrub growing 2-5 feet tall, useful in mass plantings. Flowers open in early morning and only last until 10 to 11 a.m.; in warm, humid areas, it flowers freely and continuously all day.
CULTURE Grow in full sun in warm to very warm, humid conditions. Plants are not particular and seem to do well in most soils, including rocky and dry ones. Purchase full plants with medium to dark green leaves. Propagate from seeds, cuttings, or plant division. Set out after any period of cool weather is past. Water to establish and during dry periods; plants tend to rot if kept too wet. Apply a bloom-booster granular fertilizer lightly two to three times in warm weather; don't overdo. Light mulching keeps weeds at bay. Spider mites can be a problem.

ZINGIBER SHAMPOO GINGER, BEEHIVE GINGER, EDIBLE GINGER *Zingiberaceae*

This Asian native with leafy, arching stems grows to a height of 2-6 feet from a rhizome. Its conelike flower stalks emerge separately, directly from the soil in summer. In some species, the cone holds a fluid that will lather up like shampoo. *Z. officinale* is the piquant ginger of commerce, in medicinal and culinary use for millennia, one of the species that motivated Western travel and exploration. In the landscape, ginger is a specimen appreciated for its special architecture and unusual "flowers." Smaller gingers can be grown indoors or in the greenhouse.
CULTURE Most gingers prefer light shade, although some species will grow in full sun. Conditions should be warm and humid while ginger is in full growth and cool and dry while dormant (most species die back to fleshy rhizomes for a short time); however, temperatures below 50° F can stunt plants. Rich, organic soil should be moist during the summer. Purchase firm, plump rhizomes or plants with vigorous, clean growth. Propagate from rhizome pieces or clump division; do not keep rhizomes overly wet until growth has started. Plant rhizome pieces horizontally 3-4 inches deep; plant divisions deeper than they grew previously. Slow-release fertilizer in the planting hole is beneficial, as are regular applications of fertilizer with extra potassium for established plants. Water regularly during active growth, and let the plants be dry in the winter months. Mulch heavily. Remove leafy stalks as they begin to turn yellow and die back. For better display of the flower stalks, you may remove selected leafy stalks to ground level. Pruning the rhizomes by making three or four cuts will promote resprouting.
OUTSIDE THE TROPICS *Z. officinale* is often grown indoors, and the root, which is the gingerroot used in cooking, is harvested. It can be started from fresh ginger purchased in the produce market. *Z. zerumbet* performs well indoors also.
SELECTIONS *Z. spectabile,* beehive ginger, grows to 4-6 feet tall; its display of yellow and orange cones punctuated with black flowers lasts for nine months or more. *Z. zerumbet,* shampoo ginger, is somewhat smaller; its cones start out green and age to crimson red; it was used by the early Hawaiians as shampoo. *Z. z.* **'Darcy'** is similar but smaller, with variegated foliage.

Above: Ananas bracteatus displays the rosettes typical of bromeliads, plus pineapple fruit. *Top:* Unusual and attractive pink and blue flower of *Aechmea gamosepala.*

BROMELIADS

Bromeliads are generally epiphytic plants with ornamental straplike leaves that grow in a rosette, forming a cup. The flower head emerges from this cup and is usually quite showy because of colorful bracts that may last several months. The rosettes produce generous numbers of offsets, or "pups," which can be severed when they are one-third of their parent's size and potted or replanted in the landscape. These epiphytes need air around their roots; provide a light, open, very well-drained growing medium—pine bark chips or mulch, or tree fern fiber. Any type of copper (penny coins, pressure-treated wood, fungicides) can be deadly to bromeliads. The cup of a bromeliad acts as a receptacle to hold water; it is important to maintain this water supply. Garden fauna, such as frogs, salamanders, and spiders love the wet interior of bromeliads; unfortunately, so do snails and mosquitoes. Control snails by hand picking or by setting shallow containers of stale beer; control mosquitoes by hosing out the plants' centers regularly. Scale insects can also be a problem. Lifting, dividing, and replanting every few years allows for closer inspection for scale as well as snails.

AECHMEA

Aechmeas are vase-shaped epiphytes, native to tropical America; members of the genus range in size from 4 inches to 4 feet. The foliage (usually in rosettes) is highly variable, and edges of the green, bronze, red, or banded leaves are often armed with spines. The long-lasting brightly colored flowers are usually held high above the foliage. Larger-scale aechmeas make bold, exotic landscape accents; smaller species serve well as groundcovers and as interesting houseplants and residents of tree branches. Most aechmeas develop into beautiful clumps, as they produce pups. Aechmeas may be found in flower in all seasons.

CULTURE Most aechmeas prefer full to nearly full sun, although a few species will tolerate light shade and the foliage actually looks better in light shade. Because they are epiphytes, aechmeas are not particular about soil as long as it is open and very well drained; they will root well even in pine bark chips or rocks so long as they don't wobble. Although aechmeas prefer warmth and humidity, most will tolerate some dry, cooler periods. Any type of copper can be deadly to these plants. When purchasing, look for pest- (scale-) free plants that have been kept in strong light. When planting, be sure the base of the leaves is not below ground. Water once or twice a week until the plant's center overflows. Most aechmeas are very drought-tolerant. Feed lightly with quarter-strength water-soluble fertilizer every six to eight weeks; granular fertilizer spilled into the cups usually causes burning. To minimize weeding around these heavily armed plants, heavy mulching is advisable (you may have to prop up plants to mulch). Remove older leaves and faded flowers as needed. The plant blooms once, then sends off pups and dies; the parent plant supplies nutrients to the pups before it dies, so do not remove old parent plants until they become unattractive.

OUTSIDE THE TROPICS As houseplants, aechmeas need high light and warm to hot temperatures; allow the potting mix to dry out between waterings, but keep some water in the plant's vase.

SELECTIONS *A. blanchetiana* grows 3 feet tall in full sun, forming large clumps with tall red flowers; one form has orange-bronze foliage. *A. gamosepala* prefers filtered

AECHMEA DISTACEA x QUESNELIA TESTUDO (AECHMEA) Hybrid plant to 3 feet tall, forming clumps to 3 feet wide, with thorny straplike leaves and wandlike bright pink flowers. Full sun, very well-drained soil, warm, humid conditions. Zone 10.

ANANAS COMOSUS 'VARIEGATUS' (PINEAPPLE) Plant to 3 feet tall with white-edged straplike leaves and edible fruit. Rich soil, full sun, somewhat dry conditions; do not overwater. Zone 10.

BILLBERGIA GLOISEA (VASE PLANT) 2- 3-foot-tall plant with variegated straplike foliage and large yellow-orange inflorescences with long stamens. Partial shade, very well-drained soil, warm, humid conditions. Zone 10.

BILBERGIA KANTSKAYA (VASE PLANT) 1- 2-foot tall plant with stiff green foliage and pendulous green and white inflorescences. Partial shade, very well-drained soil, warm, humid conditions. Zone 10.

PINEAPPLE

Monday, November 4, 1493: During his second voyage to the New World Christopher Columbus visits Guadeloupe, and he and his entourage are the first Europeans to taste pineapple, "the flavor and fragrance of which astonished them." Columbus's opinion seems timid compared to the praise other Europeans were to lavish on that tropical wonder. Antonio Pigafetta, chronicler of Magellan's round-the-world tour, was more exuberant, calling it "the finest fruit in existence." Others exhausted their imaginations in extolling the pineapple's virtues; Gonzalo Fernandez de Oviedo y Valdes wrote "This is one of the most beautiful fruits I have seen wherever I have been in the whole world. At least not in Spain, nor in France, nor England, nor Germany, nor Italy, nor Sicily, nor other states of Cesare, as well as Burgundy, Flanders, and Tyrol, Artues, nor Holland nor Zealand . . ." Holy Roman Emperor Charles V was the first European monarch to sample a pineapple (he found it tasty), and around 1642 a pineapple was grown in a hothouse in England and dutifully presented to Charles II, who had it immortalized by his court painter before eating it. Fully recognizing the pineapple's value, the Europeans soon began moving it around. The Portuguese brought it to St. Helena shortly after discovering that island, and then to various parts of Africa, Madagascar, and India. By the end of the 16th century the pineapple was in cultivation over most of the world's tropical areas, including several Pacific islands. Precisely when the pineapple reached Hawaii is unknown. The botanists aboard ship with Captain Cook did not report seeing any in Hawaii in 1778-79, but by 1813 pineapples were considered common there.

light and forms 10-inch-high dense green clumps with small pink and blue flowers. **A. mexicana** is 3 feet tall and very symmetrical, producing leaning flowers with large white berries; best grown in small clumps or as individual plants in nearly full sun. Twelve-inch **A. orlandiana** has small red blooms and foliage spotted and banded with maroon; needs bright light and grows best mounted on trees. **A. 'Royal Wine'** is an old hybrid whose leaves are deep wine red on the underside; makes an excellent groundcover in filtered light. **A. weilbachii** features carmine flowers and bronze foliage; grows to 15 inches in filtered light. **A. fasciata** is a popular, easy to grow houseplant. **A. x 'Little Harv'** is 3 feet tall, with chalky blue-green leaves; lemon yellow flowers with salmon-pink bracts rise 4 feet; very architectural.

ANANAS PINEAPPLE

The people of South America enjoyed the luscious fruit of the pineapple long before it became an exotic delicacy for Europeans. The plant was cultivated for its fibers and extracts that were fermented and made into liquor as well as for its fruit. Today, many varieties of pineapple are grown as ornamentals, even though they don't yield edible fruit. The straplike leaves of the pineapple plant make a good backdrop for low-growing plants, and blend well with many shrubs. The fruit, though usually inedible, can be used as table decorations.

CULTURE Pineapples require rich soil, full sun, and somewhat dry conditions. It is prone to rot in very wet areas. Amend soil with organic matter before planting. Plant well-rooted offshoots shallowly in their desired locations. Fertilize with a balanced fertilizer every six to eight weeks. Do not overwater. Little pruning, other than removing fruits and damaged leaves, is necessary. Propagate by removing side shoots and allowing them to dry for about a month until roots develop. Monitor for scale and nematodes, and especially for root nematodes. If the latter are found, remove the plant and fumigate the soil before replacing with a new plant.

OUTSIDE THE TROPICS Some smaller varieties, like **A. variegatus** and **A. bracteatus** are grown indoors for their foliage in full sun and a rich potting mix. Cut the crown off a ripe pineapple and plant in a peat-based potting mix; it will develop tiny roots, at which point it can be moved to a bigger pot. Potted pineapple plants can be brought outdoors during summer months.

SELECTIONS The species **A. comosus** yields edible as well as ornamental cultivars. The cultivar **'Red Spanish'** has red-tinged fruits that are not as sweet as the commercial varieties, but are edible. **A.c. 'Variegatus'** has striped leaves. **A. variegatus** has multi-colored foliage.

BILLBERGIA VASE PLANT

Native to tropical and subtropical America, billbergias produce plain or variegated narrow, straplike foliage that is usually spiny and, once a year, showy flowers with large bracts. Billbergias are usually small and slender, with gracefully arranged leaves that are looser than most other bromeliads.

CULTURE Billbergias prefer partial shade. Like other epiphytes, they are not particular about soil as long as it is open and very well drained; they will root well even in pine bark chips or rocks so long as they don't wobble. Billbergias transplant easily and need constant moisture; water once or twice a week until the plant's center overflows. Feed lightly with quarter-strength water-soluble fertilizer every

GUZMANIA 'SUPERAMARANTH' (AIR PINE, LIVING VASE) Epiphytic plant to 2 feet tall with long-lasting spikes projecting from brilliantly colored rosettes of leaves. Filtered light, warm temperatures, high humidity, very well-drained soil. Zone 10.

NEOREGELIA COMPACTA (NEOREGELIA) Bright red and green foliage forming flattened rosettes from which flower grow; to 2 feet tall. Bright light, warm, humid temperatures, extremely well-drained soil. Zone 10.

TILLANDSIA FUNKIANA (TILLANDSIA) Narrow silver-gray foliage, bright orange inflorescences Bright light or partial sun, warm, somewhat humid conditions, good air circulation, excellent drainage. Zone 10.

VRIESIA IMPERIALIS (VRIESIA) Epiphytic plants to 15 feet tall with 5-inch wide, 5-foot tall leaves, often striped or banded. Partial shade, warm, somewhat humid conditions, good air circulation, excellent drainage. Zone 10.

BROMELIADS INDOORS

Bromeliads are unusual indoor plants that are grown for their beautiful foliage and their spectacular flowers. Indoors, bromeliads are quite slow growing and may take several years to flower–a plant that definitely takes patience. They are generally easy to care for, however, with the only caution to avoid overwatering. They have very small root systems and will rot if left sitting in moist soil. Keep the cup filled with water and empty and change this water every couple of months. Water the soil only when it dries out. Remember–these epiphytes are used to obtaining their moisture and nutrients from the air and tiny pockets of soil. Air around the roots is crucial. Use a well-drained potting mix such as bark chips. If a plant is already in flower, medium temperatures will suffice. You can encourage a bromeliad to flower by sealing it in a plastic bag with half an apple for three days to two weeks; remove from bag and wait six months for flower.

six to eight weeks; granular fertilizer spilled into the cups usually causes burning. Remove older leaves and faded flowers as needed. The plant blooms once, then sends off pups and dies. Scale, mealybugs, and thrips are sometimes problems.
SELECTIONS *B. nutans* has spiny green leaves and long hanging flowers with blue-banded green petals and red bracts. ***B. x 'Fantasia'*** has a colorful vase or coppery green and pink spotted white and pink and blue flowers that appear to jump out of pink bracts. ***B. sanderana***'s flowers have blue and yellow petals, and rosy bracts.

GUZMANIA AIR PINE, LIVING VASE

These epiphytic bromeliads have brilliantly colored, long-lasting bloom spikes that project from the center of the rosette of leaves. The foliage is usually green, and most available species grow 1-2 feet tall. Guzmanias may be used as a groundcover or as specimens near eye level. Native to tropical America.
CULTURE Filtered light is required, although guzmanias tolerate some direct early morning or late afternoon sun. Warm temperatures (over 65° F) and high humidity are best. As for all bromeliads, plant in a light, open, very well-drained growing medium; guzmanias will root even in pine bark chips so long as they don't wobble. Space individual rosettes evenly; they will fill in, as they produce pups. Water two to three times a week, and maintain the water supply in the plant's cup. Feed lightly with quarter-strength water-soluble 20-20-20 fertilizer every four to six weeks. Periodic removal of old, dead foliage and spent flower spikes will keep plants presentable.
SELECTIONS *G. lingulata* var. *cardinalis* grows to 15 inches and multiplies rapidly; beautiful scarlet star-shaped blooms appear at any time of year, particularly in spring. ***G. l.* 'Superb'** is a variegated form. The many colorful hybrids with names like **'Cherry'**, **'Orangeade'**, and **'Grapeade'** are useful as focal points of color.

NEOREGELIA

These bromeliads, native to Brazil, produce their blooms down low in the water-filled center of the rosette of leaves. They are grown and hybridized for their bright foliage color. Leaves can be spotted, striped, or banded; ***N. spectabilis***, fingernail plant, has long leaves with bright red tips. Because the rosettes are somewhat flattened and the centers often blush brilliant colors when in bloom, neoregelias need to be seen from the top and so are most often grown in flower beds or pots even though they are epiphytes. Large species make good focal points, and smaller ones can be used a groundcover.
CULTURE Most neoregelias are best grown in bright light, but some species prefer full sun. They need extremely well-drained soil and will do well in pure pine bark mulch. Neoregelias are fairly adaptable, but they do best in warm, humid temperatures. Avoid any contact with copper. If buying a plant coming into bloom, look for one that has colored up but hasn't yet produced many flowers. Neoregelias bloom first from the outside of their pincushionlike inflorescence. The center color can last 2-6 months. Pups are ready to be severed when they are one-third of their parent's size. Cut stem off very close to the parent, then plant separately directly into the garden or a pot. Watering twice weekly is usually plenty. Mulch, and clean out center cups occasionally to prevent excess leaf build-up. Neoregelias lose color if too well-fertilized, so feed only when they are young pups. As with all bromeliads, snails and mosquitoes love these plants' wet interior; scale insects can also be a problem.

TILLANDSIA

Spanish moss is the best-known plant in this genus of over 300 species of air plants native to the Western Hemisphere, growing from ½-4 inches across. They are almost always grown as epiphytes mounted onto tree branches, cork bark, or similar structures. Use these bromeliads to add an exotic tropical look to tree canopies or almost any other firm support. The white scurffing that covers most of this genus absorbs water very efficiently, so tillandsia can add this tropical effect even to dry locations.

CULTURE Grow in bright light or partial sun, in warm and moderately humid conditions but with good air circulation. Most tillandsia thrive mounted onto trees. Soil mixtures should be mostly bark or tree fern fiber. Tillandsia will not tolerate staying wet for very long without rotting. As with other bromeliads, contact with copper is deadly. Purchase plants that are plump and green underneath the outer white scurffing. Propagate by clump division; plants break apart easily at the base. The seeds float on a light breeze and will often germinate on any rough surface they cling to. Mount plants on branches or driftwood with wire, staples, or even strips of old nylon stockings, fixing tightly enough that the base doesn't move until the plant is firmly attached by its own roots. (Some gardeners use the construction adhesive Liquid Nails to hold a plant firmly to the mounting.) Mist plants one or two times weekly; soaking is not necessary. A misting of very diluted liquid fertilizer can follow the watering. Scale and mealybugs are the most common pests of tillandsia.

SELECTIONS *T. ionantha,* blushing bride, is a compact 2-inch plant that blushes bright red when blooming. *T. usneoides,* Spanish moss, drapes over tree branches and sways in the wind. *T. stricta* (6 inches) has a bright pink inflorescence and blue flowers. *T. cyanea* (10 inches) and *T. lindenii* (24 inches) want more shade and moisture and have fascinating pink paddle-shaped inflorescences with huge blue clove-scented flowers. *T. capitata* (12-20 inches) blooms with a flattened red inflorescence; some varieties turn almost completely red at bloom. *T. streptophylla* (18 inches) forms a tight clump with unusual curled leaves and a large pink, branched inflorescence. *T. fasciculata* (24 or more inches), wild pineapple, forms a large clump and has a branched bloom spike that often looks like clusters of red candles.

VRIESEA

Vrieseas are among the most hybridized of the bromeliads, sought after for their colorful, interestingly-marked foliage, long-lasting flowers, and stature–where other bromeliads are usually measured in inches and rarely exceed 2 feet, many vrieseas grow to 3 feet and some, like *V. imperialis,* grow to 15 feet.

CULTURE Most vrieseas thrive in partial shade, making them useful as understory plants. They have the same requirements as other bromeliads–very well-drained soil, adequate moisture, warm climates–but often need to be maintained more carefully because of their large size.

SELECTIONS *V. gigantea* grows to 3 feet tall and green leaves with darker green bands and yellow and white flowers. *V. hieroglyphica* (bromeliad-king) grows to 6 feet and has wide green leaves with darker spots and marks. *V. imperialis* grows to 15 feet tall and has 5-inch-wide, 5-foot-long leaves. Hybrids include *V.* x 'Mariae' (painted feather) and *V.* x 'Chantrieri'.

Above: Vriesea imperialis growing with Bixa orellana.

Psilotum nudum is a native Hawaiian fern commonly known as moa, which means chicken. In sunlight this fern exhibits golden tips.

FERNS

Ferns are nonflowering plants that reproduce not by seeds but by spores, borne on the undersides of the leaves, or "fronds," that arise from rhizomes growing below or on top of the soil. A large percentage of ferns are tropical and grow in rain forests, although many others are native to temperate areas of the world. They are valued for the graceful, textured, and soft appearance of the usually lacy fronds in various shades of green, which can be especially useful as a cool contrast to the more showy and colorful plants typical of the tropical garden; the large, bold foliage of other plant species is often nicely complemented by ferns, which also provide a good groundcover in shaded areas. Epiphytic types can be established on trees to add that extra tropical look to the landscape.

Although some ferns are epiphytic (air plants), others are terrestrial, usually inhabiting shady, moist places. For successful culture, give ferns plenty of humidity and medium or bright, filtered light. Plants prefer well-drained, rocky, or even epiphytic soil conditions, depending on species; many are drought-tolerant. An organic mulch will keep roots moist and cool; water deeply during dry periods. Purchase well-established plants with clean foliage, avoiding newly potted, wobbly plants with few roots, which will be hard to establish. Set out in a well-drained location, perhaps tucking into openings in walls or rocks. Water to establish and thereafter during drought conditions. Groom by removing dead fronds. Once established, ferns seem to have few pest or disease problems, although if fern scale occurs, it can be difficult to eradicate.

Most ferns are propagated easily by dividing underground rhizomes; propagation of species ferns from spores is also possible but much more challenging and it may take up to a year to yield a plant that resembles a fern. Distribute ripe spores over a moist, sterile medium (a brick watered from below is traditional); cover with glass or plastic and place in a warm spot with bright light. When the surface looks as if it is covered with moss, in several months, remove the cover and keep the medium moist. When tiny ferns appear after a few more months, pot them. It is crucial to keep the humidity high during this entire process

ADIANTUM, maidenhair ferns, have lacy fronds and thin, wiry stems; some have leaflike shapes. They grow best in partial to deep shade and need generous water and deep, rich soil. Many species thrive in the tropics, others in temperate or even arctic areas. **A. capillus-veneris** (Venus-hair fern) has narrow triangular fronds to 2 feet long and 1 foot wide. **A. formosum** (Australian maidenhair fern) has broader triangular fronds, to 18 inches wide. **A. raddianum** is deeply divided and hardy only in Zone 10. **A. tenerum** is particularly graceful; Zone 10. **A. cultratum** prefers alkaline soil, **A. affine** prefers acidic soil.

ASPLENIUM, spleenwort, requires partial to deep shade, coarse, open, fast-draining soil and constant moisture. Propagate by removing plantlets from the mother plant or by spores. **A. daucifolium,** mother fern, has graceful, lacy fronds that arch to a point. **A. nidus,** bird's nest fern, has attractive, graceful, solid fronds without the typical divided patterns; it is very susceptible to snails and slugs.

BLECHNUM Blechnum ferns range in size from less than 1 to more than 3 feet, and some even develop short trunks. **B. gibbum** is a dwarf tree fern growing to about 5 feet tall. **B. occidentale** has a creeping rhizome to 1½ feet long. **B. orientale** produces a short trunk and fronds 5 feet long by 3 feet wide.

ADIANTUM TRAPEZIFORME (GIANT MAIDENHAIR FERN) Fern to 2 feet tall with many bipinnate leaves, oval to rhomboid, medium green, 1½-2 inches long. Partial to deep shade, generous water, deep, rich soil. Zones 8-10.

NEPHROLEPIS EXALTATA (SWORD FERN) Fern to 5 feet tall with many closely packed pinnae. Partial to full shade, less water than most other ferns; tolerates poor soil and some drought. Zones 9-10.

PLATYCERIUM BIFURCATUM (STAG'S HORN FERN) Epiphytic fern with sterile kidney-shaped basal leaves from which fertile thick, grayish, and forked leaves, resembling antlers, protude. Partial shade, little water. Zones 8-10.

ANGIOPTERIS EVECTA (MULESFOOT FERN) Tree fern to 15 feet tall with trunk to 3 feet in diameter and crown of lacy fronds. Deep rich soil, some shade, generous water, warm, humid climate. Zone 10.

CYRTOMIUM FALCATUM, holly fern, has scaly rhizomes and large, scattered or patterned sori; the fronds are arching with distinct segments, quite distinctive in shape. This fern needs less humidity than most and should not be planted too deeply. Holly ferns grow 2-3 feet tall, and sometimes up to 5 feet.

NEPHROLEPIS, sword fern, is native to many tropical regions and has been grown as a houseplant since Victorian times. The plants spread by runners and are easily propagated by division. They do well in partial to full shade and need less water than most other ferns; they tolerate poor soil and some drought and should be watered only if the soil is dry. *N. exaltata* 'Bostoniensis' is Boston fern, the common houseplant with finely cut leaves; it grows to 4 feet tall. *N. e.* 'Fluffy Ruffles' stays smaller than most cultivars and has attractive ruffled and cut fronds.

PELLAEA, cliff brake, is named for its dark green, black-stemmed fronds; the word *pellaios* means dark in Greek. Native to temperate and cool tropical regions, they are tougher than most ferns and can tolerate more dryness. *P. andromedifolia,* coffee fern, is native to California and Oregon and has 3-foot-long finely cut leaves, gray- to blue-green. *P. falcata,* Australian cliff brake, resembles nephrolepis, but is more compact (to 15 inches tall). *P. rotundifolia* (buttonfern) needs more watering and has darkish red-brown fronds and glossy dark green roundish pinnae.

PLATYCERIUM BIFURCATUM, staghorn fern, is epiphytic on vertical surfaces of tree trunks, tree branches, and even rock faces. The wiry roots are produced behind large, kidney-shaped sterile fronds that overlap and curve under the bottom and spread more openly on the uppermost edge, creating a kind of nest or basket. This traps falling leaves, which accumulate to become the plant's personal compost pile, retaining moisture and providing nutrients. When maturing, staghornferns produce fertile fronds that resemble antlers (hence the common name "staghorn fern"). Spores are produced in cinnamon-colored patches. As the fronds fall off, they are replaced by new ones. *P. bifurcatum* is one of almost twenty species in its genus, and one of the easiest to grow; it often becomes very large. It produces pups freely from buds that form along the roots. These pups may be severed to produce new plants. Securely tying the plant onto a pad of moss or similar substrate and onto a tree plus watering during dry spells, is often all that is needed. If no tree is available, a large basket can act as a starting point, but eventually the fern will form a large ball which will require a strong support. This species is probably the most cold hardy, enduring occasional brief frost. Other species require more care; some are extraordinarily striking in size and shape. *P. coronarium* has 6-foot fertile fronds. *P. grande's* fronds resemble moose antlers.

POLYPODIUM, polypody fern, is a rhizomatous fern most often found in lowland rain forests or in seasonally dry areas on rocks and cliffs; native worldwide. Fronds may be pinnate or strap-shaped. It makes a fine groundcover. *P. polypodiodes,* resurrection fern, is a small epiphytic plant that shrivels when extremely dry but rapidly unfurls and resumes growth once water is provided. *P. aureum,* golden polypody, is larger, with several horticultural forms.

PTERIS, brake ferns, are small terrestrial ferns, usually under 2 feet, with distinctive, delicately cut fronds. They need more light than most ferns and generous water (they should not be soaked but should never be allowed to dry out.). They provide a different effect in the landscape than most ferns. *P. cretica,* cretan brake fern, is the most common form.

TREE FERNS

Tree ferns are characterized by emergent trunks and crowns of fronds, some of which bear spores. The are indeed an asset to the landscape; providing softness and elegance with their lacy green fronds as well as vertical accents and shade. Ferns often blend into a garden, but tree ferns become focal points.

Grow in light shade, in a moist but non-stagnant soil that most ferns prefer to be slightly acidic. Many seem to do very well with low humidity if provided with enough ground moisture. Propagate from spores. Set out container-grown ferns any time of year; do not allow plants to dry out while they are establishing. Regular, light feeding with a slow-release or liquid fertilizer is beneficial; be cautious about allowing fertilizer salts to contact foliage or concentrate at roots. Apply and regularly replenish an organic mulch. Groom by removing dead fronds. Mealybugs, caterpillars, and scale insects are fairly common when growing conditions are poor; hand picking and judicious pruning are the best way to handle a small number of plants.

Angiopteris evecta, mulesfoot fern, can grow to 15 feet tall with a trunk up to 3 feet in diameter and a crown of lacy foliage. They are naturalizing in Hawaii but are hard to grow elsewhere. Zone 10.

Cyathea cooperi, Australian tree fern, is perhaps the hardiest, most forgiving of the tree ferns. Its trunk is almost black and its arching fronds are light, bright green.

C. arborea, West Indian tree fern, grows to 24 feet tall and produces deciduous scaley leaves. Zone 10.

Dicksonia includes several tree ferns that are used in California. They prefer moist, shady spots and need protection from the wind. ***D. antarctica,*** Tasmanian tree fern, grows to 50 feet. ***D. squarrosa*** has a slender black trunk and grows to about 20 feet tall. Zone 10.

ORCHIDS *Orchidaceae*

Orchids embody the essence of tropical gardening: a richness of texture and form from lovely to flamboyent to simply bizarre. Temperate gardens can harbor a few orchids, but warmer areas of the world offer the opportunity to make make full use of this wildly diverse family. In frost-free, humid climates, orchids can be used in great abundance with little effort. A conservative estimate of 15,000 species of orchids worldwide are documented, most of them in tropical latitudes; many new species are described every year. The vast majority have flowers only an enthusiast with a magnifying glass can appreciate, but that leaves thousands of species and hybrids to be enjoyed and used in the garden.

Oddly, such a huge family yields few commercial products; the vanilla orchid, source of the flavoring, is one exception. Others are salep, an edible starch once harvested from the roots of an orchid grown in temperate areas of the Mediterranean (and a popular saloon drink in Victorian times) and a few species used medicinally in Asia. Far more often, orchids are grown for their flowers.

Somehow, orchids have developed a mystique, involving the notion that they have special needs and are more demanding than other kinds of plants. Quite the opposite is true. Orchids are very adaptable and perform best if their natural adaptions are called upon. Some of their best features are tough, somewhat spongy roots that like exposure to air, hard leathery foliage that can cope with

Mulesfoot ferns.

ORCHID HUNTERS

Orchids were first imported to the British Isles early in the eighteenth century from the Bahamas. Their beauty and the romantic allure of their distant homes attracted enormous interest, and since their needs were unknown, few survived, giving them a reputation for fragility that only increased their appeal. Europe and America were soon swept by an orchid craze. Rare and expensive both to buy and to keep, orchids became a hobby of the rich, with some varieties becoming so rare they were virtually priceless. The opportunities for getting rich overnight attracted a new breed of entrepreneur, the orchid hunter. These intrepid explorers, most of them well-educated gentlemen, risked and frequently lost their lives searching for new species. They found their way through the rainforests of Brazil and Central America or along the slopes of the Himalayas using secret maps marked with no names or only with their own code, and in the far corners of the world they bribed officials, fought off or cajoled natives and bandits, dealt with wild beasts, and inevitably suffered the most from malaria and dysentery. Some of their prizes became world famous, such as the blue orchid (*Vanda coerulea*), discovered in the Khasa Hills of Assam in 1837 and brought to England, where it soon died. When rediscovered around the middle of the century it attracted so many hunters that the government of Assam was forced to pass legislation to protect it, making the blue orchid

continued on p. 156

strong light, swollen structures of many forms that allow the plants to store moisture and food. These features help orchids to adapt to life on a tree branch or in the ground. Your garden might be just the place for these wonderful plants.

Orchids ignore many of the boundaries set by botanists and horticulturists who define them. Orchid growers all over the world have freely crossed orchid species to an extent not possible in other plant families. Notwithstanding inevitable monstrosities, the results have been large numbers of beautiful progeny with good horticultural qualities.

Getting started You will most likely acquire your first orchid growing in some kind of container, possibly as an extravagant gift. After the flowers have gone, it can become a long-lasting garden plant. First find out if it is a terrestrial (ground) or epiphytic (air) plant; most fall into the latter category. If the plant is not labeled, check your library, garden club, or botanical garden; dozens of books are available. Although these books usually focus on container, as opposed to garden, culture, they may provide general information on the type of plant you have (and it's probably a hybrid) and its general habits and needs.

Terrestrial orchids, such as *Phaius tankervilliae* (nun orchid), which produces tall stems of nodding mauve, tan, and white flowers, or *Spathiglottis plicata,* with arching spikes of lavender to purple flowers, can be planted and cared for in much the same manner as other garden plants. Plant them in friable, well-drained soil that retains some moisture without remaining saturated. Full sun in the morning and broken sun in the afternoon suits them well. Under similar conditions, slugs and snails thrive, so be alert and hand pick them before they become a problem. Other terrestrial orchids you might find and try include *Cymbidium* species, large plants with long, straplike leaves that do best in cooler regions; *Sobralia* species, bamboolike plans with short-lived but spectacular flowers; *Arundina* species, bamboolike everbloomers with white or pink flowers about 2 inches across; and *Calanthe* species, evergreen or deciduous, with handsome leaves and flowers.

Chances are, your first orchid is going to be an epiphyte, adapted to non-parasitic life perched upon some other plant. Epiphytes derive their nutrients from the air; their roots are not grounded in soil. Choosing the proper host for an epiphytic plant is important if you expect it to remain there permanently. A half-rotten branch on a short-lived papaya tree, a leaf sheath of a palm that will later be removed, or a ficus or mango tree that block the sun is not a particularly good site. Oaks, on the other hand are wonderful. Citrus trees, smooth or fibrous palm trunks, and tree fern trunks are very good, too. The best time to attach an orchid to its new position is at the very beginning of its root formation season. The plant must be held securely in place until the roots are firmly attached. The area producing the roots should be closest to the new growing surface. All of this may be obvious, but it does need to be considered carefully.

Orchids tend to produce new roots seasonally. It is easy to recognize new root tips: they are translucent and green or purple, more or less pointed zones at the very end of the roots or protruding from the base of the plant or along the stem of non-clumpers (see below). Their relative length indicates the level of activity. The ideal time to attach a plant to a new host is when there are many actively emerging roots. Be careful not to crush or break root tips; they will not heal and usually die back to more mature tissue. Healthy roots can run for yards and live for many years. The orchid is able to absorb moisture and nutrients just behind the new tips

ORCHID 'HELEN VELIZ' (HYBRID ORCHID) Epiphytic orchid, 2 feet tall, with large red, yellow, and orange flowers with ruffled beards and green leaves. Very light shade, humid conditions. Zone 10.

VANDA 'IOLANI' (VANDA ORCHID) Epiphytic orchid, 2 feet tall, with small brown flowers. Full sun or very light shade, humid conditions. Zone 10.

ENCYCLIA COCOLEATA CV. (COCKLESHELL ORCHID) Epiphytic orchid, 2 feet tall, with large yellow and burgundy flowers. Full sun, humid conditions. Zone 10.

LAELIA PURPURATA VAR. WEKHAUSER 'TREASURE OF CARPENTE-RIA" (LAELIA ORCHID) Epiphytic orchid, 2 feet tall, with large purple and white flowers with ruffled beards and green leaves. Full sun, humid conditions. Zone 10.

continued from p. 154

the first flower to be protected by law. There was also the lost orchid (*Cypripedium fairrieanum*), "lost" when the only specimen died. For nearly 50 years rewards were offered, and hunters risked their necks (one lost his when forced to take part in a tribal war). It was rediscovered in 1904. The prince of orchid hunters was the Czech Benedict Roezi (1824-85), who traveled from California to Patagonia in search of exotics. He was famed for his encounters with fierce animals (once saving himself by throwing a lamp at a jaguar) and claimed he had been held up by bandits 17 times; one gang decided not to kill when they emptied his bags and found he was carrying only seeds and was thus obviously crazy. The tale of *Cypripedium curtisii* has a different moral. It was discovered in 1883 and sent to Britain, where it soon died. Hunters sought it in vain, and as the years went by it became only a vague memory. Then, in a forest of Sumatra, a Swede named Ericson, having finally decided in despair to give up the search, sat down to rest before heading back and happened to look down at his feet. There, in a rocky crevice, was the precious orchid.

and where the plant is directly attached. They do not invade the living tissue of the host nor pose any threat to it; they are not parasites or stranglers. The mature roots also contain chlorophyll and photosynthesize in the same manner as leaves and other plant parts. When they mature, the roots are white, gray, or silver, hiding the green underneath. Interestingly, some orchids have evolved into plants with neither leaves nor stems, but knots of roots that carry out all plant functions.

Attaching plant to host is easy if it is small, trickier if it is large. See page 158.

Orchids for the garden can be placed in three broad categories according to their growth habit. *Climbers* need some kind support on which to grow in a more or less erect fashion. They are generally epiphtyic and may begin life on the ground, though in nature they are more often found on tree trunks or branches. Except for vanilla, they are not true vines, but unbranched (monopodial) plants that produce one leaf after another along a stiff central core stem. *Scramblers* tend to grow by producing many wiry, sometimes elongated growths that flop over. They may be epiphytes as well, but many scramble among grasses and shrubs, forming large masses. A great many of the more familiar orchids are *clump-formers*, most of which are epiphytes and are very specialized for such a life. Many of the clumpers are terrestrials that can be grown alongside and in the same manner as more familiar garden plants.

CLIMBERS Climbers, with rare exceptions, cannot tolerate stale, soggy conditions for very long. The key to healthy plants is lots of moisture and no sogginess. Most can survive (but not thrive) in dryish conditions, but will perish if roots are kept soggy. While actively growing, a regime of wet alternated with short dry periods in rapid succession, all in relatively high humidity with good air movement suits almost all unbranched orchids. Ideal light levels vary according to species. Some produce hard, cylindrical (terete) leaves that need full sun, others have broad fleshy leaves that must be somewhat shaded to avoid burning. These orchids are tough plants and usually very adaptable. Short of actual scalding, orchids perform better with more light than less. They flower best if allowed to grow beyond their support.

The base of the plant can be in almost any coarse, perfectly drained medium such as bark chips, real charcoal (not barbecue briquets), broken bricks, gravel, or even coarse sawdust. Since these plants are epiphytes, they may be attached directly to a support such as a sturdy post or a tree. The base of the plant does not require contact with the ground at all.

Some climbers, like *Vanda* **species**, if grown in full sun and allowed to grow above their support, will bloom many times a year. Large plants can be everblooming. In addition to cylindrical and narrow-leaved vandas, climbers to try in full sun include *Arachnis* **species;** *Aerides* **species;** *Renantherea* **species;** *Vandopsis* **species,** and any of their multi-generic hybrids. Many of the large-flowered vandas are carefully made and selected hybrids of many species; literally thousands of hybrids between vandas and closely related species exist. These, and the broader leaved varieties like a little shade from the hottest rays of the sun, while luxuriating in the very brightest light. *Vanilla* **species,** which are true vines, also prefer a bit of light shade.

SCRAMBLERS Either as pure epiphytes mounted on a tree or wall or as semi-terrestrials growing in some kind of loose, perfectly drained medium on the ground or in a container, scramblers form large colonies in time. Information about climbers

ONCIDIUM CV (POPCORN ORCHID) Epiphytic orchid, to 4 feet tall, with abundant yellow flowers with brown centers. Can be grown in beds, in loose growing medium (moist but not wet), full sun, humid conditions. Zone 10.

PHAIUS TANKERVILLIAE (NUN'S ORCHID) Terrestrial orchid, 4 feet tall, with large graceful purple and white flowers with nodding petals and green leaves. Loose soil (moist but not wet), full sun to light shade, humid conditions. Zone 10.

PHALENOPSIS VIOLACEAE CV. (MOTH ORCHID) Epiphytic orchid, 2 feet tall. Fine to medium epiphtic potting medium; medium to deep shade, humid conditions. Zone 10.

CATTLEYA CV. (HYBRID CATTLEYA ORCHID) Epiphytic orchid, 2 feet tall. Fine to medium epiphtic potting medium, light shade, humid conditions. Zone 10.

ATTACHING AN EPIPHYTE

Large limbs and tree branches are often the best spots, but sometimes difficult to tackle. Your aim is tying the plant to the host. Biodegradable material is preferred so that it does not have to be removed once the plant is established. The material should be strong, nontoxic, non-damaging, and inconspicuous. Many people find strips of pantyhose work well; David Bar-Zvi prefers jute rope or butcher string. Insulated wires can also be used, but must be removed; fishing line is inobtrusive but often hard to work with and must be removed.

Tying the base of the plant that is to grow to the host can usually be done by encircling it with the tying material. if the limb or trunk is very thick, creating a nest or cradle against the face of the tree using nails or galvanized staples is possible. (It's never a good idea to drive nails into trees and it should *never* be done on palms for any reasons, but staples will usually be okay on a thick-barked tree.) Sometimes, just wedging the plant into natural crevices is sufficient; play with it, but take care not to injure the host.

The object is to hold the plant still until it can produce enough roots to secure it in place. Some growers use pads of moss or other fibrous material near the base of the new plant to help retain humidity around newly emerging roots; other growers find this unnecessary. Until the epiphyte is established, irrigate during dry spells. Addition of orchid fertilizer dissolved according to instructions can be beneficial, but only after the plants are established. After a while, if the plant is suited to the microclimate of your garden, you will not have to worry about it again.

is true for scramblers, except the need for support. Scramblers with tough or small foliage prefer or even require full sun (or at most very light shade during the brightest, hottest hours of the day). Softer, more succulent foliage is an indication of a preference for shadier locations.

Scramblers recommended for the home gardeners for full sun include reed-stemmed **Epidendrum species,** with balls of red, orange, yellow, pink, or white flowers; some *Vanda* species and hybrids that naturally grow as scramblers; and several **Dendrobium species** that form large colonies by producing plantlets along stem-like pseudobulbs. In light shade, try **Ascocentrum species** (similar to small *Vanda* species) or other *Dendrobium* species, particularly those with pendant pseudobulbs. Fan-leaved **Oncidium species** can also be grown in light shade. Several of them will form colonies that produce intriguing sprays of "dancing ladies." They can be grown on small branches; plantlets produced on old flower stalks will take root when contacting a branch. In deeper shade, **Phalaenopsis species** are recommended; some, like **P. luddemaniana,** form large colonies over time.

CLUMPERS The majority of orchids fall into this category. They are epiphytes and can be grown in pots in an appropriate medium, on living hosts such as trees, or on non-living bases like posts, plaques, walls, or rocks.

Clumping species include *Dendrobium* species with bulb- or canelike stems, **Cattleya species** and multitudes of intergeneric hybrids between *Cattleya* species, **Brassavola species,** and **Laelia species** (each of which offers clumping plants)—these are corsage orchids and among the easiest to grow.

CONTAINER ORCHIDS Growing orchids in containers allows mobility and control of immediate conditions for plants that need special treatment at different times. For orchids in pots, less is more; what would be considered underpotting for most other plants is good or even necessary for them. Constantly wet soil is a death sentence for epiphytic roots. If the pot is too large, the medium will stay wet too long. Fortunately for tropical gardeners, many of these orchids grow wonderfully on trees with little attention. You may, in time, wish to divide the plant, potting a portion and mounting a portion; remember that plants in containers require more care. Pots can be clay, plastic, teak, cedar, wire, or other substances; sides can be perforated or not. The orchids don't care as long as the roots can thrive.

Many commercial potting materials are available, usually mixtures of coarse to fine perfectly drained non-soluble substances such as bark, charcoal, tree fern fiber, styrofoam, perlite, baked clay, and various gravels. Whatever the substrate, it must drain immediately and perfectly and it must support and hold the plant. The medium should hold moisture so that the roots can be damp for a period, yet be completely exposed to air; it must never be soggy. In general, the thicker the roots, the coarser the potting material. The potting material must not be loose enough to allow the plant to fall out, injuring new roots or growth.

OUTSIDE THE TROPICS Several orchid species can survive in Zones 8-9; the one most often seen is **Bletilla striata,** with delicate nodding pink flowers, small but exquisite. It is a staple of Oriental herb gardens, used in Chinese medicines. Orchids can be grown indoors in bright light. It is important that nighttime temperatures be about ten degrees warmer than daytime. Keep the soil moist but not wet and repot only when potting medium begins to break down. Popular indoor orchids include cattelyas, phalaenopsis, and dendrobiums.

PALMS *Arecaceae*

Palms are the plants that first come to mind when we think of the tropics; a garden or landscape without palms would lack the essential tropical feel. The fascinating variety of palms adds delightful appeal to the landscape. Most palms have large pinnate (feathery) or palmate (fanlike) fronds. Stems vary widely: some palms grow sturdy trunks, solitary or clumped, which can exhibit a variety of interesting textures, colors, and spines; others produce only leafstalks until very mature. Size varies as well, from tall and stately to miniature. Most palm flowers are small and inconspicuous, but some are spectacular and fragrant. Fruits may be large and intensely colored. Most palms need an abundance of water and filtered bright light when they are young (mature specimens tolerate full sun) but a few require partial to deep shade.

ARCHONTOPHOENIX KING PALM, PICABEEN PALM, BANGALOW PALM, ALEXANDRA PALM

Only two species of *Archontophoenix* are widely known in cultivation, **A. alexandrae** (alexandra palm) and **A. cunninghamiana** (picabeen palm). Both are tall, beautiful, stately, graceful palms, native to Australia, with stout ringed trunks and feathered fronds. *A. alexandrae* has become naturalized in Hawaii to such an extent that it is commonly known there as Hilo palm. Archontophoenix is a wonderful palm for that "tropical paradise" look in a small garden, used as single specimens in a small space or in groupings to provide some shade in larger areas.

CULTURE Grow in shade when young, in full sun to partial shade when older. Soil may range from neutral to acidic and from sandy to loamy; the presence of organic material is beneficial. *A. cunninghamiana* is the better choice where cooler weather may prevail for part of the year, like southern California, while *A. alexandrae* prefers the more tropical conditions of Florida. When purchasing, avoid older plants with undersized trunks in small containers; choose plants with medium to dark green foliage color. Plant from containers any time of year if you can provide regular irrigation; otherwise, plant at the beginning of a warm, wet period. Field-grown plants may be transplanted during the most active growing period in spring and summer. Space 10-15 feet apart. Supplemental irrigation may be needed in dry soils. This is a self-cleaning palm, so pruning is not necessary or recommended. In alkaline soils, nutritional deficiencies may occur, but a sprayed or liquid application of micronutrients will eliminate this problem.

ARENGA SUGAR PALM

These moderate to large clumping or solitary often have black fibrous trunks and dark green fishtail-shaped leaflets on the fronds. They are native to Southeast Asia and Australia and some produce sugar, edible starches, and strong fibers used to make ropes. Sugar palms mature only after the trunk is fully developed and only then begin to flower and fruit; when the last inflorescence is mature, the plant dies—though a multiple-trunked specimen will continue to live as it produces new trunks. Single-trunked species are useful as specimens, but bear in mind that they may have to be removed. Clumping species serve as shrubs.

CULTURE Small sugar palms need some shade; larger ones adapt to full sun. They

PALMS

The Swedish botanist Linnaeus, founder of the binomial system of nomenclature and originator of modern scientific classification, called palms the "princes of the Vegetable Kingdom." The American botanist and plant explorer David Fairchild called them "the greatest single glory of the tropics," adding, however, that the naturalist "learns to have a reverence of them and a love of them which is perhaps in direct relation to the difficulty he experiences in telling the different species apart." There are, in fact, more than 200 genera of palm with as many as 4,000 species, most of them tropical. Of these, fourteen species in nine genera are native to the United States and are found in California along the Colorado desert, in Arizona and Texas, and most of all in Florida. The palms of the United States, like those of other temperate areas, are of limited use, but their economic importance in tropical regions is second only to that of the grasses, for palms furnish food, shelter, clothing, timber, fuel, building materials, fibers, paper, starch, oil, sugar, wax, tannin, dyeing materials, resin, and even wine.

do best in moist, well-drained organically rich soil and moderately to very warm conditions under high humidity. Look for vigorous, disease-free plants that are not overgrown or flowered-out. Water to establish and then during dry periods; fertilize four times a year with palm fertilizer and mulch root zone with organic matter. Propagate by seed. Though usually pest-free, these palms are sometimes susceptible to woolly scale; follow general scale control methods.

SELECTIONS *A. pinnata* (sugar palm) has a single trunk; moderate size. *A. undulatifolia* looks like a gigantic maidenhair fern and needs space. *A. enlgeri,* Formosa palm, is one of the hardiest clumpers, 9-15 feet tall. It does well in containers.

BISMARCKIA NOBILIS BISMARCK PALM

Bismarckia is a large, solitary palm with fan-shaped fronds, growing to 25 feet or more. The color of individuals varies from blue to gray-green; the silvery blue forms are highly prized and can be very showy with a complementary background. Where space permits, a grouping of bismarckia can provide pleasant shade. While bismarckia is widely cultivated as an ornamental in the tropics, its natural habitat in its native Madagascar is being destroyed, and these palms could soon become endangered. Bismarckia is dioecious—male and female flowers are produced on separate trees.

CULTURE Once established, bismarckia is easily grown in full sun. It tolerates humidity ranges from moderately low to high, but will stand no freezing. Purchase plants with healthy, nonspotted fronds and a trunk of a suitable size for the age of the palm. Since plant color can vary among individuals, choose the color you want from plants grown in full sunlight. A plant that is truly blue-gray

Fairchild Tropical Garden holds one of the world's largest collections of palms and cycads. At right: tall *Roystonea regia* with *Cycas circinalis. Livistona rotundifolia* is in the background.

ARENGA PINNATA (SUGAR PALM) Single-trunked palm to 30 feet tall. Some shade, moist, well-drained organically rich soil and moderately to very warm conditions under high humidity. Zones 9-10.

BISMARCKIA NOBILIS (BISMARK PALM) Solitary, fan-shaped fronds, blue to to silver-gray. Once established, bismarckia is easily grown in full sun. It tolerates humidity ranges from moderately low to high, but will stand no freezing. Zone 10.

COCOS NUCIFERA (COCONUT PALM) Single-trunked palm to 80 feet tall with large, pinnate arching fronds. Full sun; tolerant of a wide range of soil conditions and salt. Zone 10.

DICTYOSPERMA ALBUM (HURRICANE PALM, PRINCESS PALM) Single-trunked palm to 30 feet tall or more with graceful deep green fronds. Full sun; well-drained, organically rich soil, warm to very warm and humid conditions. Zone 10.

Though often hidden by foliage and too high to see, palm inflorescences are very ornamental. *From top to bottom: Caryota mitis; Latania verschaffeltii; Ptychosperma Macarthurii.*

when young will mature with this color. Plant from containers at any time, and provide irrigation only until established. Locate so the large, stiff fronds can develop without interference from walls or other structures. Pruning is not recommended.

BUTIA CAPITATA JELLY PALM

This hardy, moderately-sized palm has arching fronds in gray- to silver-green on a stout, rough-textured trunk. It produces edible orange or yellow fruit. A single specimen usually looks best, and should be given space and not planted near similar-looking speces. The silver or gray cast of the foliage contrasts well with dark green backdrops.

CULTURE Jelly palms need full sun. They have few requirements other than perfectly drained soil, which is a must. They easily endure some frost and low humidity, and some seem to prefer cool winter weather. Buy plants with a full crown of healthy, non-yellow fronds; avoid those that have overgrown their containers. Once well-established, no watering is needed, but application of palm fertilizer three to four times a year is beneficial. Light mulching helps reduce weeds but is not absolutely needed. Some specimens look better if spent fronds are removed. The leaf bases can be trimmed to uniform size. As they age, some specimens will easily shed old leaf bases; in any case, never rip them off the trees as damage to trunk may occur. Propagation is by seed. No serious pests or diseases.

CARYOTA FISHTAIL PALM

Named for their fishtail-shaped, two-pinnate leaves, palms in this genus vary from single-trunked to multistemmed plants; the trunks are often clothed with fibrous leafstalks. Fishtail palms flower and fruit only once.

CULTURE These palms thrive in light shade or full sun in any reasonably fertile, moist soil. They are hardy only in Zone 10 and will not survive freezing. They are easily propagated from suckers or seeds planted in sandy, peaty soil and kept in a humid spot, protected from direct sunlight for a few days.

SELECTIONS C. urens, wine palm, is the source of beverage called toddy; it grows to 100 feet tall and has pendulous inflorescences up to 12 feet long; its leaves are up to 20 feet long and 12 feet wide. **C. mitis** grows no more than 40 feet tall; its flowers and leaves are much smaller than those of *C. urens.*

CHAMAEDOREA PARLOR PALM, BAMBOO PALM, CAT PALM

This is a variable group of small, elegant palms, with slender stems and pinnate or bifid fronds. They may be solitary, clumping, or even vining in habit. Clustering types can be effective screening, especially in shaded areas, and most are very forgiving house plants.

CULTURE Native to the understory of tropical American rain forests, most of these palms are shade-loving, although some tolerate full sun. Moist, well-drained soil is best, and many chamaedorea tolerate alkaline soils. Most species need warm, humid growing conditions, although some tolerate freezing and many thrive indoors. Propagate from clump division or fresh seed. When roots are produced above soil level, air layering may be used to shorten overly tall plants–the bottom portion will not resprout after the top is removed. When purchasing, choose vigorous plants with medium to dark green color. Plant out from containers any time of the year, irrigating to establish and during drought periods. Transplanting seedlings from the ground is best done when weather is reliably warm and moist. Removal of the dried leaf sheaths reduces availability of hiding places for pests. Mites and mealybugs can be a problem, particularly in dry situations such as indoor container growing. Cool, wet weather can sometimes lead to leaf spots caused by fungi. Grown indoors, these palms perform well in low to medium light, and should be allowed to dry slightly between soakings.

SELECTIONS Clumping types include *C. microcarpa; C. seifrizii,* bamboo palm, growing to 5 feet and popular in the home; and *C. cataractarum.* Solitary types include *C. elegans,* parlor palm, the reliable, elegant favorite with small yellow flowers followed by black fruit, growing to 6 feet; *C. metallica,* miniature fishtail palm, growing to 3 feet and very useful for small spaces; and *C. ernesti-augusti.*

COCOS NUCIFERA COCONUT PALM

This is the quintessential palm, with large, pinnate fronds gracefully arching from a single, often sinuously leaning, very tall trunk. The large, globular fruits are produced in clusters at the base of each frond. Coconuts are perhaps the most utilitarian plants in the tropical world. Every part of the plant provides something useful–food, shelter, medicine, clothing, tools, and on and on. Coconuts have been in cultivation for so long that their origin is unknown; the nuts float excellently and so have been carried by ocean currents around the world to new areas where they easily colonize. This is a bold, tropical palm for low-lying coastal areas. If there is room, plant in groups spaced 12-15 feet apart; young plants need a lot space for the wide-spreading fronds while the stems are still short. When planting, consider where fruits will fall if they are not pruned off–you will not want them positioned over a parked car, a patio, or a bedroom roof.

CULTURE Coconut palms need full sun, but are very tolerant of a wide range of soil conditions, including salty. They cannot bear more than brief cold and are badly damaged by freezes. When purchasing, avoid undersized trunks in older plants. Propagate from fresh, ripe seed shallowly sown in very warm, moist soil. Field-grown palms are best planted at the beginning of a warm, wet season; container-grown palms may be set out at any time of year. Water regularly to establish and later during very prolonged dry periods. Application of a palm fertilizer three to four times a year will enhance beauty and growth, although coconut palms are quite tolerant of nutrient-poor soils. In dry areas, mulching is helpful. Do not prune off green fronds; dead fronds are usually shed soon after they turn brown. Lethal yellowing, a fatal disease, is the most serious problem for coconut palms; the only solution is to plant only resistant varieties.

SELECTIONS Although there is only one species of coconut, several horticultural varieties have been selected over time, including dwarfs with green, yellow, or orange fruits. Maypan hybrids and Malayan dwarfs are resistant to lethal yellowing; Malayan dwarfs are tall trees but fruit at a small size, hence the "dwarf" name. **'Fiji Dwarf'** is a short but very handsome variety that unfortunately is not resistant to lethal yellowing. **'Red Spicata'** has smaller fruits.

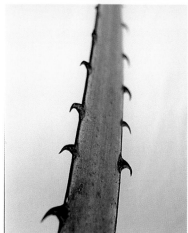

Above: Petiole of hyphene palm. *Top: Arenga pinnata.*

NEODYPSIS DECARYI (TRIANGLE PALM) Single-trunked plant to 15 feet tall, with 12- to 15-foot erectly arching silvery fronds held in three ranks. Full sun; wide range of soil conditions (moist and well-drained is best). Zones 9-10.

PHOENIX CANARIENSIS (CANARY ISLAND DATE) Single-trunked plant to 50 feet tall or more with a dense crown of pendulous and arching fronds that form a rounded shape. Full sun; wide range of soil conditions (moist and well-drained is best). Zones 9-10.

PRITCHARDIA GAUDICHAUDII (LOULOU PALM) 6- to 8-foot-tall plant with silvery green fan-shaped pleated leaves. Partial shade, evenly moist soil. Zones 9-10.

RHAPIS EXCELSA 'VARIEGATA' (LADY PALM) 15-foot-tall plant with pointed, puckered leaves. Partial to deep shade, moist, fertile soil. Zones 9-10.

COPERNICIA CARNAUBA WAX PALM, PETTICOAT PALM

Copernicia are medium to large palms, mostly solitary, native to the Greater Antilles and South America. Their fan-shaped fronds are characteristically armed with spines on the outermost edges, so care must be taken when considering placement in the landscape. Stately specimens and even avenues are a good use for the large species, such as *C. baileyana*. Several species are sculpturally interesting, with a petticoat effect of retained dead fronds, and several others have silvery foliage. The hard wax on the fronds of *C. pruinosa* is the carnauba wax of industry.
CULTURE Grow in full sun. Warm, humid conditions are best for copernicia; most species fare poorly in cold weather. These palms are adaptable to a variety of soils, but most seem to prefer well-drained yet moist soil. Propagate from fresh seed, or purchase plants with clean, healthy foliage and normal trunk size. Set out container-grown plants at any time the weather is warm and moist. Place carefully, as copernicias are difficult to transplant once established. Water to establish and during dry weather. Pruning is not necessary or recommended. *Ganoderma* fungus can be a serious problem. Avoid injuring a palm in any way to help prevent the infection of healthy specimens.
SELECTIONS *C. baileyana* is massive, with a thick, clean, columnar trunk and erect, gray-green fronds; an avenue of these palms is reminiscent of the huge pillars of ancient classical architecture. *C. macroglossa* has a relatively thinner trunk hidden by a "petticoat" crowned by green fronds on very short petioles. *C. alba* is a beautiful palm with silver-gray fronds.

CORYPHA TALIPOT PALM

Talipots are massive, solitary palms growing up to 80 feet tall with huge, fan-shaped fronds up to 16 feet across that are used as 7- or 8-person umbrellas. Native to tropical Asia and Australia, this palm reaches maturity at about 60 years and then produces a single gigantic flowering and fruiting stalk stretching up as much as 35 feet above the foliage, with up to 10 million flowers in the spike–the largest flower cluster in the plant kingdom. By the time the flowers have produced mature seeds, the tree is exhausted and dies. This dramatic palm is suitable only for a large space in a public garden or estate.
CULTURE Grow in full sun. Talipots are adaptable as to soil but prefer available moisture. While warm, humid conditions are best, talipots are known to tolerate at least brief periods of cold. Propagate from fresh seed, or purchase plants with healthy, clear to dark green foliage. Irrigate well to establish. Digging large plants from the ground may stimulate flowering and thus death of the palm. Irrigation during drought periods is worthwhile. Pruning of dead fronds will expose the interesting booted trunk and help to keep the palm attractive; do not remove live fronds. No serious pests occur in the United States.
SELECTIONS *C. elata* has a very attractive spiral arrangement along its booted trunk. *C. umbraculifera* is particularly massive, and the boots on the trunk appear as a basket weave. *C. utan* is somewhat less massive and also less elegant.

DICTYOSPERMA ALBUM HURRICANE PALM, PRINCESS PALM

Though cultivated throughout the world, hurricane palms are now quite rare in nature. Botanists now place all of them in one species, and note color variations as different varieties. These are moderately-sized solitary palms with dark trunks to 30 feet tall or more. Their graceful heads of deep green fronds emerge from a

Above: Hyphorbe lagenicaulis. Top: Latania lantaroides.

PALMS INDOORS

True palms make a large group of plants, many of which are favored for indoor use. They are tropical in nature and conjure up images of Caribbean islands and hot climates. Most palms have large pinnate or palmate fronds and varying types of stems. Some grow tall, sturdy trunks in the wild but remain short and succulent when grown indoors. Some, such as howea, produce only leafstalks until very mature. Palms have only one growing point on each stem and generally produce only one or two fronds a year. Mature palms will produce clusters of flowers, but this is seldom seen in the home (except on chamaedorea).

There are indoor plants referred to as palms that are actually members of other families. The tendency is to call anything that looks palmlike a palm, when in actuality, these plants may need very different cultural conditions to thrive. Cycas, the bread palm, and nolina, ponytail palm, are in different families than the palms and are quite a bit more tolerant of low light and cool conditions than true palms.

Most palms need an abundance of water and filtered bright light when they are young (mature specimens can tolerate full sun). Palm seeds can take from one month to two years to germinate.

prominent crownshaft; leaflets on the fronds are closely spaced. It makes a handsome specimen and is useful where a large mass is not wanted, especially near water.

CULTURE Hurricane palms are very salt tolerant and able to withstand strong wind without damage. They do best in full sun and well-drained, organically rich soil under warm to very warm and humid conditions; they do not withstand freezing. Choose vigorous plants with dark green foliage; avoid those that have overgrown their containers. Pruning is not needed. Keep weeds away from the base and apply a layer of organic mulch over the root zone but do not bury the base of the trunk. Although they do not suffer from any special pest problems, they are susceptible to the palm disease lethal yellowing which occurs in some regions. Propagation is by seed.

HYOPHORBE BOTTLE PALM, SPINDLE PALM

Once abundant these handsome palms are now rare in nature; only one *H. amaricaulis* remains in the wild. The species in cultivation have a few stiff, arching fronds emerging from a distinctive crownshaft atop bottle- or spindle-shaped light gray trunks. They look marvelous in small groves or singly.

CULTURE Bottle palms need full sun. They tolerate a wide range of soil types, so long as the soil is well-drained; they thrive in warm, humid conditions and are somewhat sensitive to freezing. Buy plants that have clean, healthy foliage and are not too overgrown in their containers. Once established, they need watering only during dry periods and fertilizing four times annually with a palm fertilizer. Organic mulching is beneficial, but do not bury the base of the trunk. No serious pests or diseases. Propagation is by seed only.

SELECTIONS *H. lagenicaulis,* bottle palm, has a very broad base that narrows some distance above the soil to a narrow neck, producing a remarkable and very sculptural resemblance to an old-fashioned milk bottle. *H. verschaffeltii,* spindle palm, is a handsome erect palm with arching fronds on a blue to purple-gray crownshaft.

NEODYPSIS DECARYI TRIANGLE PALM

This native of Madagascar is a distinctive palm among its species, medium-sized and single-trunked, with 12- to 15-foot erectly arching fronds held in three ranks at the top of a 15-foot trunk 2 feet in diameter, giving three flat planes as seen from the ground. The fronds are silver-gray with overlapping bases, covered with a gray and rusting flocking-like surface. A relative, *N. lastelliana,* teddybear palm, has recently become popular, with its wax-coated trunk surmounted by handsome green fronds with a dense, cinnamon-colored base covering. These palms are so individual in their character that they must be planted away from other palms of similar color or texture. They can serve as distinctive specimens or can create an attractive avenue.

CULTURE Grow in full sun. While triangle palm will tolerate a wide range of soil conditions, moist and well-drained soil is best. A warm and humid climate is preferable; trees will tolerate some cool weather but will be injured by freezing. Purchase a plant that is not overgrown in the container with healthy, gray-green foliage; for field-grown plants, choose those with the largest diameter and most

Left: Howea fosterana, kentia palm.

fronds. Propagate from seed. Set out at any time of year when the temperature remains above 65° F at night. Stabilize, and water well to establish and thereafter during dry periods. Mealybugs can sometimes be a nuisance in damp conditions.

PRITCHARDIA LOULOU PALM

Most of the 35 species in this genus are native to the Hawaiian islands and thrive there. These palms have unusually attractive fan-shaped pleated leaves and produce edible fruits. This is an excellent specimen palm for a small lawn.

CULTURE Grow pritchardia in any average garden soil in partial shade with protection from direct sunlight. Biweekly fertilization with liquid fertilizer is beneficial. Propagate by seeds.

SELECTIONS *P. gaudichaudii* grows 6-8 feet tall and is silvery green. *P. pacifica,* grows up to 30 feet and has leaves up to 5 feet in diameter.

RHAPIS LADY PALM

The name *rhapis* is derived from the Greek word for needle; lady palm's leaves are pointed and somewhat needlelike. These low-growing plants have unusual leaf sheaths and leaves that grow like the fingers of a hand. Short clusters of flowers appear several times a year. Lady palms are excellent backgrounds to flower gardens, blending and adding texture.

CULTURE Lady palms are fairly easy to grow. They require moist, fertile soil and partial to even deep shade. Mulch to keep roots moist. They are easily propagated by division in spring.

SELECTIONS *R. excelsa* has puckered leaved and grows to 15 feet tall. *R. humilis* is lower and more compact.

ROYSTONEA ROYAL PALMS

This native of the Caribbean basin is a majestic palm with a solitary, tall, columnar, clean, and white to gray trunk surmounted by a prominent, smooth, green, crown shaft from which the 10-foot or more dark green fronds erupt. Depending on the species, the trunk may be variously swollen for some of its length. This is a massive palm for use in large areas, with a stately grace perfect for avenues.

CULTURE Grow in full sun in very warm and humid conditions. Rich, moist, and well-drained soil is best. Some will grow well but will not fruit if the temperature is not high enough. Purchase plants that are not seriously root-bound, with deep green and not yellowish fronds. Propagate from seed. Plant out container-grown palms at any time when the weather is not cold. Field-grown palms are best moved during the warm, wet periods. When a tree crane is used to move a large specimen, care must be taken not to injure the crown shaft by compression or impact. Jerking the palm sharply while moving it can damage the bud. The planting hole should be large enough to accommodate the root ball easily. Plant at the same level at which the palm was previously growing. If many roots are damaged during the move, reducing the number of fronds will help to reduce water loss. Irrigate well to establish; thereafter, watering is needed only during periods of drought. Royal palms are self-pruning. Few pests or diseases bother these palms, although palm weevils can infest and kill a tree from the inside; a spray of a predatory nematode seems effective.

CYCAS REVOLUTA (SAGO PALM, KING SAGO) Graceful, ferny palm-like plant to 10 feet tall but usually smaller. Full sun or partial shade, well-drained soil. Zone 10.

DIOON SPINULOSUM (GIANT DIOON) Palmlike plant to 20 feet tall, with sharply pointed 6-foot leaves; large, tough cones. Partial shade, moist soil. Zone 10.

ENCEPHALARTOS GRATUS Palmlike plant to 10 feet tall with stout trunk and rounded crown of fernlike foliage. Full sun, well-drained soil. Zone 10.

ZAMIA PUMILA Spreading plant, to 2 feet tall. Full sun or part shade, well-drained soil. Zone 10.

CYCADS

Some species of cycad that appear today in Florida gardens were once nibbled by triceratops and other plant-eating dinosaurs. The cycads are the most primitive of the living seed-bearing plants, having first appeared in the Permian period. Their appearance reveals their age, for they are truly ancient plants, between ferns and palms, both of which they resemble (they're often called fern palms). Some cycads have tuberous underground stems and a crown of leathery, glossy–fernlike–leaves springing from ground level; others have a columnar stem and are thus often mistaken for palms. They are pollinated by beetles and weevils that carry pollen to the female cone. The cycads, ginkgoes, and conifers are the three major orders of gymnosperms, or cone-bearing plants. There are nine genera of cycad (some sources cite ten or eleven) with fewer than 100 species, some seldom found.

The fact that cycads have survived so long would lead one to believe that they are tough plants that adapt to their surroundings and need little care; one would be right. These plants are built to last and once planted in a suitable environment–well-drained soil is the most important requirement–they will thrive in full sun or partial shade indefinitely. Most cycads are slow-growing and take up to several years to achieve cone-bearing maturity. Some cycads have taproots and coralloid roots. Shaped like coral, they contain a bacteria that takes in nitrogen; these coral-head roots grow up instead of down.

Plant cycads in early spring, before new growth begins; water well, but do not allow ground to become soggy. Transplanting cycads with trunks needs to be done carefully so as not to bruise the trunk. Seeds can also be planted, but take up to a year to germinate. Cycads benefit from a general palm fertilizer applied after planting and three to four times a year thereafter. Cycads are prone to armored scale; use of a systemic insecticide (just before a new flush of growth) is sometimes necessary. They sometimes suffer from iron deficiency (indicated by yellow leaves) or magnesium deficiency (indicated by brown spots on the leaves) which can be alleviated by adding those elements to the soil. Pruning off spent or damaged foliage keeps them looking fresh.

Cycads are excellent landscape plants, providing a truly tropical accent wherever they are placed as well as a graceful presence. They work well in both formal and natural settings, particularly in small gardens. They can also be used as borders. Cycads can be grown in pots and brought indoors in winter. Repot frequently to avoid soil compaction that would prevent good drainage.

Cycas revoluta (sago palm, king sago) are the most hardy and tough of this tough group of plants, often surviving in Zone 9. In a sunny location it can grow to 10 feet, but usually stays smaller. In dry climates, it prefers some shade. Sago palms form extremely graceful rosettes of shiny, deep green leaves up to 4 feet long. ***C. circinalis,*** queen cycas, grows faster and sometimes reaches 20 feet; its dark green leaves are stiffer and up to 8 feet long.

Dioon edule is a squat, palmlike plant, to 6 feet tall, with sharply pointed 6-foot leaves. It prefers evenly moist soil and some shade. ***D. spinulosum,*** giant dioon, grows to 20 feet. Both bear large, tough cones.

Encephalartos gratus, resembles a palm but has a thick, rounded trunk. ***E. horridus*** has gray-green leaves and sharp spines.

Zamia pumila is the source of a laundry starch used by Florida pioneers for baking; it is good border plant. ***Z. furfuracea*** (cardboard palm) is good specimen in sun or half shade, large, spreading, and medium green.

Top: **Ferns and cycads are major components of the Prehistoric Glen at Foster Botanical Garden in Honolulu.** *Above:* **Frond of** *Cycas circinalis.*

Cool-season annuals
Ageratum
Arctotis
China aster
Begonia
Brachycome
Browallia
Caladium
Calliopsis
Candytuft
Coleus
Dianthus
Globe amaranth
Godetia
Gypsophila
Helichrysum
Lobelia
Nasturtium
Nictoiana
Nierembergia
Phlox
Poppy
Salvia
Schizanthus
Snapdragon
Warm-season annuals
Balsam
Cosmus
Gaillardia
Gazania
Marigold
Portulaca
Rudbeckia
Zinnia

Below: A morning glory vine, run wild.

SEASONAL BLOOMING PLANTS

Even amid the lush year-round bloom of the permanent landscape, tropical gardeners sometimes need a splash of concentrated color that only the plants usually called "annuals" can provide. Many of the plants used for this purpose are the same ones that gardeners in temperate regions rely upon—begonias, impatiens, marigolds, phlox, sweet alyssum. In the tropics, however, the seasons for planting and blooming are altered. There are two groups of plants that bloom seasonally, and they are generally called warm- and cool-season annuals. Cool-season annuals, which perform from October to April, should be able to accept nighttime lows down to 40° F, and even a touch of frost now and then. Warm-season annuals should to be able to cope with the heat and humidity of a tropical summer.

In most tropical areas of the United States, warm-season annuals are planted out from February to April to bloom from May to September. Cool-season annuals are planted out from October to January and bloom from January to April. Many annuals, including begonias and impatients, need rich soil to grow quickly, but some (especially marigolds) will produce copious foliage but few flowers unless the soil is poor. In the poor soil that is characteristic of much of the tropics, at least some fertilizer at the beginning of the season is usually necessary. If possible, provide some shade for the first few days after planting if the weather is extreme. Once the plants are in the ground, pinching off new growth and deadheading helps keep them neat, bushy, and full of flowers. When the bloom has passed, cut back the foliage or pull up the plants. Or, take cuttings or collect seeds from the plants to use for the following year.

The list at the left is but a small sample. There are hundreds of plants that can be used in this way, providing every color in the rainbow and a full range of sizes and shapes. From the intense golden yellows and oranges of gazania, portulaca, and tithonia that blaze through the hottest weather to the elegant pastels of brachycome and sweet alyssum that brighten the cooler months, from the tall globes of gomphrena to low, spreading foliage plants like coleus—it's a wonder that so many people stop at the admittedly useful impatiens, begonias, and petunias. And because these plants are not permanent, you can experiment endlessly, creating shapes and color combinations you wouldn't dare try with flowering shrubs. Will six different bright colors in a small area look rich and complex or just too busy? Does hot pink pentas look good with lime green coleus? If not, you only have to look at it for one season.

One important note to remember when you're putting out seasonal plants is that some of them may want to stay longer than you want them. Some of the plants that are used as annuals in temperate regions are noxious weeds in regions where they can overwinter or reseed themselves. Morning glories have escaped gardens in Hawaii and covered all over vegetations; fountain grass is taking over wild areas in Arizona; some species of lantana are hard to eliminate once they've become established. Before you plant, look around your area and ask at your local botanic garden.

Caladium x hortulanum 'Frieda Hemple'.

Coleus x hybridus cv.

Evolvulus glomeratus 'Blue Daze'.

Gaillardia pulchella 'Yellow Sun' (blanket flower).

Gomphrena globosa 'Lavender Lady' (globe amranth).

Impatiens wallerana 'Dazzler' series (busy Lizzie).

Pentas lanceolata cv.

Setcreasea pallida 'Purple Heart'.

Tithonia rotundifolia (Mexican sunflower).

Choosing plants for this volume turned out to be one of the most difficult tasks. No sooner had we whittled our list down to a manageable size than we came up with new plants that we couldn't possibly leave out. On this page and the next five pages, another 54 plants are described. Most are extremely useful in tropical landscapes. Some, like gardenia and dieffenbachia are also easily found. Others like *Triplaris americana* and *Cochliostema odoratissimum* are rare but worth seeking. Still others, like the cannonball and sausage trees can only be described as oddities. Even this list does not begin to cover the available and soon-to-be-available plant material of the tropics.

OTHER PLANTS

Adenium obesum (desert rose) is a low-growing, succulent plant with a swollen, often gnarled trunk; it produces exquisite flowers in many shades of pink and red, often striped in white. It is only hardy in Zone 10, but works beautifully in containers that can be brought indoors in cool weather. Keep it rather dry.

***Asparagus densiflorus* 'Myersii'** (asparagus fern, foxtail fern) is not a true fern. It produces bright green tapering taillike stems that jut out from the center of the plant. It needs a lot of water and space, and can be weedy.

Beaumontia grandiflora (Easter-lily vine) is an evergreen vine that bears abundant, bell-shaped white flowers up to 4 inches long and fragrant. This vigorous vine sometimes becomes woody and needs support.

Brachychiton (bottle tree) This genus includes several very useful trees ranging from 40-100 feet tall; most produce showy flowers. *B. acerifolus* (Australian bottle tree, flame tree) has a swollen, bottle-shaped trunk and bright red flowers in loose racemes. *B. populneus* is only 30-40 feet tall and produces clusters of white flowers.

Cochliostema odoratissimum is an herbaceous plant that produces very showy lavender to purple flowers, up to 5 inches across. It requires a light shade and water.

Coffea arabica (coffee), source of the world's morning beverage, is an ornamental evergreen shrub, to 15 feet tall, with wavy, dark green leaves, small fragrant white flowers, and red berries. It is also grown as a houseplant.

Cordia boissiere is a small evergreen tree to 25 feet tall with abundant, showy creamy white flowers. It tolerates dry conditions well.

Couroupita guianensis (cannonball tree) is a good example of how bizarre tropical plants can look. It is a very large deciduous tree with fragrant pink flowers and 8- to 10-inch fruits with hard shells that appear in groups and truly resemble cannonballs.

Crossandra infundibuliformis (firecracker flower) is a small shrub, to 3 feet tall, with bright, showy flowers.

Curcuma longa (hidden lily), a member of the ginger family, produces green and white cones with waxy yellow flowers similar to beehive ginger. It is the source of the spice turmeric.

Dietes bicolor (African iris) produces narrow, grasslike foliage and small yellow flowers with brown spots; it forms an attractive, open clump.

Dieffenbachia maculata (dumb cane) is often used a houseplant, but is an excellent landscape plant in warm regions. It produces very large leaves in various patterns of green, cream, and white; many cultivars exist with particularly showy markings.

Eucharis grandiflora (Amazon lily) is a bulbous plant that produces fragrant, white, daffodillike flowers and broad, arching shiny green leaves.

Euphorbia This large genus includes many succulent plants used in the tropics; particularly useful in dry areas. They include *E. pulcherrima* (the popular Christmas poinsettia, often used as a hedge or border) and *E. milii,* crown of thorns.

Feijoa sellowiana (pineapple guava), an evergreen shrub, grows up to 20 feet tall, produces white flowers, gray-green foliage, and edible fruit that resembles avocado and has a pineapple scent.

Adenium obesum, desert rose.

Asparagus densiflorus 'Myers', asparagus fern.

Crossandra infundibuliformis, firecracker flower.

Couroupita guianensis, cannonball tree.

Cochliostema odoratissimum.

Dietes bicolor.

Eucharis grandiflora, Amazon lily.

Euphorbia pulcherrima, poinsettia.

Hoffmania refulgens, taffeta plant.

Ilima.

Iochroma cyaneum.

Kalanchoe pinnata, air plant.

Kigelia pinnata, sausage tree.

Medinilla cumingii 'Kinabalu'.

Nymphaea 'Blue Beauty', tropical water lily.

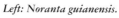

Passiflora coccinea, red passionflower.

Left: Noranta guianensis.

Pseuderanthemum laxiflorum.

Gardenia jasminoides is a common and popular shrub with glossy green foliage and very fragrant white flowers. It can be clipped as a formal hedge. It requires acid soil.

Harpephyllum caffrum (Kaffir plum) is an ornamental evergreen tree, to 30 feet tall, with white flowers; its dark red fruit can be made into jams and jellies.

Hoya carnosa (wax plant) is a climbing evergreen vine with dull green leaves and pink and white flowers in spring and summer. It tolerates shade and dry conditions.

Ilima is the common name used in Hawaii for *Sida fallax*, a low-growing shrub with tubular yellow flowers.

Iochroma cyaneum is a 10-foot tall shrub with clusters of deep blue to purplish blue flowers.

Kalanchoe pinnata (air plant) is one species in a large genus of succulent plants popular in the Southwest. It produces yellow and reddish brown flowers with inflated, papery calyxes. Other useful landscape plants in this variable genus include *K. blossfeldiana*, a branching herb to 1 foot tall that produces abundant small flowers in many colors, and *K. beharensis,* feltbush, to 12 feet tall (usually grown in pots and much smaller) with felty leaves.

Kigelia pinnata (sausage tree) is another novelty; it grows to 50 feet tall and produces dark red flowers, but is known best for its unusual, hanging, sausagelike fruit, up to 3 foot long.

Lagerstroemia indica (crape myrtle) is a common plant in all warm areas, used as a shrub or small tree and grown for its profuse flowers. It is hardy to Zone 7. *L. speciosa* (pride of India) is hardy only in Zone 10, and is a tree to 60 feet tall.

Liriope muscari (lilyturf) is an extremely useful grasslike groundcover that produces spiky purple and white flowers, used in both tropical and temperate regions. Attractive variegated cultivars are available.

Macadamia integrifolia is an excellent garden tree in Zone 10, to 60 feet tall with dense glossy green foliage. Don't count on nut production unless you've purchased special grafted varieties.

***Medinilla cumingii* 'Kinabalu'** (Malaysian orchid) is an epiphtyic plant that produces very showy pendulous flowers in pink or light red.

Mucuna bennettii (red jade) is a woody climbing vine with spectacular red flowers, in hanging clusters; flowers are similar to strongylodon.

Myrciaria cauliflora (jaboticaba) is a small shrubby tree with dense foliage and small white multi-stamen flowers; its grapelike fruits are used for making wine and jelly.

Nymphaea (water lily) is usually used as a container plant submerged in pools. Some types are hardy to Zone 5; others, known as tropical water lilies, are hardy only to Zone 10. Tropical water lilies are distinguished by height (they rise up a foot or more from the water), fragrance, and attractive lily pads. Hundreds of cultivars in every color (including blue for tropicals) exist; some are night bloomers. They do best in full sun.

Noranta guianensis is a shrub that can grow to 10 feet tall with support and produces spiky red inflorescences and glossy green foliage.

Ochna serrulata (Mickey Mouse plant) received its common name for small black seeds that appear in pairs. The plant also produces bright yellow flowers. Evergreen shrub, to 12 feet tall.

Ophiopogon japonicus (mondo grass) is a clump-forming grass that tolerates

Bamboos are used throughout the tropics, including *Phyllostachys* and *Bambusa* species and low-growing *Sasa* species (bamboo grass). Bamboos perform best in warm, moist soil. They will tolerate poor soil but not poor drainage. Most thrive in partial shade although some species will do well in full shade. Water well while establishing (can take two to three years). Bamboos are somewhat invasive by nature, so fertilization is generally unnecessary. Prune by removing the largest stems to let in more light and appreciate more fully the grace of mature plants. Shorter varieties should be cut back to the ground in early spring, much the same as ornamental grasses, to allow fresh new growth to emerge. In order to confine running species, sink a non-degradable barrier at least 20 inches deep.

CHOCOLATE

Cortés's gold-thirsty men were disappointed when the first Aztecs they encountered offered them handfuls of beans. The Spaniards were more impressed when they witnessed the ceremonies involved in the growing and harvesting of these beans, which included human sacrifices and, on the day of the harvest, orgiastic, erotic games. The beans were cacao, of course, used to make chocolate. The gold cups the Aztecs drank their chocolate from caught the eye of the Spaniards, but more interesting still was the taste. The Spaniards soon agreed with the Aztecs that drinking chocolate made you know that the gods were good. To the Aztecs chocolate was a drink, and it was part of their political life, its use encouraged in the hope it might replace alcoholic drinks, and it was given to warriors for energy. It was also part of their religion, the original recipe having been a gift to humans from Quetzalcoatl, the "feathered serpent" himself. Cortés was but the first European to fall for chocolate; for the rest of his life he kept a full pot on his desk. Soon it caught on throughout Europe, with those who could afford it sipping it all day long and even having it served to them in church; scholars opined that the ambrosia of the gods had at long last been identified, and when Linnaeus classified the cacao tree, he put it in the genus *Theobroma,* "divine food." Chocolate was used as a drink for three hundred years before the notion caught on of evaporating it and molding it into solid shapes.

shade and is an excellent groundcover under trees or palms.

Passiflora coccinea (red passionflower) is one of several species of ornamental vines in this genus. It produces red or orange 3- to 5-inch flowers, and, if pollinated, edible fruit. *P. caerulea* is also ornamental, but does not fruit. These plants are sometimes weedy.

Podocarpus graciolor (fern pine) is a coniferous evergreen tree, to 75 feet tall with a particularly graceful shape. Some species in this genus, such as *P. marcrophyllus*, are hardy to Zone 8

Pseuderanthemum reticulatum can be grown as a shrub or kept small. It produces attractive yellow-green variegated foliage.

Psidium littorale (strawberry guava) is an evergreen shrub or small tree that grows to 20 feet tall and produces leathery dark green foliage, white flowers, and 2-inch, dark red spicy fruit.

Rondeletia amoena is a small shrub or tree with 1- to 6-inch panicles of small flowers with pink corollas.

Schefflera (umbrella tree, rubber tree, starleaf) includes many plants that are useful in tropical landscapes. They are small shrubs or trees with compound leaves; many produce ornamental drupes. *S. actinophylla,* also known as *Brassaia actinophylla,* is also used as a houseplant.

Schinus terebinthifolius (Brazillian pepper tree) is an attractive ornamental tree that bears greenish flowers in summer and bright red berries in early winter. It is notoriously weedy and can be toxic.

Tabernaemontana divaricara (crape jasmine) does well in sun or shade. It produces clusters of fragrant noctural flowers and grows quickly to about 10 feet tall.

Terminalia catappa (tropical almond) is a very ornamental tree with bright green leaves that sometimes turn red in fall. This useful plant provides shade, lumber, and edible nuts.

Theobroma cacao (chocolate tree) is the source of cocoa beans. This evergreen tree grows to 25 feet or more and is usually grown under smaller trees, particularly mother-of-chocolate, *Gliricidia sepium.*

Tibouchina urvilleana (glory bush, princess glory bower) is an open shrub, to 15 feet tall, with bright green foliage and bell-shaped dark purple flowers. It can be grown as an annual in cooler climates, allowed to die back or dug up and brought indoors for winter.

Triplaris americana (palo santo) is a columnar tree, to 70 feet tall that produces abundant pink, red, and white flowers.

Typhenodorum linleyanum, an aquatic plant, becomes woody and grows huge leaves in the tropics. In temperate regions, it is often used in containers submerged in water and stays small.

Warszewiczia coccinea (wild poinsettia) grows to a treelike 20-25 feet tall and produces 2-foot clusters of bright red bracts. It is very cold sensitive.

Wikstroemia uva-ursi is a useful groundcover that produces small leaves and yellow flowers.

Wedelia trilobata is an excellent groundcover for tropical areas in sun or shade. It produces abundant bright yellow flowers, about 1 inch across, and dense bright green foliage on trailing stems. It tolerates salt well and can even be mowed.

Rondeletia amoena.

Schefflera sp.. umbrella tree.

Tabernaemontana divaricara,
crape jasmine.

Theobroma cacao, chocolate tree.

Tibouchina urvilleana, glory bush,
princess glory bower

Triplaris americana, long john,
palo santo.

Typhenodorum linleyanum.

Wikstroemia uva-ursi.

Warszewiczia coccinea.

GARDEN DESIGN 3

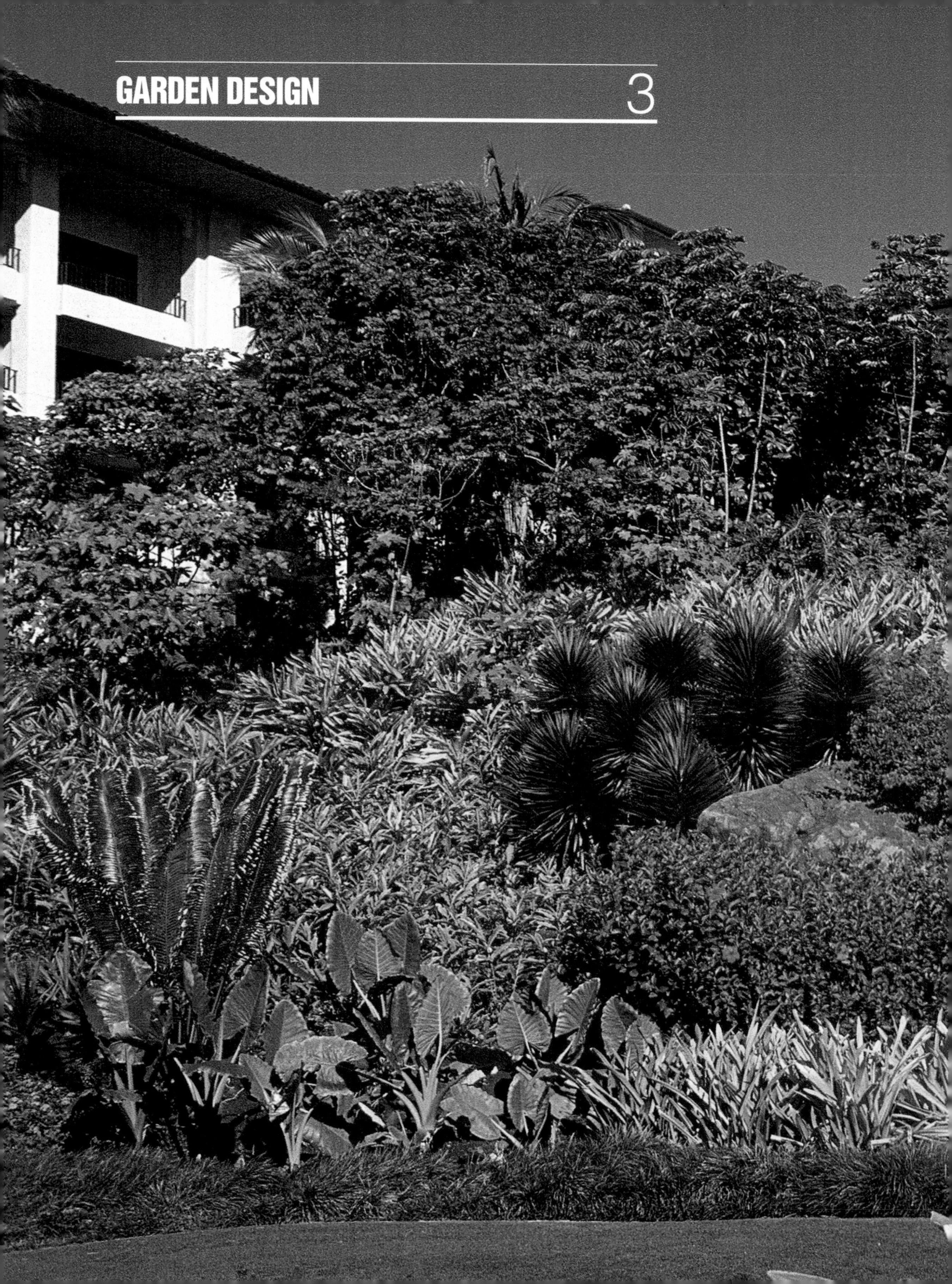

Above: A small pool is surrounded by foliage plants. *Right:* A standard of Eugenia is the focal point of this patio garden. *Opposite bottom:* Bauhinia shrub. *Opposite top:* Royal poinciana, crotons, and and traveler's palms against a backdrop of jacarandas at Waimea Falls Park on Oahu.

Planning your tropical garden or landscape encompasses many possibilities and an enormous variety of plants. With over 200,000 species native to the tropics and subtropics, you have a huge array of textures, forms, colors, and fragrances from which to choose, and you'll be challenged to combine these in ways that allow for displays of individual flamboyance balanced by less visually demanding but equally attractive interplantings. Often, the temptation of enjoying exotic flowers that bloom for a short time or lush plants that tend to overtake the landscape—at the expense of the garden as a whole—is great. Designing a tropical garden involves restraint. Tropical shrubs and trees can grow to a large size quickly; in many cases, you will not want to move them once they are established. So creating or renovating a tropical garden demands careful preplanning.

GARDEN TYPES First, consider what type of garden you want. Tropical plants are often grown in formal beds and borders with a linear or geometrical layout, providing a structured look that complements houses with a formal, classical architectural style especially well. Tropicals suitable for a formal garden would be those with a controlled and structured rather than rampant growth habit such as palms and cycads that won't require an excessive amount of maintenance to keep a well-groomed appearance. On the other hand, you might prefer an informal garden, with a free-flowing, relaxed look, which easily incorporates the enthusiastic growth habits of many tropicals, especially the vines. Individual specimen plants are also typical of the tropical landscape—a decorative cycad, a dramatic heliconia, a majestic palm, a delicious grapefruit. You could combine formal and informal elements in your landscape—for example, formal plantings around the house and patio, specimen trees and

shrubs in the lawn, and informal tropical woodlands areas around the borders of the yard.

The best choice of garden type is what pleases you and best complements your home and yard and also fits the amount of maintenance you are willing to do yourself or pay someone else to do for you. Visit botanical gardens and observe the plantings around homes in your area to identify what is pleasing to you.

THE RIGHT SITE Choose the site or sites for your tropical garden(s) carefully. Of primary importance is sunlight. Does a site receive sunlight all day or for just part of the day? Is the shade heavy, from buildings or thickly leaved trees, or is it dappled? While many tropical plants, such as bougainvillea, thrive in full sun, others like alpinia or allamanda appreciate protection from the hours of most intense sunlight each day, and yet others are native to the shaded tropical forest understory and thrive in dappled, filtered sun and even deep shade. Remember that as trees and shrubs grow, their shade will encroach on areas that are sunny today. Keep large trees away from the swimming pool, so their leaves don't drop into the water and their roots don't crack the pool's walls in search of moisture. Tender tropicals will benefit from being planted near warmth-absorbing walls, and others will appreciate protection from buffeting,

Bold foliage plants–purple colocasias, huge philodendron, and
white-veined alocasias are softened by feathery cyperus in this
garden. With a small waterfall
and an edging of stones, a lush
jungle effected is created in a
small space.

drying winds provided by structures or larger surrounding plants.

Be sure to consider access to water when siting your tropical garden(s), especially if your growing area experiences an annual dry spell. (Also see the information on xeriscaping in Chapter 5, Special Conditions.) If you are planting in
a very sloping site, you'll have to level it out, terrace it, or break it up into
smaller individual areas so the heavy tropical rainstorms don't wash away the
enriched soil and mulch.

PLANNING ON PAPER Now you're ready to draw up a garden plan on paper. First,
figure the exact dimensions of your site (or sites) with a tape measure, and
draw these to scale, preferably on graph paper; a scale of 1/4 inch to 1 foot is
useful. Next, fill in the existing structures—buildings, pool, patio, deck,
walls, permanent paths and walkways. Then mark in semi-permanent elements such as arbors, trellises, fences, and benches, plus major existing trees
and shrubs. Consider, too, the area beyond your own property. Do you want
to screen out neighbors' yards for privacy or to hide an eyesore? Do you want
to frame a vista?

Consider structural edgings for your garden beds, especially formal beds.
They give a clean, more defined look and keep invading vegetation out but
your improved garden soil and mulch in. Edgings can range from bricks to
attractively placed rocks to rot-resistant woods such as locust or cedar. Once
you know how much space will be taken up by pathways, edgings, and permanent and semi-permanent structures and elements, you can figure out just

how much space you have for your tropical plants in each site.

STRUCTURING THE GARDEN In designing your tropical garden, start with the larger elements first–trees and shrubs–to provide the basic skeleton, or "bones," that will provide the backdrop for smaller perennials and annuals. Tropical trees and shrubs, either as background plantings or individual specimens, add flowers, fruits, shade (for you, your home, and/or other plants), and drama to your landscape. They can also serve as hedges. Many of these trees and shrubs give your garden the quintessential tropical look: palms, cycads, bauhinias, mangos. Choose these elements carefully, so their ultimate height or overall size doesn't overwhelm the site where you plant them and so you will not have to prune them constantly to keep them within bounds. Create groupings that vary in size and shape–different heights, and a combination of rounded and thin, upright forms. Most gardens benefit from a focal point, a plant that is so architecturally interesting or flamboyant that it causes the viewer to come to what English garden designer Gertrude Jekyll called a full stop. In the tropics, this is easily achieved: specimen trees like mangoes, palms, heliconias, and alpinias can provide this easily. Then add perennials to your plan, filling in the spaces between and beneath the shrubs and trees and adding further variations of shape and size. Annuals for both winter and summer bloom can finish off the plan. A bonus in the tropical garden is provided by epiphytes–aroids,

Here, too, water (and a bridge) add to the effect of a garden. In this instance, flowering plants, (are combined with tree ferns and cycads.

When planning a tropical garden, consider using the design techniques shown in these pictures. Top: Mix flowering and foliage groundcovers, such as lobularia and alternanthera. Center: Combine a foliage plant (cordyline) with a flowering plant (dietes). Bottom: drape a flowering vine along a fence or wall (petrea in this case). Above right: Combine foliage plants of different colors and textures. Shown are pilea, san-sevieria, philodendron, and various bromeliads.

bromeliads, orchids, ferns—which you can add to trees and shrubs for visual interest and depth. Groundcovers, such as wedelia, alternanthera, and smaller philodendrons fill in any empty areas; in the tropics, these plants grows quickly and add another layer to the landscape.

COLOR AND TEXTURE Tropical plants offer a much wider range of colors and textures than species native to cooler climates, and the most effective and pleasing tropical landscape will display a well-coordinated variety of, especially, foliage hues and textures. While many tropical plants provide a brilliant splash of vivid color during their period of bloom, the permanent, year-round color interest in your tropical garden comes from the foliage. Leaf color ranges from all shades of green to reds, purples, and yellow, often in variegated form; crotons and cordylines provide some of the most interesting foliage colors in the tropics, but the leaves of alocasias, colocasias, and calatheas have some of the most intricate markings. Vary this permanent display of color by choosing plants that bloom during different seasons so your landscape will sport flowers of various colors, often astonishingly vivid, all year.

Texture, too, adds great interest and variety to the tropical garden. Lacy fern fronds contrast with the sharp, swordlike agave leaves; the soft-leaved rosette of a bromeliad clings to the rough bark of a live oak, next to the drooping leaflike stems of Spanish moss; the tangled multiple branches of centipede plant create a self-contained ball of texture. The huge leaves of philodendrons, monsteras, and colocasias can be softened by feathery foliage like eugenia and malpighia. Palm trunks are varied and beautiful: smooth or heavily booted, covered by a woven bark, encircled by horizontal bands of color, slender or swollen. Vines add sinuous grace, and ficus exhibits its roots for a unique design element. Flowers offer a multitude of form, from the bottlebrush blooms of calliandra to the tubular flowers of firecracker vine to the classic shape of the orchid and the unusual form of the bat plant flower.

When choosing plants, consider their requirements as well as your own. Plants that need a lot of water should be planted together, and at some distance from those that would rather stay dry; this saves water during dry spells and avoids drowning plants that don't need it. Ask about insect pests and diseases at your local botanic garden or county extension service; try to choose plants that are not susceptible to pests that are active in your area. Unless you enjoy cutting back constantly, avoid plants that are invasive.

PLANNING FOR YEAR-ROUND INTEREST Gardeners in temperate regions have learned to live without their gardens for a good part of the year. Although Northerners may talk of the beauty of a sprig of holly or a stick of colored bark against the snow, it is only gardeners in the tropics and subtropics who know the pleasure of year-round growth. It is, however, not always easy to achieve. The calendar is different in most of the tropics, with the plants used as summer bedding plants in the North serving as winter-flowering seasonals in the tropics (see pages 170-171 for information on using seasonal plants). For early spring, bulbs like amaryllis provide color after most shrubs have finished flowering. Include some plants that thrive in the heat of summer, like gingers, heliconias, and spathiglottis orchids.

Since Victorian times, gardeners have been fascinated by tropical plants. For those who live in temperate climates, using exotic plants is a fantasy they can only dream of—but gardeners in the tropics have the opportunity to create lush paradises with relative ease. Combining the almost overwhelming variety of size, shape, texture, color, and growth habit offered by tropical plants into a coherent, pleasing whole is admittedly a challenge but one you will be infinitely rewarded in working to meet. Remember that no garden is ever finished; don't be afraid to experiment and to change things around if your initial design doesn't quite please you. Tropical plants love to grow, and if you meet their minimal needs, you'll soon be surrounded by a thriving landscape.

Key
A=*Setcreasea pallida* (purple heart)
B=*Neoregelia*
C=*Bismarckia*

This bed at Fairchild Tropical Garden, designed by Raymond Jungles, a student of Robert Burley Marx, uses only three plants, but combines them so that the best features of each are highlighted. The bismarckia palm can be seen from all sides and provides the focus of the garden; the groundcover of setcreasea provides color that blends with the markings of the neoregelia; and the neoregelia bridges the gap in height between the two. This formal effect is startling in color and shape.

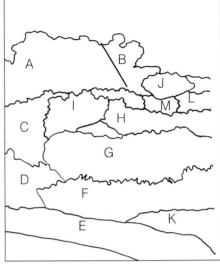

Key
A=*Aleurites moluccana* 'Kukui'
(candlenut tree)
B=*Schefflera actinophylla*
(umbrella tree)
C=*Alpinia darceyi* (variegated
ginger) and *Alpinia purpurata*
(red ginger)
D=*Alocasia macrorhiza* 'Ape'
E=*Ophiopogon japonicus*
(mondo grass)
F=*Crinum* sp. (dwarf spider lily)
G=*Hibiscus rosa-sinensis*
H=*Bougainvillea spectabilis*
'Miss Manilla'
I=*Yucca alnifolia*
J=*Pritchardia pacifica*
K=*Impatiens wallerana* 'Dazzler'
L=*Cycas circinalis*
M=*Cuphea hyssopifolia*

This hillside garden at the Hyatt Regency in Kauai uses many more plants and, though just as impressive, is softer than the one on the previous page. An edging of mondo grass separates the garden from the lawn beyond it, and candlenut tree and umbrella trees provide a backdrop. Within the garden, pritchardia palms and cycads (*Cycas circinalis*) are focal points. Flowering plants, such as red hibiscus, bougainvillea, and crinum provide color at different times of the year. Alpinias, not in flower when this photograph was taken, are showstoppers when they bloom; impatiens and pentas are planted out when extra color is needed. Cuphea is used as groundcover to bridge gaps. Natural stones are left in place to contrast with the soft, blending effect of the plant material.

TECHNIQUES 4

Making things grow in the tropics does not require much effort; moist, humid, and hot conditions promote rampant growth in thousands of different species. Making things grow how and where you want them is a different matter. In the tropics, gardening skill is often a matter of impeding rather than causing growth and of choosing plants that will work well together without overpowering one another. Gardeners new to the area often have to contend with a whole new set of pests. in addition to the ones they left behind in cooler regions, as well as new methods of planting and pruning. Although the region has the advantage of a long gardening season, the time frames are often reversed; planting "annuals" (seasonal bedding plants) in the spring, for example, is rarely a good idea because tender young plants will be subjected to the brutal summer. In this chapter, guidelines and techniques for gardening in tropical areas are presented; information about using tropical plants in other climates or indoors appears in Chapter 5, Special Conditions.

We refer to "guidelines" rather than "rules" for tropical gardening, because every garden presents different conditions. The subtropical climate of southern Florida is a far cry from the dry region of southern California, although many of the same plants will thrive in both. Even the short distance from Miami Beach to Boca Raton requires a significant change in gardening expectations. Even within a single garden, microclimates make procedures useful in one area damaging in another. The information in this chapter, therefore, is general. As you apply it you will learn through trial and error the techniques that suit your landscape best.

CHOOSING AND IMPROVING THE SITE Many of the tropical plants you put in the ground will stay where you plant them for a long time. Other than seasonal flowering selections, your plants will be perennial, and you will not remove them when spent or replace them every summer. So it is important to set them in the right place the first time. The gardener's' first task is to find the right spot for each plant, the spot where it can use its own innate ability to thrive. It takes time, experience, and experimentation, but a gardener who wants to succeed must acquire an understanding of the site. Whether you are planning an elaborate shrub border, a bed of orchids, or a single specimen plant, you should be aware of the following factors, their relationship to your site, and how they affect the plants you choose to grow.

Sun/shade When considering sites for your tropical plants, observe all possible areas over a period of time. Is the site sunny, and if so, how much sun is there and at what times of day? Is there shade, and if so, what kind and how much? While we might first think of tropical plants as sun-lovers, this is not always the case. Many tropical plants grow naturally in the filtered light of the forest floor below the forest trees' canopy, so in the garden, these plants appreciate a similar situation, with either high-light intensity but no direct sunlight or dappled sunlight filtering through a light layer of tree branches swaying overhead. Other tropical plants want some sun but need protection from the most intense afternoon rays. especially during the hottest months of the year. Plan your garden areas accordingly, using larger sun-lovers (as well as structures in your landscape) to provide the needed shade for their lower-growing companions..

Soil Although you cannot change the type of sunlight your garden receives (without altering major structures), you can change the composition of your soil. Soil improvements can be made for the short run with the addition of chemical fertilizer, but serious gardeners manage their soil to attain peak production over a long period of time.

The medium in which tropical plants root is very different from that in temperate regions. Outside the tropics, the word used is soil, a mixture of small particles that can be sandy, loamy, or clayey. Soil is only one element of the growing medium in the tropics. In most tropical areas, the surface has been covered with fallen leaves and branches from the lush canopy of trees, shrubs and vines. This debris does not disappear or blow away; it quickly decays, becoming part of the earth and a source of nutrients. This is fortunate, for much of the soil is often rocky; the coral rock and limestone of Florida would be an inhospitable medium if the plants could not take advantage of the thick layer of decayed material that covers it.

Another consideration about your soil is its levels of nutrients. Like all living things, plants require a variety of nutrients, primarily, nitrogen, phosphorus, and potassium, for healthy growth. These and other trace nutrients occur naturally in the soil where they are absorbed by the plant's root system and metabolized for growth. Alas, few soils are perfectly nutrient-rich. Tropical soils, in particular, tend to be somewhat nutrient-poor.

To identify the level of nutrients in your soil and the additions that are needed requires a soil test. A small but representative amount of garden soil is analyzed for nutrient deficiencies and excesses. Simple home soil test kits are available, and a full analysis can be done by a county extension service, an agricultural university or perhaps even a local garden center. The analysis will generally be accompanied by recommendations for needed nutrients and their application rates.

Most soil-test analyses will also report on the pH level of your soil—its acidity or alkalinity. You can also test pH levels yourself with a simple home kit. The pH level is measured on a scale of 1 to 14. A measurement of under 7.0 indicates an acid soil; above 7.0 indicates alkaline soil; 7.0 is neutral. Like most other plants, tropicals typically grow best in a neutral to slightly acid soil. You can correct overly acid soil by adding limestone; do this several months before planting, and work the limestone into the soil well. Overly alkaline soil, typical of south Florida, can be corrected by adding organic matter and compost. The pH level can also be altered with sulfur (but be aware that sulfur can also turn limestone soil into a claylike material). However, these improvements will not last over time and must be done over a large area for larger tropical shrubs, vines, and trees whose roots will spread. In most cases, amending the soil pH around a large perennial plant actually does it more harm than good, because it prevents the plant from sending its roots past the immediate area of the "good" soil. Unless you are prepared to amend the soil heavily each year, it is advisable to choose plants that can grow well in the existing soil, or to plant in raised beds or containers.

To meet the nutrient needs indicated by your soil test, add the recommended organic materials, such as compost and well-rotted manure for nitrogen, bone meal or powdered rock phosphate for phosphorous, and wood ashes for potassium. Organic soil amendments will create the well-balanced, friable, well-drained, yet moisture-retaining soil in which most tropical plants thrive, and unlike the "quick fixes" of chemical fertilizers, will not harm your plants or the environment and will build the soil for long-term fertility. An added bonus is that

Drainage is the ability of soil to move water so that the roots don't get too waterlogged and nutrients can percolate through the soil to the roots, where the nutrients are used. While most tropical plants require a lot of moisture, most also require very well-drained soil, which is also critical for areas that experience heavy tropical rainfalls. To test for drainage, dig a one-gallon-size hole and fill it water; if it does not drain within an hour, you may have drainage problems. There are several ways to correct poor drainage:

1. Add sand and organic matter to the soil. Sand plus clay results in cement, but sand, clay, and organic matter will give you friable soil.

2. Use raised beds, which provide better drainage and also allow you to mix better soil from elsewhere into your site.

3. Insert a drainage pipe. These pipes, usually plastic, are sold at most garden supply or hardware store and move water to a place where it will do less harm.

4. Grade the area with terraces or retaining walls.

5. If your problem is serious, or if you think it is worth the investment, talk to a professional landscaper about installing a drainage system, such as tile, gravel beds, or more elaborate drainage ditches.

in warm tropical soils, organic matter breaks down relatively rapidly, so their nutrients will become available to your plants much more quickly than in temperate-climate soils.

There are many ways to maintain good soil; simply adding a lot of chemical fertilizer is not one of them. It take experience to understand what your soil needs and to provide it. It is important to match the proper plant to the soil; the wrong plant will usually fail, and it may also damage the soil. Use organic matter generously for plants that need it. Adding compost and fertilizers will keep your soil rich in organic matter. Use fertilizers that add missing ingredients, including trace elements, only when you have reason to suspect that they are necessary. If you manage your soil properly, it will increase in fertility after several years of cultivation and provide the best possible home for your plants.

One group of tropical plants requires no soil at all. The epiphytes, or air plants, extract the nutrients they need from atmospheric moisture and air. All epiphytes need is a congenial base to attach themselves to, such as a stones, a roof, a tree, or a tree stump.

CLIMATE Tropical plants vary in their tolerance of and requirements for temperature ranges and humidity levels. Some, for example may not tolerate any temperatures below 50° F, while others will withstand light freezes; some species thrive when the temperature is above 90° F, while other delight in temperatures in the 70's F.

MICROCLIMATES No matter how small your site is, it probably encompasses several sets of conditions. The area near the protection of a wall or building is probably warmer than the open space in front. The strip that faces the street receives more pollution than the yard behind the house. The spot near the wall of the house may be affected by limestone in the foundation.

SITE IMPROVEMENT Your plants will grow better if you take the time to improve the ground in which you put them. The first step in preparing a garden site is a general cleanup, the removal of rocks, sticks, stumps, or other debris. Once the area is relatively clean, lay out the boundaries of your site using string, garden hose, or spray paint.

If the site is a grassy area, skin the turf off using a shovel or spade. Take the top 2 inches off—grass and roots—and knock the soil loose from the roots. Don't throw away the turf—use it to start a compost pile, If the area is covered with brush or weeds, mow first and then skin off the vegetation. Once you have bare ground, you're ready to begin improving the soil for a productive garden. Don't delay at this point; the exposed soil will become degraded and eroded quickly.

In tropical areas, gardeners often face competing growth from weedy plants. If you are starting a new garden, consider using a weedkiller such as Roundup that will remove all weedy vegetation before you start.

PREPARING THE SOIL Under ideal conditions, loosen and turn over the soil to a depth of 4-6 inches. If tender vegetation is growing on the site, turn it into the top part of the soil. Pull out any woody stems. Wait at least two weeks after this tilling to allow the tilled plants to decompose, and again turn the soil under to a depth of 4-6 inches to ensure the breaking up of dead plants and to loosen the soil further. After the second tilling, apply soil amendments such as fertilizer, lime, sulfur, compost, or sand. Till once again, this time to a depth of 8-10 inches with a tiller or 12-18 inches by hand with a spading fork.

However, ideal conditions rarely exist in much of tropical United States.

1. Dig a shallow hole, wider than deep.

2. Scatter fertilizer or other necessary amendments; recent research has shown that it is better not to use amendments in the planting hole, and it causes the plant to stay within the planting hole and not spread out its roots.

3. Place the tree. Find the root flare, the place where the trunk of the tree hits the roots. Nurseries sometimes cover this up and you may have to remove burlap or soil. Place root flare at a point ⅓ of rootball higher than existing grade in heavy soils, level in light soils.

4. Fill in the hole.

5. Firm up the soil before you water. If you water first, you will compact the soil.

6. Create a 3- to 6-inch mound, called a berm, around the outer edge of the roots to hold water that can soak in deeply.

Vigorous, unmarked foliage is a
sign of a healthy plant.

Gardeners in southern Florida contend with coral rock that passes for soil here. In
this enviroment, you will probably be able to dig only 2-3 inches with a trowel or
shovel. It is then necessary to use a digging bar or other implement to loosen
stones as much as possible, removing them if you can.

Planting in a raised bed solves this problem, as well as providing excellent
drainage. To create a raised bed, mound soil to a height of 2-3 inches; soil for a
raised bed can contain a mixture of topsoil and compost or soil additives such as
vermiculite or bark chips. Water well, then plant.

Double digging is a process by which two spadesful of dirt are lifted and loos-
ened to create a loose, well-tilled bed. It is time-consuming and back-breaking,
but it is greatly beneficial to the future health of your plants. To be effective, it
should be done in an area several square feet around the planting site. Although it
seems complicated, the procedure simply required digging down an extra shovel-
depth. As you dig, place the soil you've removed alongside the trench; fill each
trench with the soil from the trench before it. Break up all clods in the soil and
amend as necessary. This method is popular in some regions, but is rarely used in
Florida, where coral rock soil makes digging almost impossible.

BUYING PLANTS The most important aspect of choosing plants for your garden is to
select those that are vigorous and healthy. The best growers have a healthy,
robust appearance. The plants have received enough but not too much fertilizer;
they show strong growth that has not been forced in a hot greenhouse or stressed
as a result of inappropriate conditions; their color is rich green with no sign of
chlorosis. No pest infestation or damage is present.

Another significant consideration in choosing plants is to understand your own
conditions and to buy only plants that will thrive in those conditions. For example, if you have extremely sandy, dry conditions, then you would not consider
buying heliconias or ferns, since they requires moist soil.

Take care to purchase plants at the correct stage of growth and in good health.
If they are too young, they will be weak and easily killed. If they are too old, often
they have experienced a great deal of stress (such as too much or too little water)
from which they may never recover. Here is what to look for.

• Plants should be well established in their pots, in appropriately sized containers, and have an overall appearance of vigor.

• Plants should be established beyond the seedling stage and have developed
into good, sturdy individuals—a minimum pot size of 3 inches is recommended.

• If the plant is a rooted cutting, it should have been pinched when young,
which creates bushy and full growth, with more than a single stem.

• Plants that are repotted divisions should have been given ample time to
establish themselves in the container.

• Foliage should be turgid (full, slightly swollen) and solid green.

• Leaves should be upright and undamaged.

• No infestation or damage by insects or disease should be evident. Pick the
plant up for a close inspection. Mottled leaves could be a sign of infestation or disease. Yellowish stripes or stunted or distorted shapes could be signs of virus. You
do not want any plant that has little white flies hovering it. If you add plants with
insect or disease problems to your garden, these unwanted guests could spread to
the soil or to other plants.

• A potted plant should have a sturdy root system. This is harder to check, but some buyers knock the plant out of the pot to be sure a healthy root system has been established. Often the top growth is an indicator of the health of the root system.

• Many yellow leaves at the base of a plant are often an indication that the plant is pot-bound. After an extended period of time in a pot, a plant can lose its vigor, often because it has used up the available nutrition in the container. If replanted with care, and if the root system is spread out at planting time, a pot-bound plant may recover. (This problem is much more severe with woody plants because their roots are sometimes impossible to redirect, and if they continue to grow in a circular pattern, they will eventually girdle themselves and make the plant unstable in the ground.)

• Many roots growing out of the bottom of the pot is another indication that the plant is pot-bound. A few roots is no problem, but many roots out the bottom is not a good sign.

PLANTING Planting is a gardener's most rewarding task and also one of the most crucial. Without the right start, even the most carefully tended plants will languish. When setting out, whether the plant is bought bare-root, containerized, or balled-and-burlapped, the roots need to be kept moist before planting. The maxim is simple, but apt: if they dry, they die. When digging the planting hole, make sure it's large enough to fit the roots without crowding. Prune any crushed or damaged roots back to sound wood. Finally, be sure to plant at the proper depth; too deep is just as wrong as too shallow. The hole should be at least as wide as it is deep, and the sides should be roughed up so that the soil around the roots does not become solid. Recent research has shown that the hole should be 2-3 times as wide as deep and that the plant should be placed at the same level as it was in the container. Never dig when soil is very wet or very dry, as this will damage the soil structure.

To plant bare-root shrubs and trees: Remove packing material, clods of earth, and broken or dead roots. Prune off dead or broken branches, and soak the plant for at least one and not more than four hours. Mound soil in the bottom of the hole so that the center of the plant can be placed on the mound with the roots resting below it. Fill in half the soil; pack the soil firmly enough to avoid large air pockets, but not so firmly as to compact it.

To plant containerized shrubs and trees: Remove the container (even if the manufacturer suggests leaving it on). It is important to loosen the rootball, which may have become pot-bound. Using a sharp knife or pruning shears, make cuts into the roots on all four sides of the rootball. Fluff out the roots with your fingers. Place the plant into the hole, and fill in soil. Create a rim above root level in the hole to hold water around the roots.

To plant balled-and-burlapped shrubs and trees: Fill in half the hole and firm up the soil. You do not need to remove the burlap (unless it is synthetic) but fold it back so that it does not stick out of the soil and act as a wick for moisture; take off all string, twine, and other packing material. Place the plant in the hole and make sure it is at its proper depth by placing a rod across the hole; if the top of the rootball is not level with the rod, put in more soil, or dig deeper. Fill in remaining soil, and firm.

Perennial vines, flowers, and other plants are set out in much the same way as

This plant has overgrown its pot and is probably stressed; it has less chance of success when transplanted.

1. An overgrown, ready for division, has been removed from its pot and its roots exposed.

2. The main clump is divided into several smaller clumps, each with at least a few healthy roots.

3. An appropriate pot is chosen and filled 1/3 full with potting mix. One tablespoon of slow-release fertilizer is added.

4. A division is nestled into the new pot and roots (in this case rhizomes) are spread 2 inches below pot rim.

5. The pot is overfilled with good soil, then pressed and thumped to settle soil.

6. Soon, four plants will be available for transplant.

shrubs and trees. Seasonal flowering plants require care, even though they are not permanent. When the plant is in place, water well. During the first few months (and up to a year) after establishment, check frequently to make sure that the plant is kept moist. Yellowing leaves or dry soil indicate that the plant needs more water. You can dig a shallow depression around the plant to hold water. Mulch will also keep the soil around the plant moist and will help control root nematodes.

PROPAGATION To the avid gardener, nothing is as exciting as receiving a cutting of a long-sought plant, and nothing is more frustrating than watching it fail, often in a glass of water on the kitchen windowsill. With understanding and a little planning, you can avoid this kind of disappointment with relative ease, but you must keep in mind that no single method works for every plant all of the time.

Plant propagation is the art and science of reproducing plants. Plants can be propagated in several ways, including seeding, grafting, layering, division, cutting, and tissue culture. The method selected is determined in large part by the plant's genetic characteristics and growth habit, the available facilities, the number of plants desired, and the skill and knowledge of the propagator. For home gardeners looking to produce a few favorite tropical plants without great expense, cutting, layering, and division are generally the most appropriate techniques.

Softwood Cuttings Many popular tropical plants, including gesneriads, coleus, and pentas, and other plants in the Acanthus family can be propagated by softwood cuttings; it is a good idea to try this method while you are gaining experience in propagation. The optimum time to take cuttings can vary somewhat among species, and for certain plants, such as mussaenda and jade vine, the period available may be limited. However, most tropical plants will root well from cuttings taken in early summer, at the beginning of the growing season. At this time, the new growth is soft enough to root rapidly but is sufficiently ripe to prevent premature wilting and deterioration. Ideally, you should collect the cuttings in the cool early-morning hours from vigorous, healthy, insect- and disease-free plants. Using secateurs (pruning shears) or a sharp knife, take cuttings from terminal or lateral shoots of the current season's growth. To prevent the possibility of spreading disease, clean cutting tools with a solution of one part household bleach to six parts water before moving to the next plant. Cuttings are usually 4-6 inches long and have several sets of leaves. Moisten the cuttings immediately, place them in a plastic bag, and store them in a cool place out of direct sunlight.

To prepare the cuttings, first remove flowers, buds, and seed heads; strip all leaves and flowers from the lower half of the cutting. Next, make a fresh cut one-eight to one-quarter inch below a node (where the leaf joins the stem—the site at which most rooting activity takes place). Strip the leaves from the lower half of the cutting. Usually two or more sets of leaves will remain on the upper portion; if they are very large, reduce them by up to half to lessen water loss from the cutting and conserve space in the rooting container. Then dip the bottom inch of the cutting in a rooting-hormone/fungicide mixture. Several liquid and powdered formulations of varying strengths are available, each with its own merits; experience will suggest which is more effective for specific plants (or check a manual on plant propagation).

You can use almost anything as a rooting container, provided it is well

Staking a palm for the first few years after planting helps avoid problems. Never nail the stakes to the palm; use braces as shown.

drained, clean, and appropriately used. For most tropical cuttings, a clay or plastic 6-inch bulb pan works well and will accommodate six to ten cuttings. You must wash and rinse recycle pots with a bleach solution to ensure sterility.

Rooting media should be light and well drained. They may contain peat moss, vermiculite, perlite, coarse sands, or even polystyrene beads, alone or in combination. Experienced propagators alter the composition of the medium to suit the growing conditions and needs of specific plants, but a 50-50 mixture by volume of peat moss and perlite is a good general-purpose starting point. Before filling containers with the selected rooting medium, moisten the mixture to the consistency of a wrung-out sponge.

Insert the prepared cuttings to a depth of one-third to one-half their length, and space about 2 inches apart; spacing will vary depending on the size of the cutting, but avoid the temptation to overcrowd. Mist the cuttings lightly and place the entire cutting-filled pot inside a clear plastic bag. Seal the bag and move it to a shady location in the garden. Particularly soft cuttings may wilt initially but should soon recover. Check the cuttings once a week and remove any leaves that have dropped or cuttings that begin to rot. If the initial moisture content of the rooting medium was correct and the bag is properly sealed, no additional watering will be required throughout the rooting process. Depending on the type of plant being propagated, rooting can take two to ten weeks.

When the cuttings are well rooted, remove the bag. At the first required watering, use a water-soluble transplanter (or "starter") fertilizer. Continue to grow the cuttings in the rooting container for two to three weeks, then transplant to a protected nursery site in the garden where the plants can grow until they are large enough to be moved to a permanent location.

Hardwood Cuttings Propagating deciduous tropicals from hardwood cuttings is a useful method for home gardeners, since the cuttings are relatively nonperishable, easy to prepare, and require no special equipment or facilities for rooting. Unlike leafy softwood cuttings, which are prepared at any time of year when plants are actively growing, hardwood cuttings are made in the beginning of the growing season.

Cutting wood is collected in the form of long, healthy, vigorous stems of the past season's growth. These will vary in length depending on the species, and diameters will range from ¼-1 inch. In most cases, each stem will be sufficiently long to yield more than one cutting. To prepare the cuttings, first remove and discard the thin terminal portion of the stem. Then cut the balance of the stem into 4- to 12-inch uniform lengths so that each cutting has at least two sets of buds. Where possible, make top cuts just above a bud and ½ inch below a bud at the base. Dust the lower inch of the cuttings with rooting-hormone fungicide mixture formulated for hardwood cuttings, and secure with elastic bands in conveniently sized bundles.

Pack the base of the cuttings with damp sphagnum moss and place them in a plastic bag. Seal the bag with a twist-tie and attach a label that indicates the date, name of plant, and required treatment. Store in a dry, cool but not cold area until planting time. It is usually considered advantageous to plant tropicals out at the beginning of the warmest, wettest season. Select a particularly well-drained area of the garden, and plant the cuttings deeply, but make sure that some buds are above the soil. The location and spacing of the cuttings must be adequate to allow the plants to grow undisturbed for a year.

Not all deciduous tropicals will root from hardwood cuttings, but for those that will–including caesalpinias and gumbo-limbos–the method provides a simple, low-cost form of propagation.

Division A number of tropical plants, including freycenetia, heliconias, gingers, orchids, and some palms, naturally spread and colonize by producing upright-growing shoots, known as suckers, from roots and underground stems. Division is simply the removal of these from the parent plant. For small plants it may be advantageous to dig the entire plant and sever the desired number of suckers with secateurs. For parent plants that are too large to dig, detach the suckers with a sharp spade. Do this in early spring before the period of active growth. Root systems of the suckers are usually not extensive, and pruning back the top by one half will help to compensate for the loss of roots.

Layering Some popular tropical plants—brugmansia, litchee, and mussaenda are good examples—are difficult to root from cuttings without the aid of specialized, often costly equipment beyond the modest means and needs of most home gardeners. In such cases, a technique known as layering provides a viable alternative means of propagation. Layering is simply the development of roots on a stem while it is still attached to the parent plant. Once rooted, the layer is severed from the parent to become a new plant. A few tropical plants, including brunfelsia, barleria, russellia, and pseudanthemum, do this naturally. Gardeners may opt to use layering even for easy-to-root tropicals because of its simplicity.

There are several forms of layering, but simple layering is the technique most often used. After growth has begun, select a long, low, supple branch. Sharply bend it to an upright position 6-12 inches from the tip. Often this is all that is required to begin the process, though in some cases a small notch is cut on the underside of the branch at the point of the bend; dusting with rooting hormone will also aid in rooting. Next, insert the bent portion into the soil and cover to a depth of 3-6 inches. Use a peg or wire over the bend to help hold it down and in place, and stake the upper part of the layer as it grows to keep it upright. The layer will be well rooted and developed by the following spring (and for some plants in only a few months), when it may be detached from the parent plant.

Simple layering is a low but nearly foolproof method of propagation; it can be applied to almost any shrub, although it is most easily accomplished on plants with long, arching branches.

Starting from Seed Many tropical plants can be started from seed. Not only can it be cheaper to start your own plants from seeds, but also it makes a much wider selection available to you. Many containers are suitable for starting seeds. Some of the best include small, 2- to 3-inch pots or a 3-inch-deep corrugated fiberboard or plastic tray. The potting mixture should be lightweight and sterile to prevent seedlings from damping off and to avoid weed seeds. Several "soilless" mixtures are available commercially, containing perlite, sand, and peat moss.

PRUNING There are three basic reasons to prune a plant: to keep it healthy, to promote flowering and fruiting, and to shape and maintain its size. Pruning for health entails the removal of dead, diseased, and weak wood; pruning for flowering and fruiting encompasses thinning, root pruning, deadheading, and the

Vigilant clipping and pruning will help keep your plants from running rampant in your garden. Remove leaves close to, but not at root level; remove yellowed or dead leaves as they appear.

A properly pruned strelitzia follows the plant's natural shape but keeps it open. Handpulling individual leaves is usually better than cutting them.

removal of old wood; pruning for shape and size is essentially the selective removal of both old and new growth. Many gardeners view pruning as an arcane art, difficult to learn and taxing to practice. In fact, it is a relatively simple process, given a modicum of knowledge and the right tools, properly maintained.

To prune effectively and safely, you will need a few basic pieces of equipment: hand shears (which perform a clean cut that doesn't promote a way for disease to enter the plant), hedge shears (electric or manual), lopping shears (wooden-handled or steel with ratchet) a hand saw (sheathed or folding), gloves, and eye protection. Store all tools out of the reach of children, and maintain them regularly. Whatever your reason for pruning, a few general caveats apply. When removing branches, cut as close to the branch collar of the main stem as possible, but do not cut into the branch collar. Do not paint over the pruning wounds; this once-popular practice only promotes rot by providing a moist, sheltered environment for fungal organisms. Spring-blooming plants should be sheared directly after flowering, since next season's flower buds will be formed on the new wood.

To maintain a larger tropical plant's optimum health, prune regularly to removed dead, diseased, and weak wood. Old multistemmed deciduous tropical shrubs often profit from rejuvenation, the practice of cutting all the main stems back to within a half-inch of the ground during winter dormancy. Though it may take more than one season, rejuvenation produces spectacular results; in the year following rejuvenation, however, be attentive to mulching, fertilizing, watering, and weeding. With most larger tropicals, it's best to remove all main stems over a period of three to four years, cutting back the two or three oldest canes to the ground the first year, taking out another two or three of the old ones the year after, and so on.

Three techniques encourage heavy bloom. Root pruning is the practice of spading around the plant; it is rarely practiced by home gardeners. Deadheading is the removal of spent flowers shortly after the blossoms fade, conserves the energy that would normally be spent on fruit production; it is commonly practiced on tropical plants with profuse floral displays and nonornamental fruit, including dombeya, tabebuia, and ixora. Selective removal of old stems coupled with shortening and thinning of the remaining growth not only helps to maintain flowering tropical shrubs but also is the key to better yield in fruiting plants. It can be done at any time, but the best time is after flowering and fruiting. Winter-blooming shrubs that bloom on new wood, like brunfelsia, should be cut back to encourage branching. Pollarding (cutting off all of previous years' growth to the main trunk) works well on lagerstroemia.

Pruning to shape need not be daunting, especially if you practice it regularly. To prune an ornamental tropical shrub or tree, begin directly after planting by cutting out all dead, diseased, and weak wood. Then evaluate the branching structure and consider removing branches that overlap and rub, and those that form V-crotches that are likely to split apart; branches that have a crotch angle of less than 45° should usually be removed. Retain branch collars. Branch stubs can be sites of disease entry as they rot; remove at branch collar, but be careful not to cut into branch collar.

Shape formal hedges at least four times a year, informal hedges at least two times. Remove one- to two-thirds of the new growth at each pruning until the hedge nears mature size, then prune more severely. Hedges should be narrower at the top than at the base, so that adequate sunlight can reach the lower leaves.

To reduce a shrub's size without shearing, reach into the canopy and selectively prune branches back to a major limb, standing back from time to time to assess your progress. This method not only hides the cuts behind the remaining foliage but also gives the shrub a more open and natural appearance.

ROUTINE CARE

Weeding Rare is the gardener with an affection for weeds. Not only are they unsightly, but also they compete with desired plants for available water and nutrients. By their very nature, weeds are prolific and tenacious, and in the tropical garden they can be positively rampant. Few tropical gardens can be weed-free, but with a bit of knowledge and some assiduous elbow-bending, gardeners can maintain the upper hand. There are two approaches to weed control: chemical and manual. In home gardens, chemical controls are usually unnecessary and often hazardous—not just to the environment, but to the health of the garden itself. In the tropical garden, mulching is often the best way to reduce and control the ever-sprouting weeds. A good hoe, a cultivator, and a little exertion also provide effective weed control. The trick is to cultivate regularly and eliminate the weeds when small. Large, established weeds require a great deal of effort to remove and if allowed to go to seed provide an endless source of future aggravation.

Though rare, there are times when chemical controls are the only alternative. Perennial grasses with rampant root systems, for instance, can be particularly difficult to dislodge. Often the only practical method for ridding the garden of such stubborn interlopers is the application of a systemic nonselective herbicide containing glyphosate; these will kill anything that is green. Fortunately, these products are quickly degraded and have no residual effects.

Watering Water is becoming an increasingly precious resource, and restrictions on its use are already in force in many areas. It is therefore sensible when designing a garden to select plants that are adapted to grow with the moisture that nature provides. Nevertheless, some watering to help establish new plants or compensate for unexpected droughts is inevitable. Many tropical plants require large amounts of water, and many must have soil that is kept evenly moist at all times. If your area experiences a wet season or frequent heavy rainfalls, these moisture requirements may not be a problem. Otherwise, you may need to select plants that are drought-resistant once established or that appreciate a dry season of little or no growth.

The key is to water only when necessary, but then to do so very thoroughly. Frequent light sprinkling, especially in the evening, is a waste of water and often does more harm that good by encouraging the growth of shallow root systems and creating ideal conditions for the spread of disease. The frequency and quantity of irrigation will be determined by a number of factors, including soil characteristics, exposure, the type of plants being grown, and the time of year (wet or dry season).

You can apply water in a variety of ways, from a simple watering can to a fully automated time-controlled system. Most home gardeners opt for driplines, soakers, or an ordinary garden hose fitted with an overhead sprinkler. Each method has its relative advantages and disadvantages with respect to convenience, mainte-

When is the best time to prune? Whenever the pruners are sharp! Prune vines to remove obtrusive branches. To prune a small palm (bottom) cut off old fronds close to the trunk, being careful not to injure or tear the trunk, or to injure yourself on sharp spines.

VIEWPOINT

PEST CONTROL

Choosing proper sites for specific plants will cut down insect populations. For example, keeping brugmansia and other plants susceptible to red spider ants out of hot spots will keep them in check. Good air circulation and wise plant spacing is another good IPM practice–plants with continued insect problems should be moved and tried in other exposures and completely removed if insects are still a problem. We have no regular pest-control program because we don't want to hurt our butterflies; when necessary, we spot-treat for insects.
LINDA GAY, MERCER GARDENS, HUMBLE TEXAS

We garden to attract birds and butterflies, so we use an IPM system with spot treatments of problems only when necessary.
DOUGLAS WILLIAMS, MERCER GARDENS, HUMBLE TEXAS

Spray only when necessary! When plants are cared for properly–given proper nutrition and pH, full sun plant in full sun, shade plants in shade, adequate moisture–they rarely succumb to pests and diseases. Sharp streams of water will dislodge aphids, pyrethrum will work on most others.
ROBERT BOWDEN, HARRY P. LEU GARDENS, ORLANDO

The only regular program we use for pest control is on hibiscus, for mites and bud weevils.
KEITH WOOLLIAMS, WAIMEA FALLS PARK

We spot treat pest problems and have no regular spraying program. We advocate IPM for home gardeners.
DAVID BAR-ZVI, FAIRCHILD TROPICAL GARDENS

nance, and cost. Whatever your method, however, you can conserve water by: 1) watering only when necessary, 2) selecting plants that will thrive with the moisture nature provides, 3) using mulches over the soil, 4) watering in the early morning or evening and avoiding midday, when evaporation is greatest, and 5) collecting rainwater for future use. Automatic, timed lawn irrigation can be wasteful unless the system is sensitive to rainfall and shuts off when extra irrigation is unnecessary.

Mulch The practice of mulching—covering the soil with protective and sometimes decorative materials—is as old as horticulture itself. Indeed, the first mulcher was Mother Nature, who wisely devised a way to spread leaves and other plant litter across the forest floor, thus creating an insulating, nutrient-rich, biologically active "duff" layer between bare soil and the elements. Mulches help to conserve water, suppress weed growth, moderate soil temperature, reduce erosion, and, in the case of organic mulches, improve the soil structure and add nutrients as they decompose. In the tropical garden, mulches can be especially valuable. Most tropical plants want a soil that remains evenly moist, and mulch creates that condition. It also suppresses the weed growth that can be so rampant in warm weather and provides a continuing source of the nutrients needed by ever-growing tropical plants. Organic mulches also foster important microrhizal fungi which help certain plants flourish by assisting in the absorption of otherwise inaccessible nutrients.

The list of suitable mulches is virtually endless and includes such organic materials as wood chips, bark, and pine needles, as well as inorganic products like marble chips and pea gravel. Limestone gravels can raise soil pH, which can be detrimental to some species. Gardeners can also choose among several weed-barrier landscape fabrics; these are suitable as underlays for inorganic mulches but should be avoided if an organic mulch is being used, since they prevent much of the beneficial interaction that takes place between the decomposing mulch and the soil.

Just before applying the mulch, cultivate the surface of the soil to eliminate existing weeds and break up any hardpan that has built up. Two to four inches of mulch are usually adequate, but be careful not to pile the mulch around trunks or plant stems; this can lead to basal rotting. Mulches should remain light and porous; too heavy or compact a mulch can prevent water and air from reaching the plant's root system. Because organic mulches use nitrogen as they decompose, they can produce a temporary nitrogen deficiency in plants. You can avoid this problem by applying a light dressing of all-purpose garden fertilizer when you mulch. Mulch breaks down and disappears quickly in the tropical garden; a thick layer may be gone in four to five months, so be prepared to renew your organic mulch regularly.

Fertilizer Tropical plants grow fast and continuously, and organic matter in warm tropical soils break down swiftly; nutrients from both organic materials and manufactured fertilizers are absorbed by plants—and the atmosphere—quickly. Therefore, plants in a tropical garden benefit most from regular, moderate applications of natural or manufactured fertilizer about once a month during their periods of active growth to provide a steady supply of nutrients.

Fertilizers fall into one of two basic groups: organic and manufactured.

Organic fertilizers include such naturally occurring materials as compost and well-rotted manure; they have the advantage of being environmentally friendly and providing organic matter and microorganisms as well as nutrients, and they can generally be applied without fear of damaging plants. Unprocessed organic fertilizers, however, may contain weed seeds, can harbor disease, and have unknown nutrient value. To avoid these problems, choose pasteurized and tested manures and composts, available bagged at many nurseries and garden centers. Simply mulch your plants with these materials, or work them shallowly into the soil with a cultivator. Nearly all new plantings will benefit from a generous application of organic fertilizer or compost mixed directly into the planting hole.

Manufactured fertilizers can be granular or water-soluble. Their nutrient values are clearly stated on the label, with the percentages for nitrogen, phosphorus, and potassium listed in that order. A product marked 5-10-5, for example, contains 5 percent nitrogen, 10 percent phosphorus, and 5 percent potassium, with the remaining 70 percent nonnutrient filler. If trace elements like iron and sulfur are present, they will also be listed as percentages. Most manufactured fertilizers contain little organic matter and they must be used at recommended rates to avoid burning the plants. Work the recommended amount into the soil around your plants with a cultivator, being careful to keep the fertilizer away from direct contact with stems and leaves.

Because each plant responds individually to fertilization, only experience will show you what modifications may be necessary for your specific situations. Chapter 2, the Plant Selector, will guide you.

PROTECTION In many areas where tropical gardening is carried on, there come times when all seems to be at risk. Occasionally, a severe cold spell will affect some of the tropical and subtropical areas; and every few years a hurricane threatens (and sometimes arrives).

Panic is the least helpful reaction. Your plants are not helped by it and you only get to feel bad. It is totally unnecessary to panic.

If the freeze is of short duration, as it usually is, a surprising number of plants will come through relatively unscathed. A few will be noticeably damaged but in time will recover totally. A very few will die. These unfortunately tend to be our most cherished possessions in the garden. There are steps which are useful to take which will help you protect your garden.

Obviously the aim is to keep the plant from experiencing damaging conditions. With that goal in mind, here are some observations about subfreezing conditions and your garden.

Irrigation: The ground water temperatures (50° F or higher) are warm relative to the 32° F of ice. If you can keep ground water running over your plants until the freeze has passed, it can work to save everything. The grave danger on this is the possibility of water pressure drop or even loss due to power failure often caused by the greater demand for electricity at the most critical hours of the feeze. Water pumps often simply shut down, creating spectacular icicles and terrible damage caused by the ice weight and subsequent freezing. If you happen to have an independent water source and a generator to assure continuous operation of the water pump during the freeze, this might be a good option. You must wait until all danger of the freeze has passed before turning off the water. In the after-

HURRICANE PROTECTION

Your ability to protect your garden during a severe hurricane is limited. Since many areas where tropical plants can be grown are prone to hurricanes, it is important to plan for them before they happen, and to react properly after they strike.

The best planning is choosing plants with strong root systems and avoiding those with shallow brittle roots; hurricane palms are known for their ability to withstand winds. The treecanopy should be thinned sufficiently so wind can blow through it.

Before a storm, follow direction on general safety precautions. If possible, move to safety any items that are likely to cause damage. Don't try tying trees up; they're better off allowed to sway with the wind.

When the storm has passed, if water is available, hose down the garden to remove salt. Cover exposed roots and clean up debris. Then assess the damage calmly. Some trees will be destroyed and stumps will have to be removed eventually. Others can be righted or pruned to regain vigor. If you right fallen trees, water and fertilize them as if they were newly planted.

Remember that hurricanes are an important part of the ecosystem; they spread seed and remove weak plants. The tropical landscape would not be what it is if they did not play their part.

math it will probably be necessary to drench and spray with fungicides and bactericides to limit disease.

Heating: In limited areas it has sometimes been proven useful to try to heat up the air around the plants. Large grove heaters have been used for decades. They use kerosene as fuel and keep the air circulating so that frost does not settle. The effect in the immediate area around the heater can range from good to scorched disaster. Grove heaters are largely out of favor now because of their polluting effect on the environment; they are illegal in many areas. Burning tires during freezes, a common practice pre-EPA, is totally forbidden now. Electrical heaters or infrared heaters may be useful in very small spaces such as patios. Of course, they are useless if there is a power failure and can cause fires and short circuits. Using a barbecue pit or portable barbecue (hibachi) is not very useful and the carbon monoxide produced is harmful to plants and animals alike.

Covering and natural heat: A natural canopy of trees will often be sufficient protection for most plants by itself. In some cases, it is practical to cover exposed plants until the frost is gone. Use paper or cloth in preference to plastic and try to minimize any direct contact between plants and cover, if practical–frost damage may occur where covering touches plant. Large, potted specimens can be laid on their sides and covered with mats, paper, blankets or even staw or leaf litter. Plastic has its uses but can cause overheating unless removed in a timely fashion. The insulating with plastic requires air space over plants.

Prior to a freeze, the soil should be irrigated well, early in the day. The foliage should go into the cold period as dry as possible. Pulling back heavy layers of mulch will allow heat to be released from the soil.

After a freeze, don't be compulsive about removing dead foliage quickly. If there is more than one period of subfreezing temperatures during a severe cold spell, you will simply be exposing the undamaged foliage to damage. Also freeze damage might take a while to show itself. A plant that looks fine a few days after the freeze may start losing leaves after a week or so. Sunburn might be an unexpected consequence of a freeze due to canopy leaf drop. When all danger of freezing is only a memory, clean up should begin. Watch for signs of disease. Delightfully, many plants that look like goners will show renewed life if given time and care. "I have had several "dead" palms surprise me by pushing up a new spear from an apparently dead crown," says David Bar-Zvi. "Thank goodness I didn't discard them!"

TRAINING TROPICAL VINES There are nearly as many ways to grow a vine as there are vines themselves, and though most have a natural urge to clamber skyward, nearly all benefit from some initial training. Vines usually flower and fruit better when they are trained. The sooner you start the vine on its desired path, the sooner you achieve your goal. With the exception of those grown as groundcovers or used to soften the sides of containers, vines usually require a structure on which to start their clambering. Whether that structure is a trellis, pergola, wooden fence, latticework, or masonry wall depends largely on the vine's method of climbing. Plants like passiflora and gloriosa have slender tendrils that usually coil easily around string, wire, or the stems of other plants. Twiners like mandevilla, jade vine, and tecomanthe, on the other hand, send their stems around supports such as trellises and arbors. Clinging vines climb by rootlike holdfasts that attach

Where possible, twine and tie errant branches to their desired location. Tie into stable position until it creates its own frame. Here the vine is held in place by a strip of material (pantyhose) attached to thin rope. These are kept in place until the vine has developed enough to be held in place by its own weight.

themselves, with great stubbornness, to masonry or tree bark. Finally, there are procumbent vines, like allamanda, and vinelike plants, like bougainvillea, that will not clamber upwards at all unless planted very close to or anchored directly to a support. However, these vines are effective in softening containers or the sides of raised beds.

For twiners, the best structures have horizontal crossbars, placed at 8- to 12-inch intervals, to help support the vine's weight and relieve stress on the anchored branches. They are also helpful in training stems in a horizontal fashion, which is beneficial in developing a visual screen. Structures include trellises, crisscrossed wires, and fences. Aluminum and plastic trellises offer the advantage of low maintenance, and some are even adjustable, expanding, accordionlike, either horizontally or vertically. Wood has an undeniable aesthetic appeal, especially if the vine has an open habit, but in the interest of upkeep, choose a decay-resistant variety like cedar or redwood and if possible leave the wood unpainted. (You can extend the life of the wood with a clear sealer or colored sealer stain, but remember that the color will fade, and it will be difficult to restain the wood after a perennial vine is established on it.) For wire supports, the best choice is thin stereo speaker wire, or you can use thin-gauge plastic-coated electrical wire, which comes in a variety of colors (the darker the better), and it won't heat up like bare metal.

To encourage the vine to climb, you'll need to secure it occasionally to the support (once every week or two during the early season of growth is a good rule of thumb). For tying, any stringlike material—preferably green, for the purpose of camouflage—will do, as will bread-wrapper twist-ties, but don't tie them too tightly or leave them on for more than a season, since the wire inside can do damage to the expanding vine. If you're training the vine to a wooden fence, you can thread the string through nonrusting cup hooks (C-shaped hooks mounted on screws available at most hardware stores). Or you can add matching horizontal wooden lattice boards for support.

To train a vine to grow up the sides of a pergola or arbor, you can simply use galvanized nails 12-18 inches apart (depending on the vine; add more nails if you think they're necessary) and/or strings that match the color of the structure attached with nails or wrapped around the boards. On white stone pillars, clear fishing line is very effective, since it is virtually invisible. Another approach is to wrap the posts with a thin strip of wire or plastic netting or, for twining vines, to stretch three or four single wires from top to bottom spaced about 6-12 inches apart. Avoid expanded metal, since it cuts down on air circulation, which is essential for keeping the vine cool and for dissipating fragrance.

Though many climbing vines are relentless ascenders, nearly all benefit from some initial training, especially to keep them in aesthetic bounds. For brick and limestone structures, there are brick- or limestone-colored hooks, equipped with wires for loosely twisting around the vine's stems. These attach with heavy-duty glue or resin (don't twist the wires too tightly, since they have a tendency to break).

PEST AND DISEASE MANAGEMENT The best time to begin a program of pest management is before you plant. Carefully sited, well-tended plants require a minimum of intervention; weak or stressed plants, however, will be predisposed to the ravages of opportunistic insects and diseases. In fact, a whole host of horticultural

VIEWPOINT
TRAINING VINES

I use 35-50 pound-test fishing line. It will train the limbs/stems to go where you want, but even from a few feet away, you can't see it. Tie it to the base of the plant and use small nails to anchor the other end. It's like magic!
ROBERT BOWDEN, LEU BOTANICAL GARDENS

We plant vines at the bases of native trees (oaks, pines, yaupons) and allow them to climb. Initial training is sometimes done with fishing wire. We've also allowed vines to climb trellises attached to brick walls with mortar nails and stainless steel wire.
LINDA GAY, MERCER ARBORETUM, HUMBLE, TEXAS

I prefer vines planted at the bases of structures such as arbors and poles so that their flowers, leaves, and other interesting features can be seen.
DOUGLAS WILLIAMS, MERCER ARBORETUM, HUMBLE TEXAS

Our vines are tied with single wire, waxed string, or Kwikstem tie. or trained through chicken wire. We try to encourage vines to grow up trees and guide them to the first branches.
KEITH WOOLLIAMS, WAIMEA FALLS PARK

Often, pests must be captured with traps to diagnose the problems they've caused.

disorders are caused not by living organisms but by poor cultural practices or environmental problems. Known as physiogenic diseases, these disorders commonly result from winter injury, poor drainage, air pollution, road salt, nutritional deficiencies, mechanical injuries, improper application of herbicides—even lightning and strong winds. Their symptoms—including stunted growth, yellowing or spotted leaves, and twisted stems—often resemble those of organically afflicted plants. The good news for gardeners is that, once identified, these physiogenic diseases can usually be corrected, or at least accommodated.

To keep organic pests and diseases at a minimum, begin by practicing proper hygiene; a clean garden is usually a healthy garden. Fallen leaves, weeds, and other litter are more than just unsightly; they provide the perfect breeding ground for disease. Of course, given the daunting list of potential pests (which includes insects, mites, fungi, bacteria, viruses, and, of course, mammals), even the most carefully tended plant can succumb. To detect problems at an early, manageable stage, you'll need to monitor the garden on a regular basis, remembering that pests and diseases—like weeds—can proliferate at a positively alarming rate in warm tropical conditions. Make it a habit to stroll through the yard weekly, carefully examining plants for signs of trouble; don't forget to check the undersides of leaves, where pests and diseases often hide. Many insects, including aphids, beetles, scales, and caterpillars, are easy to spot, but you'll need a magnifying glass to detect smaller pests like mites and thrips. Borers and leafminers, which spend most of their life cycle inside stems and leaves, are difficult to see, but the damage they cause if obvious. Keep a record of the trouble you encounter. With experience, it's possible to anticipate problems on specific host plants. Carefully inspect plants you are considering purchasing to be sure you do not introduce new pests or diseases into your garden via your new acquisition.

Some insects can do serious, life-threatening damage to plants, while others are simply unsightly. Every gardener has to determine for himself or herself an appropriate and tolerable level of infestation. When control is deemed necessary, you have a number of choices, including soaps, oils, synthetic chemicals, and hand-picking. Whatever the product you select, it's essential to follow label instructions carefully, both to ensure the method's efficacy and to protect the health of the plant and the environment. One of the most promising new areas of insect management is biological control, which enlists the services of natural predators like parasites, diseases, and other insects. (Ladybugs, for example, prove to be voracious aficionados of the aphid.) In controlled environments like greenhouses, these natural methods have proven highly successful; their efficacy in the backyard is still haphazard, though, since they tend to have date-limited applications.

Soft-bodied insects such as aphids, caterpillars, and slugs can be kept controlled with the use of diatomaceous earth, which is made from the ground skeletons of small fossilized animals. When spread around the plants, it forms a sharp barrier that will cut the bodies of the insects and cause them to die from dehydration. Diatomaceous earth can be expensive, but it is easily available from nurseries or from swimming pool suppliers (it is used in swimming pool filters).

In smaller gardens, it is possible to control certain insects by hand-picking or crushing them while wearing cotton gloves so as not to damage the plant. Slugs are easy to pick off, on a damp summer night, and aphids can be easily crushed by hand. Shallow trays of stale beer will attract and kill slugs. Aphids can be syringed off plants with a heavy stream of water controlled by placing your thumb over the end of a hose, and a light, frequent syringing will also help control red spider mites, which do not like water. For a very bad infestation of aphids, spray insecticidal soap onto the aphids by hand or with a small sprayer.

Scale is an insect that forms a usually brown hemispherical dome around itself. At first, this little dome is very soft; on a mature insect, it is very hard. A bad scale infestation is very difficult to get rid of, so the best protection is to catch it at an early stage when it can be wiped off or sprayed off with a strong stream of water. If necessary, spray with dormant or horticultural oil , a light oil that doesn't kill foliage but will suffocate the scale.

Mealybugs are small, soft-bodied insects covered with white, woolly, waxy filaments. Small infestations can be removed with a cotton swab. For larger infestations, dislodge the colony by scraping off or spraying with a strong stream of water. Then dab (bugs, not leaves) with a 50:50 methyl alcohol and water solution, or use a soft soap spray.

Nematodes are virtually impossible to control. These microscopic worms attack roots, causing them to appear stubby, knotted, or covered with lesions (leaves are sometimes a target as well). The roots soon lose their ability to function effectively, which results in wilted or stunted growth in leaves and stems. Alas, nematodes are very difficult to detect, and infected plants must be removed and burned or discarded. Since many nematodes are soil-borne, it's unwise to place susceptible plants in the same location. Mulching helps to lessen nematode infestation.

Fungal disease are among the most common in the garden, affecting leaves, stems, flowers, and roots. Spread by spores borne on air currents, water, or gardening tools, they can cause wilting, cankers, lesions, galls, blights, and leaf spots. Fungal infection is highly plant-specific and weather-dependent, spread generally during warm, wet, humid conditions. The most effective way to control fungi in the garden is to plant new resistant cultivars. If this isn't possible—or if your garden is established—you can prevent many fungal infections by keeping both garden and gardening tools as clean as possible. Prune plants regularly to maintain effective air circulation, and never water in the late afternoon or evening. If a plant does become infected, the application of fungicides may be your only recourse. Preventive in nature rather than curative, fungicides will protect uninfected tissue but do nothing to restore areas already penetrated by the fungi. You must therefore be vigilant and apply fungicide at the first hint of infection. Repeat applications are usually necessary during the growing season to protect new growth and replenish whatever fungicide has been depleted by rain.

Often spread by insects or gardening tools, bacteria are microscopic organisms that can cause foul-smelling rots, wilted or scorched leaves, and galls. Given the right conditions, they multiply and spread at a prodigious rate. Because no chemical controls exist, you can fight bacterial infections only indirectly, controlling possible insect vectors, removing and destroying infected plants, and replanting resistant cultivars.

Above: Yellowed and deformed leaves caused by two-spotted leafhoppers. *Top:* Browning caused by too much heat.

TROPICALS IN COOL CLIMATES

The desire to grow what one can't, or or least shouldn't, given climatic restraints of northern areas, is surely part of the gardener's nature. It is hard to avoid the temptation of the lush, encompassing feeling creating by the grand textures that tropicals or near tropicals provide. Certainly, many tricks are used to extend the range and usefulness of tropical plants. Temporary structure for winter protection (or wrapping banana trunks, which makes them hardy in the Atlanta area), planting in favorable microclimates (a bird of paradise will survive in Zone 8 if planted in a protected site), and use of tropicals as summer annuals are a few. Moreover, exploration in the the wild and garden selection continue to find hardier varieties. Many tropical plants have a natural range of some distance in latitude and/or elevation and hardiness can vary within each genus, or even within the cultivars of a species. Tropical-looking plants from subtropical or warm temperate regions are also coming into play, some with large, exotic-looking foliage or flowers as well as the advantage of some degree of frost resistance.

Cold is not the only factor; lack of summer heat and moisture, short days, and short summers also affect tropical plants. See pages 24-26 for more information.

Favorite plants—or those providing that irreplaceable touch to the garden too tender to stand a chance past Thanksgiving—can often be lifted whole and grown in a hothouse or stored in a garage or basement that doesn't freeze. The latter

This Bronx, New York, garden, takes on a tropical look during summer when indoor plants like alocasia, crotons, and dracaena are brought outdoors (after being hardened off, see page 213). Before the approach of winter, they are lifted and, after a period of acclimatization, brought indoors and kept in a sunny, humid room. These tropicals are mixed with *Hibiscus rosa-sinensis,* which is treated as an annual and allowed to die at the end of the summer, and hardy perennial foliage plants like euonymus and pachysandra.

works best for plants able to become dry and dormant in a place that's usually rather dark. Methods abound and range from burying in sawdust to hanging plants from the rafters but the object is to put the plant into limbo. Easiest is lifting the plant whole, shaking off only some loose soil, and placing into a temporary container with any exposed roots covered with a loose potting mix. The root mass should be kept on the dry side with only a dribble of water to prevent complete dehydration. Tender fuschias, any pelargoniums (geraniums), colocasias, alocasias, and other tuberous plants, abutilon (flowering maple), tender succulents, and tree ferns respond well to this treatment. Palms and some other tender species can be planted in containers, then brought indoors. A more decadent tactic is to use plants knowing they will last only one season.

The real challenge is in devising ways to bring the "almost" hardy favorites through the winter or a rare hard freeze. Of course, every species has its limits, so research is a good first step, especially with costly specimens or with plants that will be using valuable spots in the gardens. Once the decision is made, the level of protection needed must be translated into reality, taking into account that the sun is in the southern sky in North America and the south side of a wall usually retains the most heat. Protection from occasional cold wind is most important; in the Northwest, this means the east winds that carry cold, dry air from eastern deserts. On the east coast, continental air comes from the west and north, so the opposite can be assumed. One advantage of a south and west exposure however, is the reduced chance of frost damage from early morning sun on frozen foliage. Building a winter structure is also more efficient against a south wall. A covering of clear fiberglass or plastic increases the temperature by several degrees on sunny days and keeps frost, wind, and excess moisture away. It is usually best if no foliage touches the covering and a vent is included to prevent inadvertent "nuking" during a warm spell. Overhead protection–eaves or evergreens–helps too.

Mulching around the bases of woody and herbaceous plants with any lightweight material will normally keep the soil underneath from freezing to any depth and protect buds and tender stems. Some wait until later fall to mulch so that the ground is allowed to chill sooner., sending plants into a deeper sleep. Some rosette-forming plants (e.g. cabbage palm) can be tied up tight during cold weather to prevent wind damage and water entering the rosettes and freezing.

Finally, of great use to gardeners in temperate climates is the surprisingly large array of subtropical and tropical-looking species that have been proven, or are potentially, reliable garden subjects. Some have come through Portland's coldest USDA-Zone-8 winter. Many of these are from warm temperate rather than truly tropical climes, but that's just a technicality: they provide the same effect. Selections of tropicals such as oleander, banksia, gardenia, and pittosporum are much hardier than typical and have survived temperatures in the teens or even lower. In some cases, tender plants are hybridized with hardier genera, for example trifoliate orange with citrus.

Some things are impossible, even to the most intrepid gardener. But we will never know until we try. There are heliconias from higher elevations that might survive winter in a protected area in San Francisco; many palms do beautifully in coastal regions of the Pacific Northwest; bananas are seen in Louisiana and Atlanta. If you're willing to take chances, and to work a little, you might be the one to push the range of your favorite plant into your zone.

SEAN HOGAN, PORTLAND, OREGON

Above: Eriobotrya japonica, loquat, has tropical-looking foliage and sweet fruit; it is also hardy as far north as Washington, D.C. and throughout the Pacific Northwest west of the Cascades, at least as far north as Portland. A few of the many plants that can be used in some Zone-8 regions:

• *Raphidophyllum hystrix* (needle palm, from southeastern U.S.

• *Trachycarpus fortunei* (Chinese windmill palm)

• *Phormium tenax* (New Zealand flax)

• Yuccas, including many species considered tender

• *Dasylirion wheeleri* (desert spoon)

• Colocasias (taro)

• *Tetrapanax papyriferus* (rice paper plant)

Bamboos

• *Eucalyptus* species, including *E. niphophila, E. gunnii, E. periniana*

• *Hedychium greenii* and other gingers

• Citrus (usually hybrids with trifoliate oranges)

• *Feijoa sellowiana* (pineapple guava)

• *Cinnamomum chekiangensis,* a beautiful and hardy small tree

• *Musa basjoo,* a hardy banana grown as far north as Vancouver, B.C. and treated much like a canna; the ten-foot leaves die at first hard frost then sprout from the base when the weather warms.

Many tropical foliage plants thrive indoors, achieving impressive size under normal living conditions. *Above:* aucuba, dracaena, dieffenbachia, calathea.

TROPICALS INDOORS

In areas where tropical plants cannot be grown outdoors, they can enhance our indoor environment with varying shades and textures of foliage and colorful, fragrant flowers. The plants that can be grown successfully indoors are those whose native habitat resembles the conditions of common indoor settings and which show extreme tolerance and adaptability to varying light and temperature. Although plants have not evolved specifically to survive under indoor conditions, their physical characteristics allow many to survive, adapt and even thrive indoors. Origin and habitat are indicators for determining a plant's ideal growing situation. Almost every type of natural ecosystem in the world has a specific plant community perfectly adapted to it. Time and evolution dispersed plants into areas according to their ability to grow in the temperature, light, soil, humidity, and moisture available at each physical site. These five limiting factors are the basis of a plant's ability to survive in any location. Generally, plants of tropical or subtropical habitats are best suited to indoor growing since these environments do not have the extremes found in temperate regions.

Indoor gardening shares basic similarities with outdoor gardening in regard to basic plant growth and response to light, humidity, temperature, and water. However, indoor gardening involves artificial manipulation of conditions rather than gardening according to nature's whims of rain, sun, and wind. This allows the gardener to enhance the growing conditions by changing them as necessary, although there are built-in limitations, particularly concerning light. At the highest technical level, full-scale greenhouses with computer controls can recreate nearly any growing environment. It is impossible to recreate the intricacies of a complete ecosystem, but in many cases we can mimic the basic growing conditions in order to grow a plant out of its habitat.

In the average home, some conditions can be manipulated, but a smart gardener will evaluate the existing conditions and select plants accordingly. Although the environment can be changed somewhat, long-term success depends on selecting the right plant for a specific location instead of trying to adapt the indoor site to the needs of the plant. The result of poor choice is often a pathetic looking plant under constant stress, a situation that is frustrating to the gardener and a struggle for the plant. Indoor plants must have the right growing medium and light, water, and nourishment levels. The variation and manipulation of all these elements will dictate whether a plant will thrive, merely survive, or fail.

In most homes, plants share regular living spaces, usually in the area with the most light, namely, the windowsill. There are many tropical plants that will thrive on a sunny windowsill in high light–usually from the south–or even one with that gets only medium (east or west) or low light (north). Humidity is usually a key factor, but many plants can tolerate the humidity levels comfortable for humans. Among the tropical plants that can be grown in high light are bromeliads like aechmea, gusmania, and billbergia, begonias, citrus, palms and cycads, hibiscus, ixora, oleander, ponytail palm, pittosporum, and staghorn ferns. In medium light, try anthuriums, aphelandra, asparagus ferns, crotons and ti plants, dieffenbachia, fishtail, areca, and kentia palms, cattleya orchids, peperomia, rhoeo, as well as many varieties of ficus plants. In low light, you'll do well with Chinese evergreen, calathea, dracaenas, pothos, monstera, some ficuses, and rhapis palm.

The ultimate tropical plants, orchids, also are fairly easy to grow indoors, contrary to popular opinion.

Although it is certainly possible to achieve a lush, sophisticated and textured garden indoors without creating special structures, the plants will not look the same as those grown outdoors; they will probably be much smaller and flower less profusely. Today, many people are building or modifyng rooms specially for their plants—glass-houses, greenhouses, conservatories, and sunrooms in which conditions can be adjusted to duplicate outdoor conditions more closely and, in some cases, to allow plants to be set in-ground where their roots can spread more readily. In these structures, humidity and light levels can be controlled fully; the atmosphere does not have to be comfortable for humans. In conservatories at botanic gardens and some mansions, palms have grown to 80 feet tall, vines drape for yards and yards, and the lush texture of the tropics is created. Thousands of plants from rare orchids to hundreds of species of palms, flowering shrubs, and foliage plants that would remain compact and relatively unimpressive are spectacular under these conditions. A gardener can start small, with a small area of a sunporch closed off or glassed-in and a misting system with remarkable effect. Gardeners are learning that this exciting way of gardening is not only for the fabulously wealthy.

Moving plants outdoors for the summer can sometimes be beneficial for both plant and gardener. Plants often can be revived and brought back into full health by summering outdoors and provide exotic accents on decks and patios as long as they are properly hardened and cared for. Some plants, such as gardenia and hibiscus, should be moved outdoors in summer where they will receive enough light to signal the plant to flower. A plant being moved outdoors must be toughened up—hardened off—to avoid damage by wind, sun, and temperature fluctuations. Acclimatization is a gradual process that allows a plant to adapt and toughen, avoiding the damage of an abrupt move.

STEPS TO HARDEN A PLANT BEFORE TAKING IT OUTDOORS

1. Learn the needs of the plant being moved outdoors. For example, spathiphyllum, a low-light plant, will suffer in high light outdoors, regardless of how gradually you move it.
2. Select three or four locations with increasing amounts of light and decreasing amounts of protection. Move the plant to the lowest light and most highly protected situation for one to two weeks. Then move it to the next location. Look for situations that are brightly lighted but not in direct sun; protected from wind, such as an open garage or carport, under a large dense tree, under an arbor or in a shrub border.
3. Water the plant well before moving—moisture levels fluctuate rapidly outdoors and can result in drought stress if a plant is not carefully monitored. Also, water-stressed plants are more susceptible to sunburn and wind damage.
4. Cover or move plants if night temperatures are predicted to drop below 40° F—a plant may be able to tolerate more temperature extremes after it is adjusted to its outdoor spot, but when first moved out of its 65-75° F house it is extremely vulnerable to temperature change.
5. Gradually move plant into its final position and increase the amount of time in that spot every couple of days. Choose the final position according to a plant's light requirements, keeping in mind that a houseplant that does well in high light may not be suited to the intensity of direct sun. Most plants grow best in filtered sun, such as under the open canopy of a shade tree, on a patio with morning sun and afternoon shade, or under a gazebo or arbor.
6. Monitor the plant carefully, particularly for water—plants dry out much more quickly outdoors.

Above: Euphorbia millii.
Top: Agave patoni.

DRY CLIMATE PLANTS FOR THE TROPICAL GARDEN

A large group of plants that are useful for tropical gardens are native to very different conditions. Many dry climate plants—specifically cacti and other succulent plants that have adapted to their environment by developing structures that store water—blend beautifully with tropicals and often thrive under similar conditions. A succulent plant is one with thickened, fleshy leaves, stems, and/or roots; most are native to desert areas, but some come from forests and seashores. Succulence is usually a storage adaptation of plants that have evolved in situations where fresh water must be conserved—from a desert rainfall that may not reach 5 inches per year to a seashore where available water is saline, to the canopy of a tropical rainforest where epiphytes such as orchids, bromeliads, some cacti, peperomia and others must grow using only the water they may capture as rain runs down the tree branches.

Although availability of water is not a problem in most tropical areas, planting a garden of plants that do not need to be constantly moist has many advantages. Most desert plants are remarkably easy to care for; you can ignore an unplanted aloe plant for months (though we don't recommend it) and it will grow beautifully once it's in the ground. In times when rainfall is scarce, dry-climate plants are a boon; they will use their stored moisture when more typical tropicals require daily watering. Succulents add a very different, sculptural quality to a tropical garden, often constrasting strikingly with palms and flowering tropical trees and shrubs.

Few gardens in the tropics feature large plantings of mammoth cacti like golden barrels or old man cactus (though these plants do well in the dry garden at Fairchild Tropical Garden). Usually, smaller and less spiney plants are chosen. Some of the most common desert plants and succulents for tropical gardens are:

Adenium (desert rose) is either a low, grarled shrub or small succulent-stemmed tree that produces pale pink to cherry red, funnel-shaped flowers. Zone 10, Zone 9 with protection. It is often used in containers.

Agave (century plant) is an outstanding landscape feature, growing in sprawling rosettes that form large clumps, sometimes with strikingly variegated leaves and inflorescences. They are easy to find and easy to grow. Zones 9-10.

Aloe, source of a very effective skin lotion, also forms rosettes of succulent foliage; flowers can be extraordinarily large and unusual. Zones 9-10.

Euphorbia Several euphorbia species are common in the tropics, including the spiny crown of thorns (*E. millii*). Handle with care; they exude a toxic latex.

Kalanchoe Flowering forms of this plant, like *K. blossfeldiana,* popular in the Southwest, are useful in the tropics as well. Zones 9-10.

Lampranthus and other iceplants flower profusely with vividly colored daisylike flowers. They often flower on and off all year. Zones 9-10, sometimes Zone 8.

Yucca (Spanish bayonet) is a tall upright plant with sharp pointed leaves. Some species are hardy to Zone 6.

All these plants do well in full sun, though they appreciate a bit of filtered shade during the hottest part of the day. Most don't want to stay in very wet areas, though they do grow faster and more lushly if the ground is kept moderately moist and fertile. In other words, normal watering and fertilizing for other plants in your garden won't disturb them. Many of these plants are armed with sharp spines and thorns; be sure not to plant them where they might cause harm or make moving about difficult.

TROPICALS PLANTS FOR DRY CLIMATES

Many areas of the Southwest can support tropical plants' need for long, warm summers and freedom from frost. However, many tropical plants also need constant moisture and that is more difficult in the desert areas of the Southwest. During times of drought, and even when rainfall is higher than usual, most tropicals need additional watering to look their best in the Southwest.

For gardeners who practice xeriscape gardening, using plants that will, in normal seasons, require heavy irrigation is unacceptable. Xeriscaping–the word *xero* is Greek for dry–is a form of gardening established by the water department there during a drought. It promotes the following water-conserving practices:

Proper planning, to avoid inefficient use of water;

Efficient methods of irrigation;

Limiting grassy areas, and using groundcovers or grasses that are less thirsty;

Improving soil so that it retains water as much as possible;

Mulching to further retain moisture;

Using drought-tolerant plants;

Maintaining the garden so that plants can grow without being hampered by unsanitary conditions or pests and diseases.

A proper xeriscape garden takes it environment into account; since natural rainfall if markedly different in Pennsylvania than it is in Arizona, a plant that would be considered excellent in Philadelphia would be unacceptable in Tucson. Water conservation is a factor in tropical areas of the United States as well; overuse of water is wasteful no matter where it takes place. Xeriscaping and use of drought-tolerant plants is wise everywhere.

Fortunately, many tropical plants are also drought tolerant; they can withstand fairly long periods of little rainfall without harm to the plant. These plants are useful in dry climates as well as in those with greater amounts of rain.

A lush, tropical look can be achieved without copious watering. Even in Arizona, plants like bougainvillaea, antigonon, caesalpinia, and oleander flower abundantly without additional watering. Mixing these plants with more common desert trees and shrubs, like creosote and mesquite (which almost never need water) provides a sense of place without losing any of the advantages of the tropics. If a gardener wishes to include a few spectacular exotics, they can be planted close together, apart from plants that need less water. This will allow the water they need to be used only in a limited space.

DROUGHT-TOLERANT TROPICALS

Bauhinia x *blakeana*
Bougainvillea species
Bulnesia arborea
Bursera simaruba
Caesalpinia species
Cassia species
Cordia boisseri
Crescentia alata
Delonix regia
Erythrina crista-galli
Eucalyptus species
Eugenia species
Guaiacum
Jacaranda mimosifolia
Manilkara zapota
Pandanus species
Plumeria rubra
Tabebuia species

ORGANIC GARDENING

Few gardeners today are unaware of the devastating effect pesticides and other chemicals used in the past have had on our environment. Rachel Carson's searing exploration of the subject, *Silent Spring* (1962), exposed the "needless havoc" wrought by products designed to promote healthy plants. Not only were the chemicals poisoning our environment, they were also killing the natural predators of the pests we were seeking to destroy, making it impossible for nature to come to its own defense.

In the past few decades a vast and successful effort has been made to find new ways to garden without using harmful chemicals. The approach is directed at the soil and at the measures taken to control pests.

The soil is built up through the addition of organic materials, especially compost. The addition of compost, homemade or store-bought, and other organic material such as peat moss, green cover crops, and bone meal makes the soil so fertile and productive that petrochemicals are not needed.

Pest problems are handled through a practice called Integrated Pest Management (IPM), developed by the Council on Environmental Quality. IPM is defined as "maximum use of naturally occurring pest controls, including weather, disease agents, predators, and parasitoids. In addition, IPM utilizes various biological, physical, chemical controls and habitat modification techniques. Artificial controls are imposed only as required to keep a pest from surpassing tolerable population as determined from accurate assessments of the pest damage potential and the ecological, sociological, and economic costs of the control measures." In other words, gardeners must make reasonable assessments of how much damage a particular pest will do. If the pest is just munching on foliage, let it be. If controls must be taken, nonharmful ones should be tried first. Only in extreme cases is chemical warfare waged–and then in the most nonharmful ways possible.

The weapons in the IPM arsenal include:

•Careful monitoring to identify problems before they become widespread.

•Beneficial insects, such as ladybugs, praying mantises, and some nematodes, which feed on garden pests. Some of these reside naturally in your garden; others can be bought and placed there.

•Bacteria such as Bt (*Bacillus thuringiensis*) that attack garden pests. These bacteria can be bought by the pound and dusted on the plants; strains have been discovered that breed and attack many common pests.

•Insecticides such as rotenone, pyrethrum, and sabadilla and insecticidal soaps.

•Pest-repellent plants such as marigolds, which is reputed to repel bean beetles and nematodes, and garlic, which repels whitefly.

•Hand-picking pests off foliage wherever they are seen in small numbers.

See pages 206-07 for more information about pest control.

ENABLING GARDENS

Being forced to stop gardening is one of the worst fates that can befall a gardener, but the inability to get down on one's hands and knees owing to arthritis, a bad back, a heart problem, the need to use a wheelchair—or the normal aches, pains, and fatigues of advancing age—is no reason to stop gardening. By using a few different gardening techniques, modifying tools, following new criteria in plant selection, and tapping into the many resources for information and help, no one ever has to stop gardening.

Begin by thoroughly and frankly assessing your situation.
- How much time can you devote to gardening?
- Do you need crutches, a cane, or wheelchair to get around?
- Can you get up and down from the ground without assistance?
- How much sun or heat is wise for you?
- Can you bend at the waist easily?
- Is your coordination impaired? balance? vision? ability to hold tools?

Consult your doctor, occupational or physical therapist, and most importantly speak to a horticultural therapist.

Horticultural therapists are specially trained in applying horticulture in therapeutic programs for people with disabilities and older adults. They have developed specialized gardening tools and techniques that make gardening easier for every situation.

Once you've decided how much you can and want to do, the garden can be planned. For example, people with relatively severe mobility impairments should have firm, level surfaces an easy distance from the house and should use containers or raised beds to bring soil up to a comfortable working height—usually somewhere around 2 feet high with a maximum width of 30 inches if worked from one side and 60 inches if both sides of the container or bed are accessible. People with more mobility can work with easily worked, light soils mounded to 8-10 inches above grade and should use lightweight, long-handled tools. Smaller containers can be hung within easy reach on poles or fences, and an overhead structure can be used to support hanging baskets on ropes and pulleys so the baskets can be lowered for care and then replaced to an out-of-reach position.

Important considerations when planning the garden layout include:
- Start small: keep it manageable
- Use or create light, easily worked soils so less force is required to work them either by hand or with tools
- Keep all equipment and tools in accessible places
- Arrange for a nearby water source—soaker hose or drip irrigation, perhaps—to minimize the difficulties in watering
- Use mulches to cut down on weeding

SOME SOURCES

American Horticultural Therapy Association
 362A Christopher Avenue, Gaithersburg, Maryland 20879
800-634-1603

Canadian Horticultural Therapy Association
c/o Royal Botanical Garden
PO Box 399, Hamilton, Ontario, Canada, L8N 3H8
416-529-7618

Acid soil: Soil with a pH level below 7

Alkaline soil: Soil with a pH level above 7

Annual: A plant whose life cycle comprises a single growing season

Anther: The part of a flower that bears pollen

Axil: The angle formed by a stem and a leaf stalk

Balled-and-burlapped: Describing a plant that is ready for transplanting, with a burlap-wrapped soil ball around its roots

Bare-root: Describing a plant that is ready for transplanting, with no protective soil or burlap covering around its roots

Bipinnate: Having leaflets that are divided into second leaflets

Bract: A modified leaf below a flower, often showy, as in dogwood

Calcaceous: Containing calcium or calcium carbonate (lime), as soil

Cane: A long, often supple, woody stem

Capsule: A dry fruit having more than one cell

Catkin: A long flower cluster comprised of closely spaced, generally small flowers and prominent bracts, as in pussy willows

Chlorosis: A yellowing of the leaves, reflecting a deficiency of chlorophyll

Clay soil: A soil, usually heavy and poorly drained, containing a preponderance of fine particles

Clone: Vegatative produced plants from a single parent plant; clones will not grow true from seed

Columnar: Growing in the shape of column, not spreading

Compost: Decomposed organic matter, usually used to enrich the soil

Container-grown: Grown as a seedling in the container it is to be sold in

Corymb: A flat-topped flower cluster in which flowers open successively from the outside in

Cross-pollination: The transfer of pollen from one plant to another

Cultivar: A variety of plant produced by selective hybridization

Cultivate: To work the soil in order to break it up and/or remove weeds

Cutting: A severed plant stem, usually used for the purposes of propagation

Deadhead: To remove spent blossoms

Deciduous: Losing its leaves at the end of the growing season; nonevergreen

Dicot, Dictotyledon: A plant that bears two or more seed leaves (cotyledons). Most seed plants and most woody plants are cotyledons. See also *Monocotyledon.*

Dieback: Death of part or all of the woody portion of a plant

Dioecious: Having both male and female flowers

Division: The removal of suckers from a parent plant, for the purposes of propagation

Double: In flowers, having an increased number of petals, produced at the expense of other organs

Drupe: A fruit with a fleshy covering over a hard-coated seed

Epiphyte: A plant that grows on another plant rather than in soil; "air plants"

Evergreen: Retaining foliage year-round

Exfoliate: To self-peel, as bark

Fertile: Having the capacity to generate seed

Friable: Ready for cultivation, easily cultivable, as soil

Genus: A group of related species

Germinate: To develop a young plant from seed; to produce a seedling

Glaucous: Blue-hued; covered with a bluish or grayish bloom

Graft: To insert a section of one plant, usually a shoot, into another so that they grow together into a single plant

Habit: A plant's characteristic form of growth

Harden off: To mature sufficiently to withstand winter temperatures

Hardpan: Soil sufficiently clogged with clay or other particles that draining is impossible

Hardwood cutting: Cutting taken from a mature woody stem for the purpose of propagation

Hardy: Able to withstand winter temperatures

Herbaceous: Without woody tissue

Humus: Soil composed of decaying organic matter

Hybrid: A plant produced by crossing two unlike parents

Insecticidal soap: Soap formulated to kill, repel, or inhibit the growth of insect pests

Integrated pest management (IPM): A philosphy of pest management based on the idea of using escalating methods of pest control, beginning with the least damaging; incorporates the selection of resistant varieties, the use of biological and nontoxic controls, and the application of pesticides and herbicides only when absolutely necessary

Invasive: Tending to spread freely and wantonly; weedy

Leaf mold: A form of humus composed of decayed leaves, often used to enrich soil

Leaflets: the parts of a compound leaf

Liana: A fast-growing woody vine; most lianas are tropical

Lime: Calcium carbonate, often added to the soil to reduce acidity

Loam: A generally fertile and well-drained soil, usually containing a significant amount of decomposed organic matter

Lobed: Divided into segments

Microclimate: Climate specific to a small area; may vary significantly from that of surrounding areas

Monocot, Monocotyledon: a plant bearing only one seed leaf (cotyledon), and usually producing little woody tissue. Few, with the exception of palms, become tall trees. Examples of monocots are grasses, lilies, aroids, bromeliads, irises, cannas, and sedges.

Monopodial: Producing indefinite growth and elongation of the stem or rhizome, usually unbranched. Vanda and phalaenopsis orchids are monopodial.

Mulch: An organic or inorganic soil covering, used to maintain soil temperature and moisture and to discourage the growth of weeds

Naturalize: To "escape" from a garden setting and become established in the wild

Neutral soil: Soil having a pH of 7—neither acid nor alkaline

Node: On a plant, the site at which the leaf joins the stem; the area where most rooting activity takes place.

Panicle: A branched raceme

Peat moss: Partially decomposed sphagnum moss, often added to soil to increase moisture retention

Pendulous: Hanging down, drooping (also pendant)

Perennial: A plant that lives for more than one growing season (usually at least three)

Perfect: Having stamens and pistils; bisexual, as a flower

Petal: Part of a flower's corolla, outside of the stamens and pistils, often vividly colored

pH: An expression of soil alkalinity or acidity; the hydrogen ion content of soil

Pioneer: A plant that flourishes in disturbed soil, as after a fire

Pistil: A flower's female reproductive organ

Pods: Dry fruits

Pollen: The spores of a seed-bearing plant

Pollination: The transfer of pollen from one plant to another

Pome: A fleshy fruit

Propagate: To grow new plants from old under controlled conditions

Prostrate: Lying or dragging on the ground.

Prune: To cut back, for the purposes of shaping a plant, encouraging new growth, or controlling size

Pyramidal: Broad on bottom, coming to a pointed top

Raceme: An elongated flower cluster in which the flowers are held on small stalks radiating from a single, larger stalk

Rejuvenation pruning: The practice of cutting all the main stems of a tree back to within one-half inch of the ground during winter dormancy; renewal pruning

Remontant: Able to rebloom one or more times during a single growing season

Renewal pruning: See *Rejuvenation pruning*

Root cutting: A cutting taken from the root of a parent plant for the purpose of propagation

Root pruning: The act of removing a portion of a plant's roots to keep top growth in check

Rootstock: The root of a grafted plant

Runner: A prostrate branch that roots at its joint

Scarify: To sand, scratch, or otherwise disturb the coating of a seed in preparation for its germination

Self-pollination: A plant's ability to fertlize its pistils with its own pollen

Semidouble: Having more than the usual number of petals but with at least some pollen-producing stamens

Semievergreen: Retaining its leaves for most of the winter, or in warm climates

Semihardwood cutting: A cutting taken from a stem that has just begun to develop woody tissue, for the purpose of propagation.

Sepal: The part of a flower that is circularly arranged outside the petals

Serrated: Saw-toothed

Single: In flowers, having only one layer of petals

Softwood cutting: A cutting taken from a green, or immature, stem of a woody plant, for the purpose of propagation

Species: A subgroup of a genus, composed of reproductively similar plants or animals

Specimen: A plant deliberately set by itself to emphasize its ornamental properties

Spreading: Having a horizontally branching habit

Stamen: The male organ of a flower carrying the pollen-bearing anther

Staminoid: A pollenless stamen

Sterile: Unable to generate seed

Stolon: An underground shoot

Stratify: To help seeds overcome dormancy by cleaning and drying them, then maintaining them for a period of time under generally cool and moist conditions

Striations: Fine stripes

Sucker: A shoot growing from the root or base of a woody plant

Tap root: A strong, vertical-growing, central root

Terete: Cylindrical (often tapering)

Topiary: The art of trimming or training plants into decorative three-dimensional shapes

Trifoliate: Having three leaflets

Truss: A flower cluster set at the top of a stem or branch

Understock: The stock or root plant onto which a shoot has been grafted to produce a new plant

Unisexual: Having either stamens or pistils

USDA hardiness zones: Planting zones established by the United States Department of Agriculture, defined by a number of factors, including minimum winter temperatures

Understory plant: A plant whose natural habitat is the forest floor; or one that can be used beneath a larger plant in the garden

Undulated: Wavy

Variegated: Characterized by striping, mottling, or other coloration in addition to the plant's general overall color

Vascular system: The tissues that conduct water, nutrients, and other elements through plants

Weeping: Having long, drooping branches

Winged: Having winglike appendages.

Winter kill: The dying back of a plant or part of a plant due to harsh winter conditions

Woody: Forming stems that mature to wood

Xeriscaping: Landscaping with the use of drought-tolerant plants, to eliminate the need for supplemental watering

SOURCES

Exotic and unusual tropical plants can be hard to find. These sources may be helpful; try local botanic gardens and ask which nurseries they use. Inclusion on this list does not imply an endorsement, and many fine sources are not included.

Brady's Exotics
PO Box 820874
Houston, TX 77282
1-800-926-7333; 1-713-960-7117 (fax)

Brenda's Bloomers
2659 "G" Road
Loxahatchee, FL 33470
407-795-1734; Fax: 407-795-0321
Hedge materials, bird of paradise, heliconias, ginger

Dos Pueblos Orchid Co.
PO Box 158
Goleta, CA 93116
805-968-3535
Cymbidiums, phalaenopsis

Endangered Species
PO Box 1830
Tustin, CA 92681
714-544-9505
rare bamboos, palms, exotic foliage

Exotica Rare Fruit Nursery
PO Box 133
Vista, CA 92085
619-724-9393; 619-724-7724 (fax)
Mangos, lychees, sapodilla, figs, ginger, plumeria, vines, bananas

The Green Escape
PO Box 1417
Palm Harbor, FL 34682
813-784-1991
Rare palms

Harold B. Martin, Inc.
13295 SW 232 St.
Miami, FL 33170
305-258-2282, 305-258-1983 (fax)
All flowering plants

Hurov Seeds and Botanicals
PO Box 1596
Chula Vista, CA 91912
619-291-4969
Seeds for 6,000 species

Jersey Home
10195 S.W. 70th St.
Miami, FL 33173
305-270-1235
Ferns, bromeliads, palms, cycads (2,000 rare specimens)

Kartuz Greenhouses
1408 Sunset Drive
Vista, CA 92083
619-941-3613; 619-941-1123 (fax)
Flowering plants; catalog $2.00

Landscape Junctions, Inc.
7142 South Military Trail
Lake Worth, FL 33463
407-964-3323; 407-964-3158 (fax)
Flowering and foliage plants

Logee's Greenhouses
141 North Street
Danielson, CT 06239
203-774-8038; 203-774-9932
Begonias; foliage and flowering plants, houseplants, conservatory plants; fragrant plants. Catalog $3.00.

Mellingers
2310 S. South Range Road
North Lima, Ohio 44432-9731
216-549-9861; 216-549-3716
Orchids, plumeria, banana, anthurium.

Neon Palm Nursery
3525 Stony Point Road
Santa Rosa, CA 95407
707-585-8100
60 palms species, cycads, grasses, foliae plants, ferns, conifers

Our Kids Orchids
17229 Phil Peters Road
Winter Garden, FL 34787
407-877-6883
Orchids, bananas, gingers, fruit trees

Pacific Tree Farms
4301 Lynwood Drive
Chula Vista, CA 91910
619-422-2400 (phone and fax)
Mango, lychee, guava, flowering trees, palms, citrus, heliconias

Reasoner's Inc.
PO Box 1881
Oneco, FL 34264
941-756-1181; 941-756-1882 (fax)
Hibiscus, palms, ornamentals

Sunshine Greenery
4740 Deer Run Road
St. Cloud, FL 34772
407-892-4893
Hibiscus, ixora, allamanda, croton, oleander, mandevilla

Tornnello Nursery
115 12 Avenue S.E.
Ruskins, FL 33570
813-645-5445; 813-645-4353 (fax)
Bamboo

Tropical Paradise Nursery
5060 S.W. 76 Avenue
Davie, FL 33328
305-791-2029, 305-791-7858 (fax)
Large selection of flowering and foliage plants, shrubs, and trees; gingers and heliconias

Vista Nursery, Inc.
18100 S.W. 248 St.
Homestead, FL. 33031
305-246-5200; 305-246-5897 (fax)
Woody ornamentals, mussaenda, hibiscus, terrestrial orchids.

CONTRIBUTERS

Main Garden
David Bar-Zvi
David Fairchild Tropical Garden
10901 Old Cutler Road
Miami, Florida 33156

Consulting Gardens
David Price
Bok Tower Gardens
PO Box 3810
Lake Wales, Florida 33859
813-676-1408

Robert Bowden
Harry P. Leu Gardens
1730 North Forest Avenue
Orlando, Florida 32803
407-246-2620

Sean Hogan
Portland, Oregon

Robert Hirano
Lyon Arboretum
3860 Manoa Road
Honolulu, Hawaii 96822
808-988-3177

Linda Gay and Douglas Williams
Mercer Botanical Arboretum and
Botanical Garden
22306 Aldine-Westfield Road
Humble, Texas 77338
713-443-8731

June Hutson
Missouri Botanical Garden
PO Box 299
St. Louis, Missouri 63166
314-577-5110

Larry Beezley
Quail Botanical Gardens Foundation
PO Box 230005
Encinitas, California 92023
619-436-3036

Keith Woolliams
Waimea Arboretum
Waimea Falls Park
59-864 Kamehameha Highway
Haleiwa, Hawaii 96712

PHOTO CREDITS

All photographs ©Chani Yammer with the following exceptions:
  ©David Bar-Zvi: 13B, 32TR, 36BL, 55TR, 55BL, 70BL, 89BC, 105TR, 138BR, 139, 147BR
  ©Kirsten Llamos: 5, 10-11, 36TR, 44TL, 55TL, 59TL, 61R, 63, 73BL, 78BR, 82BR, 85BL, 102TR, 103, 115TR, 131BR, 134TL, 134BL, 138TL, 188-189
  ©Dency Kane: 42, 43B, 62TR, 73TL, 87TR, 95, 101BL, 118TR, 140TL, 184R
  ©Elvin McDonald: 41Bl, 59TR, 73BR, 85BR, 87BL, 96TR, 101TR, 105TL, 108BR, 118TL, 126BL, 131BL, 140TR, 180B, 213
  ©Albert Squillace: 20, 22-23, 29TL, TR, 32BL, 44BR, 47BR, 49, 50BR, 58T, 59TL, 61L, 66TR, BL, 69, 74BR, 82TR, 98, 100B, 105BR, 115BL, BR, 123BR, 125, 134BR, 147TL, BL, 151TR, BL, 161, !63, 164, 165, 167, 168, 169, 182, 183, 186, 206, 211
  ©Sylvia and Steve Sharnoff: 12, 13T, 36BR, 50BR, 91TR, 92, 93, 101TL, BR, 123BL, 145BL, BR, 153, 211
  ©Joseph Tomocik: 32BR
  ©Keith Woolliams: 44Bl, 73TR, 74TR, 94, 102BL, 123TL, 126TR, 181T
  ©Cliff Zenor: 81T, 81B, 83T, 114, 115TL, 133, 150, 166, 212

llustrations on endpapers and on pages 16-17 by Delores Bego.
Zone map on page 25 courtesy United States Department of Agriculture
T=Top; B=Bottom; R=Right; L=Left; C=Center

We would like to thank the following organizations for generously allowing photographs to be taken on their sites:
  Marie Selby Gardens, Sarasota, Florida
  Fruit and Spice Park, Homestead, Florida
  Flamingo Gardens and Arboretum, Davie, Florida
  Honolulu Botanic Gardens
  The Kampong of the National Tropical Garden
  Professor Birdsey
  Montgomery Foundation
  Hyatt Regency, Kauai, Hawaii
  The Montgomery Foundation
  The Heliconia Society
  The Bromeliad Society
  Champman Fields, USDA
  Parrot Jungle, Miami, Florida
as well as all the consulting gardens.

LEAF SHAPES

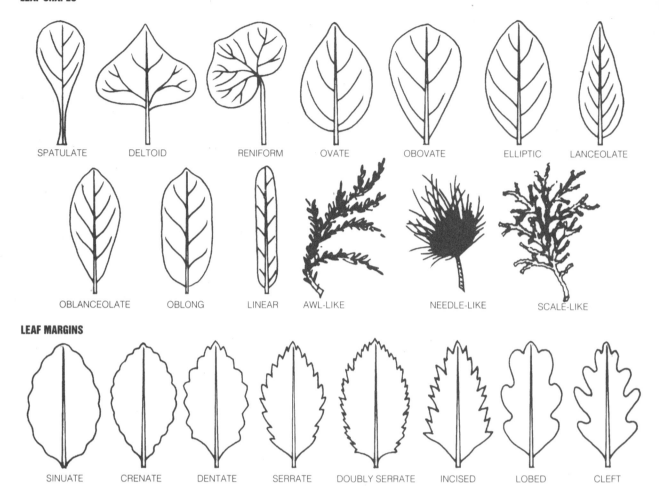

SPATULATE DELTOID RENIFORM OVATE OBOVATE ELLIPTIC LANCEOLATE

OBLANCEOLATE OBLONG LINEAR AWL-LIKE NEEDLE-LIKE SCALE-LIKE

LEAF MARGINS

SINUATE CRENATE DENTATE SERRATE DOUBLY SERRATE INCISED LOBED CLEFT

LEAF ARRANGEMENTS AND STRUCTURES

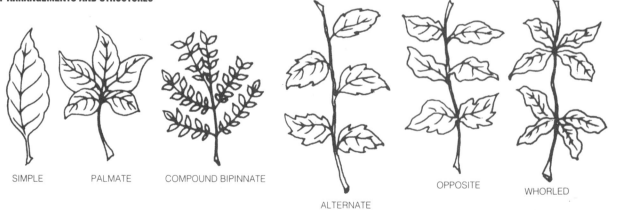

SIMPLE PALMATE COMPOUND BIPINNATE ALTERNATE OPPOSITE WHORLED